Praise for *One Call Away*

"We have all had the phone ring and our lives changed. Brenda Warner's moving and inspiring memoir reminds us all of the power of family, the miracles and misfortunes of life, and the foundation that faith plays in our all too-human existences. Unflinching and fearless, she is the woman I want in my corner: safe, smart, and savvy. A heroine for us all."

— Jamie Lee Curtis, author,
actress, mother, sister

"Brenda Warner remains a soldier fighting for faith and life in the face of unexplainable devastation. The fortitude of this 'marine mom' will grab your heart. If you think Kurt Warner's journey is moving, do not wait to read the story of Brenda."

— Elizabeth Hasselbeck, cohost
of *The View* and special
contributor for *Good Morning
America*, ABC News

"Some of the unexpected calls in Brenda's life include calls that her horse had died, that her child had stopped breathing, and that both parents died in a tornado. If I were her, I would stop answering the phone. But Brenda shows us how with faith we can face the unexpected and trust God to restore the things that the world has taken away. Honored to read her story and blessed to call her friend!"

Sandi Patty, Grammy
Award–winning
Contemporary Christian
music singer

"Brenda's courage and strength is both compelling and inspiring—a must-read."

— Peter Billingsley, actor,
director, producer

"As a mother of a child with special needs, I know how crucial yet challenging it can be to be a relentless and unyielding advocate for him. You are their best hope for a fair chance at life. I have long been inspired by the strength, conviction, and grace this mother of seven has to take on whatever challenge life presents her."

— Holly Robinson Peete,
actress, co-host of *The Talk*

"Brenda's honest and relatable story of humble beginnings and unwavering faith is one that will inspire and awaken the soul of any woman."

— Deanna Favre, author,
activist, founder of Deanna
Favre Hope Foundation

"Finally! After reading *First Things First*, I wanted to know more about what made this woman tick. This is a poignant, funny, and incredibly honest look at a very unexpected life."

— Chrissy Donnelly, #1
New York Times best-selling
author, *Chicken Soup for the
Couple's Soul*

"Brenda Warner is a woman of strength, beauty, character, and love. All of that clearly shines through in her memoir, *One Call Away*. On the outside, she may look like just another gorgeous NFL player's wife, but her story reveals the real woman of God that she is. That's the woman that I know and love. Her story will no doubt inspire, encourage, enlighten, and transform all who read it."

— Debbye Turner Bell, staff
correspondent, CBS News

"Brenda's story of her amazing faith even in times of heart-wrenching adversity is an inspirational gem of a read!"

— Pat Smith, Founder and
CEO of "Treasure You"

One Call Away

Answering Life's Challenges
With Unshakable Faith

Brenda Warner
with Jennifer Schuchmann

THOMAS NELSON
Since 1798

NASHVILLE DALLAS MEXICO CITY RIO DE JANEIRO

Published in Nashville, Tennessee, by Thomas Nelson. Thomas Nelson is a registered trademark of Thomas Nelson, Inc.

Published in association with Creative Trust Literary Group, 5141 Virginia Way, Suite 320, Brentwood, TN 37027.

Thomas Nelson, Inc., titles may be purchased in bulk for educational, business, fundraising, or sales promotional use. For information, please e-mail SpecialMarkets@ ThomasNelson.com.

Library of Congress Cataloging-in-Publication Data

Warner, Brenda.
   One call away : answering life's challenges with unshakable faith / Brenda Warner with Jennifer Schuchmann.
      p. cm.
   ISBN 978-0-8499-4719-3 (trade paper)
1. Warner, Brenda. 2. Christian biography--United States. 3. Football players' spouses--United States--Biography. 4. Warner, Kurt, 1971- I. Schuchmann, Jennifer, 1966- II. Title.
   BR1725.W325A3 2011
   277.3'083092--dc23
   [B]   2011019016

Printed in the United States of America

11 12 13 14 15 QG 5 4 3 2

For my children: you are my legacy
and for that I am richly blessed.

Contents

CONTENTS

Part One

A DREAM COMES AND GOES

1967–1992

1

Life-Changing Call

The call came in half an hour before quitting time. I was twenty-two and the lowest-ranking marine in my office. It was my job to answer the phone.

I picked up the receiver. "Lance Corporal Meoni."

"Sweetheart," said my husband. Immediately I knew something was wrong. Though Neil was at home taking care of our four-month-old son, Zack, he rarely called the office, preferring that I call him during a break. "Zack's breathing funny."

"What do you mean, Zack's breathing funny?"

"I don't know. He's just not breathing right."

"Put him on the phone." It sounds like a silly thing to say, but Neil knew what I meant. He held up the receiver to Zack's face, and I listened closely to his breathing. I heard gurgling, so I knew he was getting air.

"Do you hear it?" Neil asked.

"Yeah, it doesn't sound right. What do you think?"

"I think you should come home."

I hung up the phone and walked around the corner to talk to the staff sergeant. With his permission, I packed up my stuff and headed to the car. After his brain surgery several years earlier, Neil had suffered from seizures that left him unable to drive or work. Though the seizures were under control by now, he still had a few months to go before getting his driver's license back. Each day I took our only car to work while Neil stayed home with Zack.

———————

Neil sat in the glider, holding Zack swaddled in a blue comforter. The baby wasn't crying, and everything looked normal.

"Let me see him," I said. Neil pulled back the comforter, and I looked at Zack's chest. It didn't look like it was moving.

"We've got to go!" I scooped Zack up in the comforter and ran for the car. Neil got there first, opened the passenger door, and got in so I could put Zack in his arms. I got in the driver's side, backed out of the parking spot, and peeled down the road. There was an emergency clinic just around the block.

———————

"My baby's having trouble breathing," I told the nurse behind the desk. She took a look at him and immediately ushered us to a separate waiting room.

"Wait here. I'll be back to get you in a minute." Then she snatched Zack out of my arms and took him to a treatment room.

There was a flurry of activity in the room behind us. I heard someone call for the doctor, and then a voice said, "This child isn't breathing."

I looked up at Neil, and he stared back with a blank expression. I wasn't panicking, but I could feel the denial setting in. *This isn't happening. They've got a different child. Not my child.*

The room felt cold and antiseptic. We stood there, not speaking, just listening to the sounds from the other side of the wall. Then I prayed. *Oh, God, please help me. Please help me. What's going on? God, please make him okay.* After what seemed like hours but was probably only a few minutes, the doctor came in. "We're sending him to Portsmouth Naval Hospital."

"What do you mean you're *sending* him?"

"We're sending him in an ambulance."

"Can we go with him?"

"No, I'm sorry. You'll have to follow in your own car."

———————

The ambulance left the medical office as we got into the car. The driver turned on his siren and pulled into traffic, and I pulled in behind him. *I can't believe my baby's in that ambulance.*

While I focused on staying with the ambulance, Neil sat stone quiet. The whole experience was surreal. Just that morning, my perfect, healthy, chubby baby had smiled at me when I kissed him good-bye. Now his life was in danger. I needed to remain calm for my son, so I did the only thing I knew to do—I prayed. But words failed me. All I could say was, "Oh God, oh God, oh my God!"

I was not the crier in our relationship. But even if I had been, I knew now wasn't the time. I needed to focus on getting to the hospital and getting Zack the help he needed. Neil had always been more emotional than I, but his seizure medications made it worse. It didn't surprise me when he started crying right there in the car.

We followed the ambulance into the emergency entrance but quickly realized no parking was available there. I circled back to look for parking in the lot, but all the spaces were full. *I need a parking place now!*

"Just park!" Neil had apparently run out of tears and now, out of patience.

But I was a rule follower, a marine. I couldn't just leave our car anywhere. I needed order, especially during a crisis. Eventually I found a space, and Neil and I bolted out of the car and sprinted to the hospital entrance.

We entered through the glass doors and rushed up to the desk. "Our son was just brought in," I said, trying to catch my breath. "The baby. We need to see him."

"You'll have to wait over there." The woman behind the desk pointed to the waiting room without even looking at us.

"Can't we see him now?"

"I'm sorry. You'll have to wait."

I couldn't believe it! Frustrated, I turned toward the seating area. People filled the room. All of them were waiting to be seen, but they didn't even look sick. They looked like they had a cold or needed a Band-Aid. I wanted to scream, "People! My child is in there, and he's not breathing!"

I managed to hold myself together. Neil and I sat down in the hard plastic chairs and stared silently at the white-brick walls. I lowered my eyes so I didn't have to look at the people who didn't look sick. Half-empty cups and last month's magazines were strewn across plastic end tables. The room smelled like coffee and air freshener. I thought about my mom and dad and desperately wanted to call them, but I decided to wait until I had more information.

In a crisis, I always wanted to take action, to be the strong one. But now I couldn't do anything, so I sat motionless in the chair, my muscles tense, my mind worrying.

Eventually a clerk with a clipboard appeared. We followed her to a small room with more plastic chairs. "Have a seat," she said. "I need to get some information from you."

I wanted her to hurry up so I could see Zack, but the woman was so deliberate with her movements, she seemed to move in slow motion. She clicked her pen and poised it above the clipboard. "Names?"

"Brenda and Neil Meoni," I said. "Our baby is Zack."

"How old are you?"

"I'm twenty-two."

Neil answered, "I'm twenty-three."

All I could think was, *Why does this matter? Who cares how old we are?*

"Your address?"

We gave it.

"How old is Zack?"

"Four months."

"Any health problems?"

"No."

"Any allergies?"

"No! He's perfectly healthy. He just stopped breathing."

I knew she needed this information so they could treat Zack. I knew that. But I was worried they wouldn't treat him until we finished. So I spit out short answers as fast as I could.

"Can you tell me what happened?" she asked.

"I was at work when it happened." I glanced at Neil. "He can give you the details."

"I was giving him a bath, and he just started breathing funny."

"Can you tell me more?"

"I was giving him a bath, and when I took him out of the tub, he started breathing funny."

"What do you mean? What did he sound like?"

"I don't know. It just didn't sound right. It was kind of like a gurgle." Neil squirmed in his chair. I could tell it was hard for him to put what happened into words.

"Did he change colors?"

"Uh, no, he didn't change colors."

"He didn't get blue in the face or anywhere else?"

"No."

"So what did you do next?"

Neil walked her through it detail by detail, explaining how he had taken Zack into his room, how he'd worried about Zack's breathing, and how he'd diapered him and wrapped him in the comforter before calling me.

As he talked, all I could think was, *Hurry up. Please hurry up.* Although I convinced myself they had to be working on Zack, I felt as if every question prevented me from seeing my sick baby boy.

When she finished, the clerk told us to follow her to a private treatment room where we could wait. Over the next hour, nurses and doctors came in and out of the room, each asking the same question. "Can you tell me what happened?"

Each time he was asked, Neil told them the same thing: "He just started breathing funny."

"Do these people not talk to each other?" I asked Neil when we were alone. "Hasn't anybody put this information in the records by now?"

He didn't answer, and I knew he couldn't. I was just frustrated and impatient with the lack of progress.

Between visits by the medical staff, I paced the small room, my mind frantically searching for answers to what was wrong. No one had given us any indication of what was happening. We were left to imagine the worst.

Finally, another doctor came in, but this time he started out by giving us information. "We're not sure what's causing it, but Zack's brain is swelling at a pretty fast rate," he said. "Can you tell me what happened?"

Are you kidding me? Again?

Once again, Neil repeated the story. "He was in the tub, and when I got him out, he just started breathing funny."

"We're not sure what's wrong, so we'll have to run a few tests to determine what's causing his brain to swell. There's a small possibility it's meningitis, but we won't know for sure unless we do a spinal tap."

The doctor explained that this involved sticking a needle into Zack's spinal cord, removing fluid, and testing it for meningitis. "There are some risks with this procedure, but they're minimal. In rare cases there can be bleeding or an infection. I'll need your permission before we can proceed."

They're going to stick a needle in Zack's spine? In my baby's spine?

"If it will help Zack, do it. Please just do it," I said. "When can we see him?"

"You can see him when I'm done."

Neil and I sat quietly in the plastic chairs and waited. There were no windows in the room, and I had lost track of time. A nurse finally came in and said, "They did the spinal tap, and Zack did great. Now we just need to wait for the test results to see if it's meningitis. That could take a couple of hours. Zack is stable, and we're going to move him to the pediatric ward. You can wait for him there."

The pediatric ward reminded me of my squad bay at boot camp on Parris Island. It was one long, beige-colored room with at least twenty beds lined up in bays along the perimeter. But most of the beds here didn't look like regular beds; they looked like metal cages. There was an occasional hospital bed for an older child, but the toddlers and babies were kept in metal cribs. Some even had metal tops to keep active toddlers from escaping.

"They're not going to put Zack in one of these, are they?" I whispered to Neil.

A group of nurses and other medical professionals moved in and out of the nurses' station in the center of the room. A nurse with dark-brown hair looked up and smiled. She grabbed a clipboard and approached us.

"Are you the Meonis?" she asked, looking down at her clipboard.

"Yes," I said.

"They just called up to say Zack will be here soon. I'll show you where his bed is."

She led us to a bay on the right side of the room. Two plastic chairs faced an empty metal crib. Folded against the wall was a beige metal lamp attached to a long metal arm. A monochrome monitor waited to be hooked up. The tiled floors and beige walls made the room feel sterile. The smell of rubbing alcohol lingered in the air. "You can sit here and wait," she said. "It won't be long."

But I didn't sit. I wanted to see what was going on. Despite the size of the ward and the number of people in it, everything was quiet and calm. Nobody screamed in pain. Nurses didn't have to hurry to get to anybody. Parents held small children in their arms and swayed back and forth. A little boy wearing faded hospital pajamas and breathing into a nebulizer lay in the bed next to us. *It's going to be okay,* I reassured myself. *If they send kids here who only need an inhaler, how bad could it be for Zack?*

Neil sat down on the hard chair and buried his head in his hands. "I can't believe this happened."

I wanted to comfort him, but I wasn't sure how. He seemed confused. I sat down in the chair next to him as he repeated to himself, "How does this happen? How does this happen?"

One of the differences between Neil and me was our faith in God. My relationship with Jesus gave me strength. But Neil didn't have that kind of relationship. He had grown up in a Catholic family, but he rarely went to church anymore. At the most desperate times in my life—like now—I could turn to my faith, but Neil couldn't.

I stared at the empty metal crib and whispered my prayers. "What's going on? Please help us, God. Give us strength. Heal Zachary."

An orderly came in and rolled away the metal crib. That gave me hope. *They're putting Zack into a real bed.* But minutes later, the orderly brought the crib back with Zack inside, and my hope turned to fear. I understood why they needed to put him in the crib, but compared to his sweet blue and white crib in our apartment, this looked like a torture device, complete with tubes and wires.

As they rolled him into place, I heard Zack making a sound he'd never made before. It was like a horrible moan that came from somewhere deep inside.

I immediately went over to him, but there were so many medical people working around his bed, I couldn't get close enough to touch him. One nurse was hanging a bag of IV fluid. Another nurse had unscrewed his oxygen line from the tank and was plugging it into the wall. Yet another was checking his vital signs, while a fourth stood at the end of his crib, recording numbers. "BP? Pulse? Oxygen?"

Zack was wearing only a diaper. He'd never looked so small and frail. His head looked too big, much larger than it had at the clinic just a few hours earlier. A red light attached to his toe reported oxygen levels, and his mattress was elevated so his head was higher than his feet.

He continued to make that horrible moaning sound, and every part of my body strained to stop his pain and comfort him. I'd never felt so helpless. Several of the nurses finished and left his bedside, so I moved in closer to get a better look at my dark-haired little boy. I reached through the metal slats and rubbed his foot. There was no response. Just more of those hideous moans.

One of the nurses remained. Her name tag read, "Remi." She lowered the metal slats on one side of the bed. "You'll be able to see him better this way," she said. "You can touch him, but you can't pick him up. He's too fragile."

Zack's visceral groaning continued. Neil remained seated. I leaned over Zack's bed and rubbed his face and kissed him.

Remi asked me to take a step back so she could change one of his tubes. As I waited, I caught a glimpse through the window. Outside I saw the overpass, where two highways merged together, and watched as cars and trucks zoomed by without slowing down.

I wanted to scream, "Stop! Everybody just stop! Something is terribly wrong with my son!" My world was spinning out of control, and I needed help. So I turned to the only One I knew who could take care of things. I prayed out loud, not caring who heard me. "God, you've got to step in here. He's so sick!"

Then I heard Remi's voice. "He's starting again."

I turned back to see Zack's right pinkie finger beginning to shake, and then I watched as his face began to twitch. Nurses who had left his bedside came running.

No one had to tell me what was happening. I already knew. Just like his father so many times before, Zack was having a grand mal seizure.

That phone call from Neil on September 6, 1989, turned my life upside down. But it wasn't the first life-changing call in my life. And it wouldn't be the last. There were literal phone calls that delivered unexpected and sometimes unimaginable news. There were also metaphorical calls that challenged me to go in unexpected and sometimes unimaginable directions.

And every call brought with it a choice.

Even as a scared twenty-two-year-old, staring at my baby's convulsing body and the nurses who were trying to help him, I knew I had to choose. I could step up and do my best in the situation, or I could sit back and let life's circumstances take me out.

I can't say I've always done the right thing. But I can honestly say that when the calls came, I've done my very best to stand up and answer. There have been a lot of surprises in my life, but one thing has always held true: God has always been one call away.

2

Blind Love

In the summer of 1972, a phone call brought bad news. I was seven.

My older sister, Kim, and I, along with our four cousins, sat cross-legged on the braided rug in my relatives' great room. We called this extended part of our family our "rich relatives" because their mobile home was bigger than ours (it had additions), and, more important, they owned a boat. We spent every vacation at that huge mobile home in Arkansas. It was the only kind of vacation we Carneys could afford.

The phone rang as we were playing a board game. One of the cousins answered in the kitchen and then handed the receiver to my mom.

"It's my turn," said another cousin as she shook the dice in her cupped hands and rolled them onto the board.

"What do you mean?" Mom asked into the phone, her voice suddenly agitated. Through the doorway into the kitchen, I could see her breathing hard and trying to remain calm. "Oh no," she said.

My cousin moved her game piece around the board and then picked up the dice to go again.

"Oh my God, no!" Now there was horror in my mother's voice.

My cousin stopped suddenly before tossing the dice. We stared wide-eyed at one another, my cousin's hand suspended above the multicolored squares of the game. It sounded as if someone had died.

"Oh, Larry. What are we going to do?" my mom asked.

I had been holding my breath, but at the sound of my dad's name, I released it. Dad had stayed home in Iowa to take care of the animals while we visited Mom's family in Arkansas. He was big and strong and a former marine. I knew there wasn't anything that man couldn't handle. Whatever was wrong, he would fix it.

Mom's voice suddenly grew softer as if she didn't want us kids to hear. "But what do I tell her?" She paced in the kitchen and twisted the phone cord around her finger. "Okay, see what you can do. We'll leave in the morning and be home tomorrow. I love you too."

She slowly hung up the phone. As she walked through the doorway into the great room, her sad eyes focused on me.

"Brenda, something's happened to Flash."

Flash was my pony. My beloved pony. She was one thing in the world that I felt was truly mine. I was the only one who cared for her, and most important, I didn't have to share her with anyone, even Kim. But I could tell by the look on Mom's face that was all about to change. Tears formed in my eyes as my cousin rolled the dice again and counted off the squares on the board with her game piece. She and the others acted as if nothing had happened.

"Is she okay?" The tears pooled and then poured freely as I searched my mother's face. She took me by the hand and led me to an empty bedroom. She looked concerned. Even as a young girl, I didn't cry much, and I'm sure my burst of emotion scared her.

"We're leaving tomorrow," she said. "You'll be able to go home and see her. She's still alive."

I cried harder.

"Sweetheart, the good news is that she's still alive!"

I know Mom meant her words as comfort, but they didn't sound comforting to me.

"Your dad's got her right now. At least she's still alive."

She kept saying that over and over as if that was supposed to make me feel better. I didn't understand. *Is that the best? That she's just alive? How bad is she?*

As I lay in my cousin's bed that night, I said the same prayer I always said: "Bless Mom, Dad, Kim, Grandpa and Grandma, aunts, uncles, cousins, friends, pets, and animals." But all I could think about was Flash.

When I was little, my mom's parents, George and Ruby Woodyard, lived in a big, white house on a farm in Parkersburg, Iowa. We called my grandmother Chach—short for Cha-cha, the name a cousin had given her when he couldn't say *Grandma*. Mom's side of the family was very close; aunts, uncles, and cousins were always spilling out of Chach and Grandpa's big, white house. Including Kim and me, there were seven first cousins. Fifteen years separated the oldest from the youngest, and I was smack-dab in the middle. My parents and sister and I lived across the driveway in a mobile home, but we were often at Chach's to celebrate a birthday or a holiday. We'd ride horses, have picnics, and play games in the yard. The household was chaotic and noisy, and I couldn't have imagined a better way to grow up.

When Grandpa retired from his job at the slaughterhouse, however, things changed. He and Chach decided to sell the farm and retire to Arkansas. A rich man, Wayne Dudley, bought the farm and moved into the big, white house with his two well-dressed daughters. We stayed on in the mobile home. Dad worked the land and tended the animals for the rich man in addition to his job at John Deere in Cedar Falls.

Wayne was a bigwig at the local corn processing plant; everyone in town knew him. He owned several breeding horses, and at one point he bought two ponies so that Kim and I could each have our own. Kim's pony was a mean little red mare named Sweet Susie. Kim didn't want anything to do with her, preferring to stay inside to do her homework, help Mom in the kitchen, and watch TV.

My pony, however, had a sweet temperament. A white Shetland covered in even whiter spots, she gleamed bright, like teeth on a toothpaste commercial. I called her Flash of Light. I couldn't wait to finish my chores each day so I could spend time with her.

Every afternoon when the school bus dropped me off in front of the house, my cowboy boots would hit the dirt driveway and I'd run down the long path to the barns. I was a daddy's girl, and I loved to help Dad with the chores. I'd clean the stalls, feed and water the animals, whatever needed doing. He taught me how to groom the horses, how to tell when a mare is in labor, and how to deliver the foals. I thought he was the smartest man in the world, and I was always amazed at how much he knew. I wanted to be just like him when I grew up—living life as a cowgirl while working on a farm. There was no reason for me to think I would ever be the one who actually owned the farm or the ranch.

The best part of my day came after I finished the chores, because then I could ride Flash. I'd saddle and mount her, and together we'd be gone for hours, having adventures in the wide-open Iowa farm fields.

We'd play cowgirls and Indians. "C'mon, Flash," I'd say, squeezing my heels and calves around her side. "Let's go get the Indians."

Life on the farm was safe, and no one knew or cared where Flash and I went. They just knew we'd be home by dark, and we were. When the sun set, we would return to the barn, and I would walk her until she cooled down. Then I'd talk to her while I combed, petted, and fed her. I'd tell Flash the deepest, darkest secrets of a seven-year-old. Looking into her chocolate eyes, I knew I could trust her. A dog might be man's best friend, but Flash was mine.

———

The ten-hour drive home from Arkansas seemed to drag on forever. Most of the trip, I stared vacantly out the window, crying and desperately wanting to get home to Flash. *What's wrong with her? Why did Mom say it was good that she was still alive?*

I spent the last thirty miles or so searching intently for familiar signs of our farm. When the car finally pulled in to the dirt drive, I opened the door without waiting for it to stop. As I had done many times before when the bus brought me home from school, I ran down the path to the barn. But this time it wasn't with the same eager expectation. I dreaded what I would find.

Even before I entered the barn, I could see her inside. I froze in my tracks. Flash was no longer just white. She was white with red stains all over her beautiful coat.

Dad must have heard the car because he came running out of the barn. "Sweetheart, something's happened to Flash, but she's alive."

There was that word again. "What happened?" I asked, trying to understand what could cause the red half circles that spotted her once-gleaming coat.

"She delivered her foal while you were gone."

"Thunder?"

"Yes, I named him Thunder."

Flash had been ready to deliver when we left for Arkansas. I had asked Dad before I left if we could name the foal Thunder, thinking it was the perfect name for Flash's baby. Then I would have Flash of Light and Thunder.

"I want to see Flash."

He took my hand and slowly walked me into the barn. As we got closer, I could see that the red marks covered her entire body. "Those are teeth marks!" I said. "What would do this to her?"

Underneath Flash, Thunder was suckling. Normally, the cute baby horse would have distracted me, but my eyes and my mind were fixated on Flash. Although Dad had tried to clean her up, the bright red wounds revealed hundreds of inflamed gouges in her coat.

"It was Trouble," my dad said, referring to the black stallion, the oldest and angriest horse in the herd. "Female horses are very protective of their foals. Trouble tried to attack Thunder, but Flash wouldn't let him. The vet said Flash took over three hundred bites to save her foal."

I was shocked. I had never seen anything so violent in my young life. I wanted to hug her, but I was afraid I'd hurt her. Instead I softly rubbed her in the small, smooth spaces between her wounds. "What are the black pads on her eyes?"

"Those are patches. Trouble bit her eyes out, and now she's blind."

I started to cry. "She's blind?"

"We'll have to take special care of her. She may be blind, Brenda, but at least she's alive."

I just stood there rubbing her and talking soothingly.

"You should be proud of her," my dad said. "She took those hits to save her baby."

It was maternal instinct. My pony had been willing to fight for her child even if she died trying. Though I was only seven, I understood what Flash had done and why. I would have done the same thing to save her.

———

I was determined to do whatever I had to do to nurse my pony back to health. For weeks I came home from school and talked softly to her while I gently rubbed her body. Slowly, over time, I gained her trust, and I was able to lead her on walks—short ones at first, then longer ones. She knew me not only by the sound of my voice, but also by my smell and the touch of my hand. Her trust grew so much that eventually I could even walk under her belly without her flinching.

The bond between us continued to grow until one day I decided to try a saddle on her. As gently as I could, I eased the saddle over her back and let her get used to wearing it again. I led her around until she was comfortable, and then I mounted her, allowing her to once again feel me on her back. Then, carefully, I coaxed her to take a few steps.

It was a remarkable act of trust that a blind horse would let a seven-year-old girl ride her, but within weeks I was doing just that. Though she couldn't see, she trusted me to guide her through those cowboy-and-Indian-filled fields. Though Flash would never again be whole, she would always be mine; and just as she took care of Thunder, I would always take care of her.

Or so I thought.

———

One evening a few months after I started riding again, Dad found me in the barn, brushing my pony. "Brenda, we need to talk. Wayne has decided to sell Flash. She'll be going up for auction in a couple of weeks."

Later that night, Dad found me crying in my beanbag chair. "When we take her to auction," he said, "Wayne wants you to be the one to show her."

Thus began one of my first lessons in how to say good-bye. It would not be my last. Some good-byes would be unexpected and abrupt. Some would be wordless, just turning my back and walking out. And some, like this one, would be filled with sorrow.

———

I led Flash by her bridle as we made our slow circle around the auction arena. I had such mixed feelings. If someone bid on Flash, it would mean the bidder saw what I saw, that Flash was a desirable horse. But if Flash didn't get a bid, she would return home with me. It was the hardest thing I had ever had to do, but as I led her past the bidders and out of the show area, I held my head up high. So did Flash.

When Dad found us afterward, my head was buried in Flash's silky coat and my arms were wrapped around her neck.

"Did she sell?" I asked.

Dad picked me up and kissed me. "You did a great job, Brenda. She sold to a very nice man. A very nice man who has kids."

That night as I lay in bed, reciting the same prayer I'd said for as long as I could remember, I added something new. "Bless Mom, Dad, Kim, Grandpa and Grandma, aunts, uncles, cousins, friends, pets, and animals." And then I added, "Please let Flash be safe."

From her bed, Kim also added her two cents. "She's glue."

"Mom!" I yelled from my bed. "Kim says Flash is glue."

Mom came into the room. "Now, Kim, a very nice man with kids bought Flash."

But as soon as she left the room, Kim said it again. "She's glue."

For several weeks after Flash was sold, Kim would respond to my prayer with the same words: "She's glue." I would yell for Mom, and she'd come in and correct Kim. It got old real fast.

The rich man eventually bought me a replacement horse, a palomino that was mean and ornery. I found out the hard way that there are relationships in life that can't be replaced.

To this day, I don't really know where Flash went, but I prefer Mom and Dad's version to Kim's.

3

Centered

From the time I was about three years old, I discovered I liked attention—and when I danced, I got more of it. So I would dance around the house, wearing dress-up clothes or, sometimes, nothing but my panties. Mom and Dad would laugh, and if grandparents, aunts and uncles, or cousins happened to catch my show, they would join in the encouragement.

"Isn't she cute?"

"Do it again, Brenda."

Sometimes they'd joke, "She looks like a stripper."

I didn't know what a stripper was, but apparently strippers got attention, so that was fine with me. Even as a small child, I tried to study who got attention and who didn't so I could understand how to get more.

We didn't attend church regularly, but when we did go, I noticed that the pastor always had the congregation's full attention. I admired the way everyone watched him, listened to him, and respected him. One Sunday, during a message about God's call in our lives, the pastor took the microphone into the congregation to ask children what they wanted to be when they grew up. He put the microphone in front of me, and I didn't hesitate to answer. It was my chance to get the same respect he got. "When I grow up, I want to be a preacher," I said proudly. And then I added, "Or a stripper."

The congregation howled with laughter. But rather than being embarrassed, I loved the attention. Even today, I occasionally refer to those career choices when I am speaking: "Well, I either wanted to be a preacher or a stripper, so let's see what you're gonna get today!"

It still gets a laugh.

———————

As far back as I can remember, people told me I was pretty. Being pretty, I learned, was a valuable asset for getting more attention. So I worked to develop this asset the way my sister studied for tests. While it was never said out loud, I understood as clearly as if it had been tattooed on my wrist that my role in life was to be the pretty one, and Kim's role was to be the smart one.

When I was home sick or had a school holiday, I watched Mom's soap operas to see what made the actresses so beautiful. Later, I imitated them in the mirror—primping, posing, and practicing my best looks. Every year I watched the Miss America pageant, and for weeks afterward I worked to master the model walk and the beauty-queen hand wave. I studied the starlets in Mom's *People* magazines and spent hours in front of the mirror, trying on makeup and learning new hairstyles, like the French braid a girlfriend taught me.

Before I left for school each morning, I'd look in the mirror and ask Kim, "How should I wear my hair today? In a pony? Down and parted on the side? Maybe a French braid—but one braid or two?" Kim never answered because she hated my asking. Mom and Kim didn't worry much about their hair. They preferred to keep the same style. But I loved to change mine to create a different look.

If I stayed in my room too long, Mom would come in and check on me. She would open the door and sometimes catch me in midpose. Usually she'd roll her eyes before walking back out. But one day she just sat down on my bed and watched me walk and pose, walk and pose.

"What does it feel like to have people stare at you?" she asked.

I answered her with the honesty of a child. "I act like I don't notice them, because then they stare longer."

"I don't know what that feels like," she said. "I was never the pretty one."

"You're pretty," I said.

But she just smiled the way people do when they know you're being nice but not truthful. "They used to call me 'anteater' because of my nose," she said.

"What's wrong with your nose?"

Mom had moved from Arkansas to Iowa when she was in elementary school. Her Southern drawl and her hand-sewn dresses had made her stand out. She'd been teased about her looks and never quite fit in with the locals.

She didn't answer my question about her nose. She just said, "Kids can be cruel." Then she stood up and smoothed the sheets on my bed before heading back to the kitchen.

Mom was right. I later realized she wasn't physically beautiful like the stars she read about in *People* or later watched on *Entertainment Tonight*. She had a long, skinny nose, and her face wrinkled easily. When she let me put makeup on her, I spent more time pushing the wrinkles around than I did applying the eye shadow.

Mom smoked, so her teeth were stained yellow and her breath often smelled of cigarettes. Yet when she and Dad held hands—his grease-stained fingertips intertwined with her polished fingernails—it was obvious they each saw past the surface to something on the inside. They were more in love than any Hollywood starlets could ever be.

When they watched TV, Mom would sit on his lap. They made out a lot, and unlike our kids when Kurt and I do that, Kim and I thought their affection was normal and beautiful. But I had friends who'd never seen their parents do that sort of thing. Seeing my parents kissing and touching shocked them.

Around three each afternoon, Mom would be in the kitchen, working on a casserole for dinner, when Dad came in from his first job at John Deere. I'd hear the sound of his boots on the steps leading to our mobile home. The door would creak open, and he would enter wearing jeans and a dirty T-shirt, smelling of oil. He'd head straight to the kitchen, set his black metal lunch box on the counter, look at my mom, and say, "You are the most beautiful woman in the world."

Then he would kiss her. It was never just a peck on the cheek. It was always a deep, passionate kiss that showed how much he loved her and missed her while he was gone. They'd continue to flirt with each other as he walked back to the door to hang up his coat and take off his steel-toed boots.

As I became more focused on my looks and started to pay attention to my mother's lack of beauty, I remember feeling ashamed that I could even think she wasn't pretty. But immediately another thought entered my mind: *Dad thinks she's beautiful.* I thought my dad was the handsomest man alive. Looking back, they were probably equally attractive, but in my mind the differences seemed huge. Now, when people tell me I look just like my mom, I laugh to think how that whole issue has come full circle. But regardless of how attractive or unattractive my parents were, they just seemed to have something that drew them together.

Dad's romantic affections for Mom, however, didn't take away from his fatherly affections for us kids. Kim and I would each grab him around a leg, and he'd wrestle with us until Mom made us wash up for dinner. We ate early because Dad and I had barn chores to do, but we always ate together as a family. My mom insisted on it. I do the same thing with my family today, although it's harder to enforce that tradition with seven kids.

My parents didn't get much alone time. There was no such thing as date night on the farm. And despite their love for each other, there was still bickering. They were passionate people, after all. Often their disagreements were about money, which we never seemed to have enough of.

Sometimes when Mom and Dad fought, they used Kim and me as intermediaries. I remember a time when the four of us were riding in the truck, squeezed together in the front seat, and Mom and Dad were obviously fighting, because they weren't talking to each other. Dad started every sentence with, "Tell your mother . . ."

Kim repeated what he'd said to me: "Dad says to tell you . . ."

Then I passed on to Mom, "Kim said that Dad said to tell you . . ."

Sitting next to the door, Mom replied by saying, "Tell your father . . ." Then we passed the message back the same way—from Mom to me to Kim to Dad.

The trouble was, Kim and I were pretty young and didn't really understand all the messages we were passing back and forth, so we kept mixing up the words. After a few minutes of this, no one in the car could keep a straight face. Mom smirked, Dad laughed, and Kim and I joined in because we didn't know what was going on. That ended the fight.

As a family, we spent a lot of time talking, especially on those car trips to Arkansas. Dad loved to tell stories about his time in the marines. He had vivid memories of those years and was proud of his service to our country. "When you have that uniform on, you hold your head up high. Your shoulders go back. You just carry yourself differently . . . I was in the best shape of my life," he'd go on. "When I had that uniform on, it was the best feeling a man could have."

He especially liked to talk about the camaraderie between marines. "I haven't seen some of those men in years, but they'd still be my friends if I saw them today."

I know my eyes must have lit up whenever he talked about being a marine. Even as a little girl, I wanted to know more.

"Were you a superhero?" I asked.

But Mom would clear her throat or give Dad a disapproving look if I asked too many questions. She didn't like him talking about the marines nearly as much as I did. While she supported the military and appreciated the work they did protecting our country, she was more cautious because she didn't want her daughter going off to war.

Dad, sensing Mom's discomfort, would try to temper my excitement. "It's not all fun and games, Brenda. It takes a lot of discipline to be a marine. I remember spending an entire day doing push-ups and sit-ups."

"How many push-ups? I can do six."

"Some days we'd do hundreds of them. Then we'd have to run. There were days we had to run as fast as we could for more than an hour."

I was glued to every word he said.

"They would wake us up at five in the morning. It was still dark outside, and they would bang trash-can lids until we got out of bed."

"But after the running, you'd train to fight, right?"

"Yes, we trained all the time."

"And you got paid to do that?"

That's when Mom would have enough of the conversation. "Knock it off, Larry," she'd say. "Brenda, look out the window. Do you see those baby horses?"

My sister, Kim, and I always considered my mom a hypochondriac. She always seemed to have some kind of illness—often it was a headache or a female problem. We used to joke that she'd gotten the disease of the day after watching her talk shows. Today, when my kids don't feel well, I'll tease and call them "Little Jenny Jo," after my mom.

But even when Mom was lying in bed and hurting, I could see her eyes sparkle when Dad walked into the room. It was easy to see how much she loved him. He lit up her life, and she lit his. Kim and I both felt secure in their love for us as well.

Eventually the stress of Dad's commuting an hour to John Deere, plus the time spent taking care of the farmland and animals, took a toll on their marriage. Although they remained in love and committed to each other, they fought more and got along less. Something had to change. So when Dad got a raise at John Deere, they decided we needed to move into town so he could be closer to the plant.

I was in fifth grade when we moved to an apartment in Cedar Falls. Over the next three years, we would live in three different places—moving each time the lease expired. But one of those moves had eternal consequences, changing our family's life forever.

When I was in the sixth grade, I had a new best friend who lived across the street. One Sunday, Lynn invited our family to come to a special Sunday night service at her church. Our family didn't attend church regularly, but we weren't opposed to the idea. We gladly accepted Lynn's invitation.

Sunnyside Temple was the biggest church I'd ever been to and very unlike the small country churches I'd known. Services were held in a large warehouse-looking building. We arrived and took our seats in the middle section near the back. Interlocking rows of cushioned chairs formed three sections divided by two aisles. The floor was covered in a dark carpet.

The people in the church were energized and seemed happy to be there. When music played, they lifted their hands and faces to praise God. Then, after the singing stopped, they showed a movie from the big screen in the center of the stage.

Distant Thunder was a fictional story about the end of the world. In the movie, a teenage girl, who looked a bit like Marcia Brady, faced a terrible choice. Patty hadn't accepted Jesus as her Savior before the rapture (when all the believers were taken to heaven), so she remained behind on earth. Now she had to choose between taking the mark of the Beast or declaring her allegiance to Jesus and losing her life to the guillotine. The people who took the mark believed they had been saved, but eventually they would end up in hell.

Throughout the movie, I identified with Patty. I hadn't made a decision about my faith either. During the final tension-filled moments, while the skies turned dark and the music swelled and Patty lay in the guillotine, looking up at the glistening blade, I couldn't sit still. The scenes riveted me; it was the most intense and violent movie I'd ever seen. After the film ended, the church was completely silent, but the sounds of that guillotine echoed in my mind. Then, in the distance, I heard people crying softly.

I was terrified. The gleaming blades of the guillotine loomed in my mind as they'd loomed over Patty's throat in the movie. I did not want to be left behind. And I especially did not want to spend eternity in hell. I would do whatever it took to avoid that fate.

The pastor got up and explained that if you wanted to go to heaven, you had to be saved. You had to ask Jesus into your heart. "If you haven't made this decision yet, please stand up and come down front so we can pray with you."

Every one of us Carneys stood up, moved out from the center section, and made our way down the aisle. I was still scared—afraid someone was coming to take me to a guillotine. I wasn't sure what it meant to be saved, but I knew the alternatives were much more frightening. When we got to the altar, we knelt together as a family. All I remembered was that I never wanted to be in the position that Patty was in. The pastor asked everyone to bow their heads and repeat a prayer asking for forgiveness of our sins and for Jesus to be our Savior. I prayed the prayer with him, and so did Mom, Dad, and Kim.

That night we committed our lives to Jesus Christ as our Lord and Savior, and in doing so, we were assured that our sins were forgiven and that we'd spend eternity in heaven. That was pretty big stuff for a scared twelve-year-old. I opened my eyes and took a deep breath. *Now I can relax. I am not going to be left behind.*

People can make fun of what happened at church that night and say it wasn't real, but it was for me. When I opened my eyes from saying that prayer, I didn't feel or look any different, but in the days that followed I began to make different choices.

Church soon became part of my family's life, and Kim and I quickly joined the church's youth group. In addition to Sunday morning services, we joined Lynn at Wednesday night youth group meetings and Friday night youth activities. On Saturday, the youth group would get together and go bowling or roller-skating. I also joined the youth choir. Rehearsals, performances, and trips to places like Niagara Falls gave my friends and me more opportunities to hang out.

Our youth pastor, Pastor Rich, drove a yellow Corvette and was the only person I knew who had a swimming pool at his house. He'd invite the whole youth group over to swim and cook out. At church, he'd organize contests to see which team could bring more friends to an activity. Because I was a cheerleader and popular at school, it was easy for me to do that. It was my prayer that they would get saved too.

The youth group provided a fun environment for me to grow spiritually. But I also took my faith very seriously. When I first gave my life to Jesus, I had felt a rush of excitement. I wanted to experience God at a deeper level than I had before. I fell in love with Jesus, and I wanted to learn the Bible. So while the other girls in my freshman class were preoccupied with homework and boys, I set a goal for myself—to read my Bible for a half hour every day for a year.

When I started, I wasn't sure I could finish. It was hard to make myself pick up that Bible every day. But over time, it became a joy. I looked forward to reading, and I soaked up God's Word the way other girls my age soaked up sun at the pool.

I had an active prayer life, and when I prayed, I didn't have doubts. I believed that God would answer my prayer requests just as I prayed them, and often he did. But the more I read my Bible, the more my prayers changed. When I said my prayers at night, I no longer just asked God to bless a long list of people and animals. Instead, I asked for forgiveness for what I had done wrong. "Forgive me for stealing Kim's sweater and hiding it in my closet. I promise not to do it again." "God, I am sorry I lied to Mom. Please forgive me and help me to always tell the truth." I also prayed for sick and hurting people. Slowly my prayers were less about what I wanted and more about who I wanted to be.

———————

The things I learned during those youth group years created a spiritual foundation that supported me for the rest of my life. I look back on those days and wish I had the discipline to read my Bible now like I did then.

But my faith has also evolved.

In those days, I worried about how much time I spent reading the Bible, how many verses I memorized, or how many friends came to church and got saved. These days, I'm much more worried about living out what I read in the Bible than I am about memorizing it.

4

Called

In high school, I was popular, pretty, and a Jesus freak. At least that's what the other kids said. That was okay with me. The boys I went out with knew I wasn't going to drink or have sex. I kissed, but that was it. My first serious relationship happened when I was a senior. I dated the same guy, Brad, all year. But as much as we thought we loved each other, we somehow knew we were headed in different directions and would go our separate ways after graduation.

I believed I was attractive, because people continually told me I was. But despite the compliments, I often worried about my weight. I was the heaviest cheerleader on the squad, mostly because I was built like an ox—strong and solid from doing all of those chores on the farm. For a cheerleader, my sturdy build provided some advantages—I could lift the other girls—but it also made me feel I was fat.

Pastor Rich's wife didn't help matters when we ran into each other in the church bathroom one Sunday. "You are so beautiful," she said to me.

"Thank you," I said, flattered by her spontaneous compliment. Unfortunately, she kept going.

"Have you ever considered modeling?"

"No, I haven't."

"Well, I know they've just started using some plus-size models for women's clothes. Maybe there is a need for teenage plus-size models too. You should look into it!"

I smiled. I knew she meant that comment in the best way possible, but her words still stung.

———————

We lived paycheck to paycheck, and my parents were always anxious about money. It was the only thing they consistently argued about. Although I never felt like we were actually poor, from the time I was very young, I was very aware of our family's financial situation. Sometimes I even worried whether we would make it to the next check.

One month when money was especially tight, Mom and I sat at the kitchen table while I ate a snack and she balanced the checkbook. She took a deep sigh and then abruptly left the table, carrying an ashtray full of cigarette butts and an empty bottle of Pepsi to the garbage. I picked up the checkbook and flipped it open. A negative balance glared back at me.

"Mom, you're negative and it's only Tuesday. Dad doesn't get paid until Friday!"

"Don't worry," she said. "I mailed the phone company a check today, so it won't even get there until Thursday. They won't cash it until Friday. The one to the electric company will take even longer because I didn't sign it, so they'll have to send it back." Then she stood over my shoulder and pointed to another entry. "And I asked Helen not to cash this one until Saturday."

I didn't know it at the time, but she was teaching me how to stretch money across time and debts. It was a skill I would later have many opportunities to perfect on my own.

"I'll get your dad's check to the bank first thing Friday," she said, "before those payments even hit the account." Somehow she always made it work. We never ran out of money for food, cigarettes, or Pepsi.

———————

Kim started looking at colleges her senior year, and the topic of money came up even more frequently. Kim had worked since she was sixteen and had saved some money, but it wasn't nearly enough to pay for college. And Mom and Dad weren't in a position to do it for her.

"We're doing the best we can," Mom said. "We can't do any more."

"We could take out student loans," Kim suggested.

"We couldn't afford to pay them back. Your dad works hard just to make ends meet."

We made too much money to get grants or need-based scholarships, but we didn't make enough to take on more loans. Yet somehow Mom and Dad managed to pull together enough money for Kim's tuition. However, it couldn't have been easy for Kim; there were always additional expenses she couldn't afford.

Those conversations about money led me to my own decision about college. Kim was the smart one, after all, and if she could barely make it happen financially, there was no hope for me. I needed a different plan.

Kids in my Midwest town didn't go around dreaming big dreams. A few of my friends wanted to go to college, but just as many hoped to get hired at John Deere and make enough money to raise a family. Our parents didn't tell us we could be anybody or do anything we wanted. They were practical people and encouraged us to seek practical careers.

For me, that meant the United States Marine Corps. I'd dreamed of serving our country every time I heard my dad talk about his service. I wanted the same respect my father had enjoyed. While others struggled with what they were going to do, my mind was made up.

I was going to be a marine.

The summer before my senior year, I met with a marine recruiter.

"Why are you interested in the marines?" he asked.

"Because if I wear the uniform and serve my country, I know people will respect me."

"But you could get that from any branch of the service. Why are you interested in the marines?" he asked again, his pen poised over the paperwork on his desk.

"Because the marines demand more than the other branches. I want a challenge so that when I succeed, I will have succeeded at the hardest thing

I could do." To do something not everyone else could or would do was important to me. The fact that there were very few women in the marines made joining even more appealing.

The recruiter took notes as we talked. "What kind of job would you like to have in the marines?"

"I want to be a drill instructor."

"Okay."

I didn't know a drill instructor wasn't a job you could request. Drill instructors were selected. Chosen. The recruiter didn't clear up my mistake. He just scribbled more notes on his pad. Then he told me I was eligible for their delayed-entry program, which meant I could sign up immediately but then go back to finish high school. The following June, after I graduated, I'd be off to boot camp.

I was in.

Since I was only seventeen, however, I needed my parents' signatures before I could actually enlist. Dad had gone into the marines right out of high school, so I knew he'd approve. But I wasn't sure about Mom. She had never liked for Dad to talk about his marine days, and I wasn't sure she wanted her daughter to follow in his footsteps. She was glad someone protected the country; she just didn't want it to be her daughter.

A few weeks later the recruiter sat at our kitchen table, looking impressive in his greens. As he spoke, he flipped through the papers he'd brought with him. Dad's grin made it clear he approved, but Mom didn't look so sure. She told me later what she was thinking. *There's no way she'll go through with this.*

But my mind was made up. I was so excited I could hardly sit still. All I could think was, *Hurry up and get to the part where I sign!* When the recruiter finished his pitch and all the questions had been answered, it was my turn.

"Will you give me permission to enlist?" I asked my parents.

"Are you sure, Brenda?" Mom couldn't hide her concern. "Are you sure this is what you want to do?"

"Yes, I'm absolutely sure. I believe this is what God wants me to do."

"Sweetheart, are you sure? Are you really sure?"

"Yes, Mom, I'm sure."

Finally she picked up the pen, and I watched as she slowly and deliberately wrote her distinctive *y* on the end of both her first and last names. I didn't think she'd ever finish writing "Jenny Jo Carney." Then she carefully laid the pen down and didn't say another word.

"I'm proud of you, Brenda," Dad said as he picked up the pen and quickly signed. "You're going to make a great marine." I could tell he wanted to say more, but a glance from Mom quieted him.

I was the last one to sign. Mom may have been scared for me to become a marine, but I had no doubts. I would be following in my dad's footsteps, serving my country, and I wouldn't have to take money from my parents. All that made me very proud.

During my senior year, Mom and Dad bought their first house. With Kim's tuition, the down payment on the house, and all of the additional home owner's expenses, money got even tighter. They argued more frequently and intensely. Kim came home less. The money problems confirmed that enlisting was the right decision for me. Now I had a plan for my life, and I was able to sit back and enjoy my senior year.

When friends asked what college I was going to, I'd proudly say, "The marines." A few people teased me, but I let it go. Mostly, I got the reaction I wanted—respect.

"You're so strong, Brenda."

"I could never do that."

"I admire you."

I was certain that being a marine was part of God's plan for my life. Fortunately, it matched up well with my plan. After enlisting, I would find and marry a cute marine, and together we'd serve our country. We would raise a tight-knit family, eat dinner together every night, and upon retirement, move back to be near family. Maybe we'd even buy a horse. It was a respectable plan, and it felt good to have a solid life calling.

In the spring of my senior year, I attended a National Cheerleaders Association camp with five hundred other girls. Mom, Kim, and my grandmother

Chach came to watch the final performance. Afterward, the officials gave out awards to the outstanding cheerleaders. The top award was for "All-American Cheerleader."

While they called names over the speaker, I stood on the field, daydreaming about my future in the marines and how far I'd come. I'd never been captain of the cheerleaders, but I had stood strong and steadfast at the base of our pyramids. I should have been proud of the applause for our final performance, but my dreams weren't about becoming a college cheerleader. I was headed to the marines.

"Brenda Carney."

I looked up, startled. "Did they just call my name?" I asked Laurel, the girl next to me.

"Yes! You won—go on up there." She pointed to the makeshift platform in the center of the field.

In disbelief, I walked toward the microphone. I didn't hear people clapping or my family screaming. As the official placed the gold medal around my neck, she told the crowd that I'd been named All-American Cheerleader. All I could think was, *You have to be kidding? Me? Really? I'm better than everyone else here?*

That would have been the ideal time to pull out the Miss America wave or show off the model walk I'd perfected as a girl. It was the moment my attention-craving personality had always dreamed about. But now it didn't seem to matter. In two weeks I would be leaving for the marines. And I was smart enough to know that when I was facedown in the dirt with a boot on my back, the drill instructor wouldn't care that I was Iowa's best cheerleader.

———————

Mom couldn't stop her tears. "You're going to be so far away."

Dad didn't cry. Instead he just hugged me tighter. The more he tried not to cry, the tighter he hugged. I could feel his big, strong hands on my back, squeezing the breath out of me as he struggled to keep his emotions in check.

"I'll be back to visit. It's not like I won't see you again."

Dad kissed me and then let go.

Kim stood next to the front door, sniffling. "Are you scared?" she asked.

"Only about the plane ride." Boot camp I welcomed. But I had never flown before, and the thought of flying terrified me.

"Lynn's here," Kim said as our friend's car pulled into the driveway.

It was time to leave. I grabbed the suitcase Mom and Dad had given me as a graduation gift and kissed them both again. Kim and Lynn drove me to Des Moines to catch my flight. When they dropped me off, they were both crying their heads off. But there were no tears from me.

"Good-bye, Hard-Hearted Hannah," Kim teased, using the nickname I'd gotten because I almost never cried. Why should I cry now? I was an eighteen-year-old girl whose life was just beginning.

5

Orders

"Get off my bus! I said get off *now*!"

Apparently, we didn't move fast enough.

"Faster, faster! Get off my bus! Go, go, go!"

More drill instructors joined that first one, and they all yelled in our faces. "Get your crap and get out of here!"

It was around two in the morning. Most of us were disoriented from the flight to Charleston, South Carolina, and the two-hour bus ride over the causeway to Parris Island.

"Get on my yellow footprints!"

As we got off the bus, they took our bags and herded us to a sidewalk where row after row of yellow-painted footprints awaited.

"Are you going to cry?" a drill instructor asked one of the recruits. "Do you want your mommy?"

"Ma'am, no ma'am!" the recruit said as the DI continued to yell in her face. There was a lot of yelling, and the drill instructors were so close their spit hit our faces. We were supposed to keep our heads up and our eyes straight ahead, but I couldn't help watching the DIs in action. I wanted to see more of what I wanted to do for the rest of my life. I believed that one day soon I'd be the one doing the yelling.

"Now, move!" The recruits in front of me hustled to line up behind a table, and I followed. The DIs yelled instructions to move from one line to the next—one line to turn in our papers, another line to pick up our fatigues, yet another for equipment. There was even a separate line to get socks. We were yelled at if we didn't move fast enough—we never did—and we were yelled at while we stood quietly in line. The yelling was loud, and the DIs seemed mean.

When the initial processing was finished, the DIs led us to the barracks—our new home—and lined up all sixty-two recruits in the open squad bay next to their bunks, which they called *racks*. We had to stand there until the DIs finally gave us permission to sleep.

Private Brenda Carney reporting for duty, August 1985

I was scared to death as I got into bed. The DIs patrolled the barracks, screaming at anyone who committed the slightest infraction. We couldn't talk or roll over. If a recruit turned or made any noise as she tried to get comfortable, three DIs would descend on her rack and make her an example to the rest of the squad. I didn't want to get yelled at and vowed to do whatever it took to make sure I didn't. I knew the only way I could survive was to be the perfect recruit.

But it was hard to be perfect. As I lay on the bottom bunk, I looked up at the mattress imprint of the person above me. Private Sarah Mosley. *Who is she? Is she going to be cool? Will we be friends?* I heard a DI approach, and before I could stop myself, I glanced in her direction. Though I quickly closed my eyes, hoping she wouldn't see, she caught me looking, and the verbal onslaught began.

As I listened to her scream at me, I realized that no matter what I did, a DI would always find something to yell about. Though I was already physically strong, I would need to learn to be mentally tough to make it through boot camp. The mental toughness I eventually developed and the ability to tune out the angry voices around me would serve me well for the rest of my life.

At four thirty in the morning, we woke to the sound of banging metal trash-can lids. We couldn't have slept more than an hour or two. It was our first day, and we had no idea of the right way to get up or line up.

"You're an idiot!"

"You're the worst group of recruits I've ever seen!"

"You don't look right! You don't even breathe right!"

I was still scared, and I was definitely sleep deprived, but I was excited too. Those DIs could yell all they wanted, but this was my first day as a marine. I was just glad to finally be there.

———

The marines had strict weight limits for their new recruits. If you were my height of five foot two, you couldn't weigh more than 130 pounds. I was typically around 128 pounds, so I knew I was at risk. Although a lot of my weight was muscle, no one cared about that at boot camp.

On that first morning, each recruit stepped onto the scale, and the DI announced her weight to the whole platoon. Those who could physically handle the workouts and were near the weight limit were told they were a "fat private," and that label came with consequences, like food deprivation and humiliation from the DIs.

I stepped on the scale, and the DI announced my weight and my status. "One thirty. Fat private."

I had thought that after cheerleading I wouldn't face any more weight issues, but I faced them every day in boot camp. To be called fat was humiliating, and I was never allowed to eat in peace. The DIs yelled at me through the chow line and while I ate.

"Hurry up! You don't need to eat all that!"

"No desserts! Don't even look. You'll get fat from looking."

"You're done. Now, get out!"

I didn't enjoy a single meal at boot camp.

———

In those first days, they taught us how to make up our racks, making sure the sheets and blankets were tucked under the mattress at forty-five-degree angles and the pillow was always centered on the bed. We learned how to polish our boots, iron our uniforms, and wear both properly. Attention to the smallest details was emphasized in everything we did because in a war situation, details mattered. In the marines, it was all about discipline and unity. There were no individuals. We were a team, and we had to look and act like it.

Fortunately, other than weight issues, I was a good recruit and I knew it. I paid attention to the details, and I got along with my team. But that wasn't good enough for me. I wanted to be the best.

No matter how hard I tried, however, I always seemed to finish behind "The Blonde"—Private Holcum. I thought of her as "The Blonde" because I always stood directly behind her and stared at the back of her head.) She came in first in the running test. I came in second. She was chosen as the flag bearer. I was chosen as the line leader, which was second only to the flag bearer. But The Blonde's successes didn't stop me from trying. I was willing to do whatever it took to excel.

For example, I entered boot camp with shoulder-length hair, but I soon realized my hair got me unwanted attention when I couldn't get it pinned correctly; I solved the problem by cutting it.

Again, whatever it took.

It wasn't hard to figure out which drill instructors liked me and which ones didn't. But in my mind Sergeant Easley was in a category by herself. She was a mean little thing—just what I'd imagined a drill instructor would be like. Which made me think, *I like her. I like her a lot.* But that didn't mean I always liked what she did.

My platoon mates and I were the first women to drill with M16A2 assault rifles, so every time we marched on the parade deck, a crowd showed up to observe. Commanding officers, media, and other bigwigs came to observe how we handled holding the rifles and walking in formation at the same time. Everything we did involving rifles was heavily scrutinized; however, we felt it was an honor to show what female marines could do.

Every night two recruits were required to stay up and walk the barracks while the other recruits slept. Their job was to make sure everyone was in bed and all rifles were securely padlocked to the end of their racks. At the end of the shift, the recruits on duty would report to the DI.

At the end of my first time on duty, I reported to Sergeant Easley.

"Ma'am, Private Carney reporting. Sixty-two recruits properly secured to their racks, ma'am," I said.

"Say it again," said Sergeant Easley.

"Ma'am, Private Carney reporting. Sixty-two recruits properly secured to their racks, ma'am," I repeated.

"Say it again!" Now Sergeant Easley was yelling in my face. I knew something was wrong, but for the life of me I couldn't figure out what. So I repeated myself again, this time saying it as loudly as I could.

"Turn around! Turn around!" She was going nuts, yelling and pointing at the racks. "What do you see?"

I turned and looked, but I had no idea what she was referring to. I glanced at the padlocks, thinking perhaps one was undone, but they were all locked. Everything was secured. *What is her problem?*

"Look at me," she said, her beady little eyes glaring at me. "Now look at your platoon. Are they secure?"

I finally got it. "Ma'am, Private Carney reporting. Sixty-two *M16A2 assault rifles* properly secured to their racks, ma'am."

It was one of the few times I was called out for doing something wrong. Sergeant Easley had made me feel like a complete idiot, and I swore I'd never let that happen again.

We spent most of those first few weeks of boot camp in the classroom. We learned the Uniform Code of Military Justice, studied military history and customs, and discussed Marine Corps values. We also practiced first-aid techniques that could one day save our lives and became proficient in hand-to-hand combat skills. I loved it all.

The next few weeks involved more physical work. We practiced water survival and had to pass a water test. We learned marksmanship skills and had to demonstrate competence with a rifle. Every day we did some type of physical conditioning, taking regular physical fitness tests to check on our progress. I worked hard and did well.

In addition to the physical work, I found that I was also good at the social and psychological parts of boot camp. I respected DIs, but they didn't intimidate me, and I could be counted on to encourage other members of the platoon who struggled. Several DIs noticed I was a team player, and this led to more opportunities.

Every night before we went to bed, for instance, the DIs allowed ten minutes for prayer, and I was often selected to lead the prayer. I was also picked to read Scripture on Sundays and lead in singing the Lord's Prayer, although I wasn't really a singer. Those things confirmed to me that I was in the right place. God had me there for a reason. I was eighteen years old and doing what I was called to do. I couldn't have imagined a better life.

———

After nine weeks at boot camp, we faced our final test. To succeed, we would have to utilize everything we'd learned. I was nervous about the test, not because I hadn't done well at boot camp, but because if I didn't pass, at the very best I would have to do the whole nine weeks over. At worst—well, I didn't want to think about the worst. I didn't have a plan B.

Carrying seventy-pound packs on our backs, we began the test with a hump—a forced march—that lasted so long I thought we must be marching in circles. *It's not possible to march this far on an island!*

When we finally arrived at our destination, an abandoned airstrip, we had to set up our hootches—tentlike structures that were different from any tent I'd ever seen in Girl Scouts or church camp. It was slow going. Each recruit and her partner needed to finish before sundown, but it wasn't easy. Recruits swore and yelled at each other as they tried to drive the tent stakes into the ground. But we all got it done.

For the next three days, we split off in groups to learn how to throw a grenade, handle specialized weapons, and practice navigation. The DIs limited our sleep, and our food was limited to a couple of packaged MREs (Meals, Ready to Eat) a day.

On the last night, my bunkmate, Sarah Mosley, and I were in our hootch, listening to the DIs moving around the camp. I had succeeded at all the challenges they'd thrown at me so far, and my confidence was riding high. I was serious about becoming the best marine I could be, but I also liked to have some fun. I was in a silly mood (probably punchy from sleep deprivation), and I decided to try and get Sarah to laugh. She had a distinctive laugh that she only used when she was trying not to, so I thought it would be fun to make her try not to laugh.

When I heard Sergeant Easley pass by us, I imitated something Easley often said. It had the desired effect. I could hear Sarah trying not to laugh: "Hm-mmm-hmm-mm-mm." But she couldn't keep it in. Even with her hand over her mouth, I still felt her body shaking with laughter.

Well, that made me giggle. The more Sarah tried not to laugh, the less I could contain my own laughter, which of course caused her to laugh harder.

"They're going to kill us," I said, trying to stifle my giggles.

She couldn't hold it in any longer and laughed uncontrollably. "I'm going to pee my pants," she said.

At that point, we both lost it. It was horrible. And knowing the DIs were about to nail us made it worse.

They were on us before we could stop ourselves. They tore the tent stakes out, and our hootch immediately fell on top of us. We struggled under the weight of the fabric, but the thought of them seeing our tangled arms and legs poking out from the collapsed tent only made us laugh harder.

"Get out of my hootch!" one of the DIs yelled. That caused a fresh outburst of laughter from both of us. Though we had learned early in boot camp that nothing was considered ours—it was all theirs—occasionally their use of a pronoun was ridiculously funny.

They made us run circles and do push-ups. But it didn't help. We couldn't stop laughing. DIs know that enough physical punishment will eventually cure even the worst case of the giggles, and these DIs did everything they could legally do to make sure we were completely healed before they let us go back to bed. But I caught them laughing, too, when they thought we weren't looking.

After hours of physical punishment, they finally allowed us to climb back into our collapsed hootch and go to sleep. We attempted to raise it the best we could, but we were so tired we just slept in the partially collapsed hootch. I tried to get comfortable, but every muscle ached. Nothing was funny by then, and I doubted anything would ever be funny again. Lying there, I thought of my first night at boot camp, when I had gotten yelled at for eyeing a drill instructor. I'd come a long way since then, but I hadn't made it yet. I needed to get refocused for the next day's challenges.

For our last test, we were given a compass and five sets of latitude and longitude checkpoints. We were supposed to check in at each spot, and the last one would lead us out of the woods. Physically tired and mentally exhausted from the previous night, I got completely lost. No matter which direction I went, nothing looked like it was supposed to. All the trees looked the same. All the paths looked the same. I had no idea where I was or how to get back. I was disoriented, hungry, and terrified. I tried to breathe deeply and not panic.

Finally I stopped and did the only thing I knew to do. I prayed. *Oh God, please show me how to get back. I am so lost, and I have no idea what to do or where to go.*

I walked on. And finally, after twenty more minutes of wandering, I heard someone in the distance. I followed the sound of footsteps through the grass and eventually followed another recruit out of the woods. I had completed the exercise, and no one even knew I had been lost.

I'd done it—with a little help. I had passed the test, and I would now be a marine.

I graduated second in my company.

Right behind the very blonde Private Holcum.

One day, I was called along with four other recruits to stand before a commanding officer. I knew they would be handing out our MOS (Military Occupational Specialties) code—four-digit designators that would essentially determine our jobs and our future in the marines—I still hoped to spend that future as a drill instructor.

"You are here because each of you tested very high."

"Ma'am, yes ma'am," I said with the others. But I was thinking, *Me? I never tested high on anything!*

"We'd like for you to consider . . ."

There was no considering about it. Whatever she said next was a done deal. It wasn't a consideration. It was an order.

" . . . Marine Corps Intelligence."

"Ma'am, yes ma'am."

"You're dismissed."

As they took us away for more testing, I complained to my DI, "I wanted to be a drill instructor, not work in intelligence." That's when she explained that the only way that could happen was for me to do my assigned job so well that I was selected to be a DI. On average, it took three years for that to happen.

Fine. I'd make intelligence work.

Only problem was, I had no idea what intelligence entailed.

Over the next few days, I asked a lot of questions, and the responses I got back sounded exciting. I learned that intelligence was basically spy work—espionage, capturing enemy secrets. I still didn't know specifically what that meant, but it sounded important. I learned they had investigated my past to see if there was anything an enemy could use to blackmail me, but my years of trying to be the perfect little Christian had paid off, and they hadn't been able to find anything. I also learned I could be stationed overseas. No one had told me that before.

I graduated boot camp and had two weeks' leave at home before reporting to intelligence school in Pensacola, Florida. I spent those weeks telling friends and family that I was going to be a spy.

What an exciting life I was going to have in the Marines Corps. Though I hadn't yet gotten the job I wanted, what I did have was more than I'd ever dreamed of.

The call of duty that I had dreamed about for so many years was finally real.

6

Close Quarters

We marines were not the only servicemen and -women assigned to the Navy Technical Training Center Corry Station in Pensacola. The army, navy, air force, and coast guard also did courses there. But as we quickly learned, the facilities were not exactly equal.

The "haves" were the air force. They slept only one person per room and had cable television. The "have-nots" were the marines. We slept four to a room. But we didn't complain. We thought these conditions made us stronger and bonded us closer together. Looking back, I believe we were right.

At the intelligence school, our day started at six in the morning, when we got up and went running as a unit. We were only as fast as our slowest person; no one was left behind. We stayed together during the day as well, going to classes and eating together, and we hung out together in the evenings. We even bonded over chores. We helped each other and had each other's backs. I was beginning to experience the marine camaraderie Dad had told me about, and I liked it a lot.

But my eye was on the prize. I wanted to be the best marine I could so one day I could be a drill instructor. I looked for role models to show me the way, and I quickly found one.

A really good-looking one.

Neil Meoni was a squad leader and one of the most disciplined marines I'd ever met. He reminded me of my dad because he looked so good in a uniform. He was muscular, with a strong jawline and deep-brown Italian eyes. You couldn't help but notice him when he walked into a room.

Though his unit was only a few weeks ahead of mine, Neil had already earned the respect of everyone in the unit. He always had an entourage of people hanging around him, and I liked the way they listened when he spoke. Even those who were older or bigger did what he asked. As the leader of the pack, he just oozed power. And I wanted some of that.

"What do you know about him?" I asked a friend.

"I know he gets three hundreds on his PFTs," she said. "He's the best marine in the whole unit."

Three hundred was the highest score a marine could get on his physical fitness test.

"And he keeps staring at you," she added. "He watches you all the time."

I blushed. I was amazed that he even noticed me. But as I'd told my mother all those years before, I knew he'd stare longer if I pretended not to notice.

Although we were really just eighteen-year-old kids, we thought we were adults. We were suddenly on our own, without our parents looking over our shoulders. And for most of us, it was the first time we'd had money. It had taken only a few weeks for people to start pairing off, having sex, and getting serious about staying together as a couple.

I was still a virgin, and I planned to keep it that way. But I was also enamored with Neil's physical beauty and his charisma. We'd been watching each other for a while before he finally approached me.

After a little chitchat about our jobs, he asked, "So, do you want to work on Morse code together?" Only a marine would use that as a pickup line.

I didn't know what to say. Morse code was specialized training that the really smart people in the highest levels of Marine Corps intelligence were working on. Which meant . . . I wasn't. "Uh, I'm not doing Morse code, but you can sit here." I moved my books and papers out of the way.

As weeks went on, we started hanging out and then going out. We would begin the evening in a group, but then we'd find time to get away by ourselves and take long walks on the beach, hold hands, and kiss. Soon we were spending almost all our time together. I fell in love with him, and he fell in love with me.

For an Iowa farm girl, nothing could have been more romantic than to fall in love with her marine while in school at the beach. It looked as if my dream of becoming a marine, then marrying a marine and raising a family together, was going to happen just as I had planned.

Neil's schooling ended several weeks before mine, and he got orders to go to Guantánamo Bay, Cuba. That presented us with a dilemma.

During our nine weeks in Pensacola, we'd watched several couples get married to increase their chances of being stationed together. But we weren't ready for that. We knew we wanted to be together, but we hadn't known each other long enough for marriage. So we came up with a different strategy.

"When you fill out your paperwork, you can request three places you'd like to go," said Neil. "Just put Cuba for all three."

"That's a great idea," I said. "Who else would want Cuba?"

So that was my plan. I would follow my marine to Cuba. Then eventually we'd marry and live the life I had planned—the life I was sure God had called me to.

When I kissed him good-bye, I believed it would be only a matter of weeks before I would see him again in Guantánamo Bay.

It didn't quite work out that way.

I stared at the papers in my hand. Okinawa, Japan.

How had this happened? Japan sounded exotic, but I'd never heard of Okinawa. I was supposed to be going to Cuba. I looked at a map and found that the dot representing Okinawa was actually larger than the land underneath it. I was going to an island.

I went home on leave to celebrate Christmas with my family, and I gave them the news.

"That's so far from Iowa," Mom said with a look of concern.

"Yes, it is," I said. *Even farther from Cuba.*

I was eighteen years old and had barely traveled out of the Midwest. Now I was on my way to a foreign country. I would have been scared to death, but marines don't get scared.

I rang in the New Year with my family. Then, when 1986 was only a few days old, I left for Japan.

———————

When I arrived in Japan, a marine was waiting for me. He took me to the barracks. I was assigned to a large squad bay similar to the one in Parris Island, only this one had partitions that separated the space into tiny rooms. Sixty-three people slept in this large space segmented only by cardboard dividers that didn't touch the floor or ceiling. I shared my itty-bitty "room" with the only other female marine who worked in intelligence. We were in the same office together with a bunch of guys.

From the first day, the assignment was fun. I got a lot of attention because I was new and I was female—and I still liked attention. My relationship with Neil took a lot of social pressure off me. I already had a boyfriend, and the guys respected that, so I was able to make friends without the expectation of more. Some of the guys at the office had actually met Neil because they'd also been to school with him in Pensacola. It was amazing to see the impression he had made on people even though we were a world apart.

Telephone calls were expensive, so Neil and I wrote a lot of letters back and forth. I'd tell him what I was doing in my job, and he'd tell me about Cuba. He always wrote about how much he missed me and loved me. We were in love, and we planned to have a future together.

But even though I missed Neil a lot, I loved Okinawa. The weather was warm and sunny. Over the next few months, I learned to scuba dive and spent most of my free time diving. I bought a car from a marine who had to move because he'd been stationed elsewhere, and I learned how to drive on the "wrong" side of the road.

Work was easy, and I had a lot of free time. Occasionally we would have drills to keep us ready in case someone infiltrated our base or got their hands on information they shouldn't have. If that happened, everyone on base would have to report for duty to destroy documents. So from time to time, without warning, an alarm would sound and we were all expected to show up to practice those procedures.

I was good at my job and got promoted to lance corporal. To me, the promotion offered further evidence that I was born to be a marine. As my pay increased, I was even able to send home money to help out my parents financially. I loved being able to do that. Not only was I a marine, but I also felt like the perfect daughter. Never again would I take from them. I would only give.

One afternoon in early May, I picked up my mail before heading back to my room. Flipping through it, I found a letter from Neil. That wasn't unexpected; we'd continued to write and profess our love since I had arrived in January. I flopped down on my bed, not bothering to take off my boots, and opened the envelope.

> . . . There is no way we can have a long-distance relationship while you are in Japan and I'm in Cuba. We need to take a break. I want to see if we're really meant for each other. Let's just take a break and see if we belong together. I haven't met anyone else . . .

It was hard to make sense of what I was reading. What did he mean, take a break? What were we going to take a break *from*? Writing letters? I dropped the letter on the bed and stared at the ceiling in disbelief. I didn't need to read any further. I assumed it was obvious that he had met someone else.

I didn't cry, but I kind of wanted to. I lay on the bed, thinking about what had just happened. There had been no warning. Sure, it was hard to carry on a long-distance relationship, but it had only been four months, and we'd never even discussed the possibility of breaking things off. I lay there trying to keep the tears away and wondering who the other woman was. But finally I told myself it was his loss. A lot of guys in Okinawa would be happy to know Neil and I had broken up. I sat up, threw the letter in the trash, and decided I wouldn't look back.

Ever since I arrived in Okinawa, I'd known that a guy named Otis had the hots for me. It didn't take long for him to find out I was single and to ask me out. We started dating in May, so we'd been going together for a month by the time my nineteenth birthday rolled around in June.

In Okinawa, practically everyone was having casual sex. Hookups happened all the time among members of the military community. Everybody seemed to be doing it and having a blast doing it. But not me.

My faith was important to me. I went to church regularly, even when no one else went with me. But I was also a grown woman and a marine. I had completed a rigorous course of training in an elite corps, and I had the ego to match. As for my faith, I believed the decision I made in the church all those years ago had secured my eternal salvation. I also believed that if I confessed, God would forgive my sins. I decided it was time to lose my virginity, and I chose my nineteenth birthday to do it. I would ask God for forgiveness afterward.

And yes, there were some huge flaws in my thinking. But at the time, I thought it all made complete sense. I was about to turn nineteen, living on an island far away, and no one back in the States would ever know what happened. I decided it was my time.

On my birthday, Otis took me out to dinner, and then we went to a little local hotel so we'd have plenty of privacy. When we got into the room, I undressed and quickly crawled under the sheets. Otis took off his shirt and then unzipped his pants.

I couldn't help but be nervous. Other than in health class, I'd never even seen a picture of a naked man.

"I'm not a virgin. I've done this before," he said, nuzzling my neck. "I'll be gentle."

I don't remember the act itself, but I remember thinking afterward, *This is what everyone is talking about? This?*

Then a sudden and persistent knock on the door destroyed what little mood had been created. I crawled as far under the covers as I possibly could while still peeking out from under them. Otis got up and cracked open the door.

Standing outside the door was the little Japanese couple who ran the hotel. They motioned wildly and said something I couldn't understand. "Two ta foe! Two ta foe!"

Finally, Otis figured it out. "Telephone."

"How could it be for us? Who would know we're here?" I asked, my head still beneath the sheets.

"Stay here. I'll find out." Otis threw on his pants and ran down the stairs. It was only seconds before he returned.

"We've gotta go!" Otis said as he picked up his shirt and put it on. "There's an alarm on base!"

"Are you kidding me?"

Apparently Otis had let a buddy know where we were going in case of an emergency—and one of our drills qualified as an emergency. No matter what we were doing, we were expected to drop everything and rush to our posts.

I was mortified! This was as bad as our parents walking in on us. I just knew the whole unit would know what we'd been doing.

When we arrived at the office, everyone was busy destroying records, so no one talked. I hoped they wouldn't notice—but no such luck. As soon as the drill was over, they peppered us with questions.

"Where were you guys?"

"What took you guys so long?"

"What were you guys doing?"

And I just kept thinking, *I had sex for this?*

Otis and I continued to date, but it was a long time before we ever had sex again. I waited until our relationship was more serious, but even then I didn't really enjoy it. I just did it because I thought it was expected.

Sex, I figured, just wasn't supposed to be so great after all.

A few months later, Otis got transferred out of Okinawa. We broke up before he left.

7

A Blast from the Past

I didn't even have to read the return address. As soon as I saw the handwriting, I knew who it was from. Fingering the envelope, I felt flattered by the lengths Neil Meoni must have gone to in order to track me down. I hadn't heard from him since the breakup letter he'd sent me when I lived in Japan, and I'd moved three times since then.

I'd been living in New Orleans for almost nine months, enjoying my apartment, the camaraderie at the base, and life in general. My life was simple and stable. I didn't think I needed anything else.

But when I thought about the handsome marine I'd last seen on the beach in Florida, though I didn't want it to, my heart skipped a beat. I couldn't help thinking, *What could this mean?*

I'd saved some money while I was abroad, and when I got back to the States, Dad helped me find a truck to buy. It was a red Chevy half-ton pickup with a roll bar and lights. Smiley-face light covers finished the look. Nothing could have better represented my personality—tough, with a little flash.

I'd lived in base housing my first few weeks in New Orleans but later moved into an apartment with a girlfriend. I'd settled into a routine working an eight-hour shift on base. After work, I taught aerobics classes. This not only kept me in shape but also brought in extra money, and I was very

money-motivated at that time. I quickly paid off my truck and kept sending money home to Mom and Dad. I found a church and attended Sunday
worship regularly. For fun, I hung out with the other members of my platoon. I didn't have a boyfriend, but I didn't feel like I needed one.

When my roommate received new orders and moved out, the manager of the apartment complex asked if I wanted to teach aerobics at the
apartment complex in exchange for my rent. I was in. I'd never had such
financial freedom. I didn't think life could get any better.

But I also loved challenges, and I was ready for a new one. Once again
I started investigating my dream—becoming a drill instructor. While I
waited to hear back about that, I got the letter from Neil.

I tore open the envelope. I couldn't believe he had found me!

> Brenda,
>
> I hope this letter finds you well. I wanted you to know that I have
> never stopped thinking about you. I started dating a girl who looks like
> you and acts like you, and I am finding that I am very confused about
> her. Do I like her for who she is, or do I like her because she reminds me
> of you? I am currently living in Boulder, Colorado, and taking classes at
> the University of Denver. I would love to see you and just find out if what
> we had was real . . .

A rush of emotions ran through me when I read that. My cheeks grew
warm. I had done nothing to search for Neil. Then, out of the blue, he had
sent me a letter. Could it be God's plan to bring us back together? I was
flattered that he still thought of me, and especially that he wanted to see
me again.

I called him in Colorado, and his voice stirred up a flood of memories.
The whole situation seemed so romantic. We had met and fallen in love at
the beach. Though duty and distance had separated us, now we'd found
each other again. Only God could have made that happen, I thought.

We made plans for him to visit.

When Neil walked through the Jetway door that Friday, I ran straight into his arms.

"I missed you so much," he said, burying his face in my hair.

"I missed you more," I whispered. Until I saw those familiar brown eyes, I hadn't even realized how lonely I was.

We couldn't keep our hands off of each other as we left the airport and drove back to my apartment. Once inside, we made love for the first time.

It finally felt right.

"The only reason I broke things off was this," Neil said, pulling his hair back to reveal a large scar.

It was Saturday morning, and we were catching up over breakfast.

"Oh my gosh," I said. "What happened?"

"I had a grand mal seizure when I was in Cuba. They had to medevac me to Virginia, where they did a brain scan and found a cavernous hemangioma. It's kind of like a benign tumor. I needed surgery, so the marines removed me from active duty. Then they gave me a medical discharge because of the seizures."

"Oh, sweetheart, I am so sorry." I couldn't believe that had happened to Neil, of all people—the squad leader everyone looked up to, the guy with perfect scores on his PFTs, the best marine in his unit. He had wrapped his entire identity around serving his country, and now he had been forced out through no fault of his own.

"When I wrote you the breakup letter, I'd already had the seizure, and I knew the Marine Corps didn't want me. I was facing brain surgery, and I didn't want you to have to go through all of that." He started to cry. "I wanted to release you from the relationship because I honestly didn't know whether I was going to live or die."

"Oh, sweetheart, that's so beautiful." I kissed his tears. "I just wish you had told me!"

"Will you ever forgive me for breaking us up?"

"There's nothing to forgive. We're back together now, aren't we?" There was nothing more to say. We knew we belonged together. Fate had made it happen.

Neil explained that he couldn't drive because he still had grand mal seizures. He also took high doses of antiseizure medication that produced some pretty serious side effects.

"I get moody sometimes, and I feel like I can't help it," said Neil.

He looked different too. I noticed that his physique was different; he'd lost weight and definition because he couldn't work out after the surgery. Acne covered his face, and his teeth had yellowed—other side effects of the medication. He could no longer wear contacts, so he wore thick glasses. Neil's new appearance would have turned off a lot of people, but it didn't bother me.

As he shared his heart, I shared his pain. I felt bad because of everything he'd been through. I just wanted to take care of him and help him get better.

Mom wasn't happy when I told her Neil had moved in with me.

"It's just for a little while, until he can get back on his feet," I told her. I truly believed God had brought us together for better or worse. Now might be the worst, but things would get better. Although we weren't married, and we hadn't talked about getting married, I was committed to Neil.

"Well, I don't think you two should live together without being married, even if you are taking care of him."

At the time, I thought she was just being a fuddy-duddy. Women's roles were changing, and it was okay for me to rescue a man. I was a professional rescuer, after all. As a marine, I lived by the motto *Semper Fidelis*—"Always Faithful." And that's what I was going to be for Neil. I would faithfully take care of him because I was the strong one.

Her parting remark was the one I couldn't respond to.

"It's not what good Christian girls do."

My life found a new normal. Each day I went to work and left my boy-friend at home on the couch. He'd have dinner waiting for me when I came home, and we'd eat together before I left to teach aerobics. Neil felt bad and he tried to do more, but there wasn't a lot he could do. One day when I complained that I was too busy to get the truck tires rotated, he offered to do it for me. I hesitated because he wasn't supposed to drive. But it *had* been a few months since his last seizure. *It'll probably be fine.*

However, while driving home from the mechanic's shop, Neil had another seizure and flipped the truck. Fortunately, it was on a road that was lined with swamps, which cushioned the impact, so he wasn't hurt. He called a tow truck and had the pickup towed to our apartment. When I got home, I found it completely covered in swamp guts. Every part was a mess, and it stank. But I was just happy Neil was all right.

Having yet another seizure took a toll on him. Neil increased his medi-cations, which increased his moodiness. He often got jealous for no reason.

One Saturday we were shopping at the mall when a friendly salesman cracked a joke and I laughed. Neil grabbed the back of my arm and pinched me—hard.

"Ow! That hurt."

"Well, quit flirting."

Other times he would accuse me of looking at men when I wasn't. When those kinds of jealous incidents occurred, I would try to convince him how much he meant to me. "Neil, I love you. I would never cheat on you."

Sometimes it helped. Most of the time it didn't.

I didn't hold the jealousy against him, though. And I was convinced that Neil was the only man for me. I was absolutely committed to him no matter what his problems were.

———

I got used to my new life with Neil, but Mom never did. Every time she called, we had a variation of the same conversation:

"You mean you're *still* living together?"

"Yes, Mom. It's just for a little bit longer until he can get out on his own."

"Well, how long will that be?"

"I don't know. He can't work yet. He still has seizures."

"He can get a job somewhere. He just needs to get out and look."

But one night in February, I was shocked when Mom's call took a very unexpected turn. I was in our bedroom, lying on top of the comforter, while Neil watched a movie in the other room. "I really love him," I said. "I think we're going to be together forever."

"Then tell him to $@*% or get off the pot." Her response startled me. I wasn't used to such frank talk from her.

"Do you know what your aunt said to me?" Mom went on. "She said, 'Jenny Jo, I can't believe a daughter of yours is living with a man without being married.'"

I could tell that conversation had bothered my mom a lot. After I got off the phone, I went in to talk to Neil.

"Are we in this relationship forever?"

"Yes," he said, kissing me. "I love you. Why?"

"Mom says we should take the next step. Do you think we should?"

"What are you saying?"

"Well, we're already living together. Why don't we just get married?"

"Okay."

There was no ring or romantic proposal. This was all about taking care of business and making sure Mom wasn't embarrassed. I needed to be a good girl in her eyes again. Marrying Neil was the best way to do that.

March 17, St. Patrick's Day, was my next day off, and Neil and I took that opportunity to drive to city hall. The justice of the peace met us in the lobby, wearing a kelly green tie. He took our fifty dollars and walked us back to his office. I wore my pale-yellow dress with buttons down the front. It was from JCPenney, and it was the nicest dress I owned.

"Do you have a witness?" the judge asked me. Neil's buddy Jeff, whom he'd met in Pensacola but who was now stationed in New Orleans, was there to be our best man. My girlfriend was late.

"She's not here yet."

"Then let me get my secretary."

The justice of the peace returned seconds later with his assistant. Neil and I repeated the vows he read from a book, everybody signed the license, and Neil and I were officially married. It was what I had always wanted—to marry a marine and live happily ever after. Well, Neil wasn't a marine anymore, but I still believed in the happily ever after.

We celebrated with dinner at T.G.I. Friday's.

———

Neil and I were happy, though his jealousy and mood swings could be hard to live with. He was particularly disturbed by the time I spent away from him. He didn't like my teaching aerobics, so I cut back on the classes. He didn't like going out with my friends from work, so I stopped hanging out with them. I didn't mind making those changes. In fact, I was flattered that Neil wanted to spend so much time with me.

After we had been married a couple of months, the obvious next step was to have a baby. I went off my birth control pills in May, and by the beginning of July, I had already missed a period. On the way home from work, I stopped by the drugstore and picked up a home pregnancy test. The results were immediately obvious.

"So, what's for dinner?" I asked Neil, cuddling next to him on the sofa. "Are we having any buns?"

"Why would we have buns with chicken?"

"Well, I just thought maybe it would be fun to have a bun in the oven."

"Brenda, are you . . . ?" But he didn't need to ask. He could see the smile on my face. "We're having a baby?"

He threw his arms around me and gave me a big hug. He was excited, and I was so happy.

———

In December, I received orders to transfer to Virginia Beach—a perfect assignment. Neil's parents lived forty miles away in Hampton, so they would be able to help with the baby.

We moved to Virginia, found an apartment near a man-made lake, and made it our home. I decorated the apartment with the kinds of country knickknacks that my mom had in her house, then set to work furnishing and wallpapering the nursery as I eagerly awaited the arrival of our first child.

When my due date approached, Mom flew into town to help. She was there when my water broke and rushed me and Neil off to the hospital. The marines hadn't offered prenatal classes, so I wasn't quite sure what to expect, but from friends I'd heard about something called an epidural. I wanted to make sure I got one, so after I got settled in my room, I asked the nurse, "When do I get my epidural?"

Her answer was quick and to the point. "You're a marine. You don't get an epidural."

Once again, it seemed, the marines were the have-nots. I wasn't terribly disappointed, mostly because I didn't really understand what an epidural was. But I did know there would be no medication and I would be having this baby the old-fashioned—and painful—way.

Mom stayed by me the whole time, doing what she could. When I was hurting, she held my hand and wiped my forehead. Neil stood across the room, watching Mom take care of me. "I don't know what the big deal is," he said. "Indians just squat behind the trees to have their babies."

If there's such a thing as good-son-in-law points, Neil didn't just lose all of his that day—he went deep into debt. After that comment, Mom didn't seem to care if he was a part of the birth or not. She was going to take care of me with or without him. And Neil let her.

On April 25, 1989, after ten hours of labor, Zachary Taylor Meoni was born. He had his father's Italian coloring, with olive skin and thick, black hair. His big, brown eyes looked like almonds, and he had dimples on both cheeks. Neil was excited. Mom was proud. And I was head over heels in love with my chunky little boy. The nurse weighed him and took his vitals. He was healthy and perfect in every way. They let me hold him for a few minutes; then they took him to the nursery.

Forty-five minutes later, they still hadn't brought my baby back, and I couldn't stand being separated from him any longer. I got up and started walking to the nursery.

A nurse tried to stop me. "No, no, no. You just gave birth. You can't get up."

"I'm fine!" I insisted, and she let me pass.

"There's a marine for ya," she muttered under her breath.

I wanted to say, "You're the one who told me I couldn't have an epidural." But I secretly liked her affirmation. I was strong. I was a marine. I'd just given birth without any pain medications. And now, at twenty-one, I was finally a mother.

Twenty-four hours after giving birth, I was released from the hospital. Mom, Neil, baby Zack, and I all went back to the apartment. I had the nursery decorated with a Kmart wallpaper border, bumper pads, and matching comforter. I'd hung a special calendar on the wall so I could record the baby's first smile, his first word, his first tooth, and so many other "firsts" I looked forward to.

Dad flew in so he could see Zack, and I'll never forget the image of my dad's big, gnarly hands holding Zack's tiny body. Mom and Dad were thrilled with their first grandchild. I had done good.

Mom and Dad went home, and Neil and I settled into a happy routine. My dreams, though a little different than I imagined, had basically come true.

That is, until the day Neil called me at work.

8

Prayer and Seizures

Zack experienced multiple seizures within his first couple of hours in the pediatric ward. Each seizure started the same way. The little pinkie finger on his right hand would shake. A nurse would notice and say, "He's starting." She would glance at her watch to note the time. About then, Zack's little face would start to twitch. The energy would build as nurses came running and took positions around his bed. It seemed like they were purposely trying to block my view of what was happening. I would pray, silently at first but then out loud, as if more noise would help God hear my desperate plea. Neil would stand behind me, crying softly and resting one hand on my shoulder or lightly rubbing my back.

At the height of each seizure, Zack's whole body convulsed. I'd catch glimpses of him between the nurses closing in around his crib. When he finished, a nurse would say, "It's done. Time?" The nurse who had been observing her watch would call out the length of the seizure so it could be recorded in his chart.

My panic intensified each time it happened. I didn't care who saw me crying or who heard me praying; I had to help Zack. After one particularly severe episode, I asked the nurse named Remi what was happening.

"His brain's misfiring, and it's causing his body to react."

"I know, but are the seizures hurting him?"

Remi paused and took a breath as if she was trying to figure out what to say. "Every time he has a seizure he could lose brain cells. If the seizure lasts too long, he could die."

"Can't you make them stop?"

"We're giving him medication to regulate them. But too much of it could be dangerous, so we have to go slow."

A million questions filled my mind. *Just how dangerous is the medicine? Is it more dangerous than the seizures? And what does "slow" mean?*

I thought about the past year with Neil on the couch, unable to drive or work because of his seizures, embarrassed when he had one even though he couldn't help it. *Is this what Zack's in for? Will he be on medication for the rest of his life too?* That was not what I'd planned for my sweet baby.

"The shorter the seizure, the better," Remi said.

I nodded. But all I could think was, *None of this sounds good.*

Between seizures, Zack just lay there making that horrible moaning sound. I sat there praying silently. Neil sat next to me, weeping. After a while, his sobbing began to get on my nerves. I wanted to say, "Step up and do something! Let's deal with this. Stop crying and start believing that God is going to heal our baby." But Neil didn't believe what I believed, and his lack of faith left him with few options. It also forced me into action. *If you're not going to be a man and take charge, then I will.*

When the next seizure started, I stood and cried out, "God, please, please, in the name of Jesus, God, heal this child!" I knew Jesus had said that with just a little faith—faith the size of a mustard seed—anything was possible. "God, please, I know you're a healer," I said, laying my hands on Zack. "Heal my baby."

If the curtain around Zack's bay was open, someone would usually close it when I prayed. But I didn't care about privacy or about being embarrassed. I only cared about God answering my prayers.

But I also wanted someone else to pray for Zack. I left Neil with Zack and found a pay phone. With shaking hands, I dialed the operator and asked to make a collect call.

As the phone rang and I thought about telling Mom, my emotions overwhelmed me. When she answered, all I could do was sob.

"Calm down, Brenda," she said. "Take a breath and tell me what's wrong."

"It's Zack. Something's wrong with Zack. We're in the hospital, and I don't know what I am going to do."

"What happened?"

She must have been shocked, because as I told her, she didn't give me the reassurance I expected. Instead, she kept talking to Dad. "Something's happened to Zack. He's in the hospital. Oh my God, Larry. Oh my God!"

"What do I do, Mom? What do I do? You've got to help me." I don't know what I expected her to do; she was a thousand miles away. But I knew I needed help.

"Oh, Brenda, sweetheart . . . what can I do to help?"

I wanted her to jump on a plane and come out, but she and Dad had just been out a few months earlier. I knew there was no money for another flight.

"You need to pray," I told her. "You need to have other people pray."

"We'll all pray, Brenda."

"I've got to get back to Zack. I'll let you know what happens."

Once Remi told me that shorter seizures were better, I started timing Zack's. Every seizure seemed to last an eternity, but if the current one was shorter than the one that preceded it, I was momentarily comforted. Timing the seizures didn't do anything to help Zack, but it gave me something to do so I felt like I was contributing.

The nurses and doctors who stopped by Zack's crib often touched the crown of his head. Sometimes I overheard them talking about it: "It's feeling a little bigger" or "It feels harder than last time."

The next time I saw Remi, I asked her why everyone was so interested in my baby's head.

"They're feeling his soft spot." She pointed to where a slight indention used to be on Zack's head. Now a lump was there. "His brain looks like it's swelling. We need to keep an eye on his soft spot because that will tell us how fast the fluid's building up." She gently touched it. "His soft spot is a little bigger now. That means the brain is swelling and pressing against his skull. In an adult, there wouldn't be room for it to swell, so we'd have to open it up in surgery. But in a baby, the skull hasn't fused completely, so there's room for the bones to expand. The soft spot gives the brain room to swell. Would you like to feel it?"

She took my fingers and guided them to the spot on Zack's head. I felt his pulse throbbing through his silky hair.

"Right now, it's okay. The soft spot's still giving him room to swell. But if the swelling continues, we may have to do something different."

"Like what?"

"Let's just wait and see what happens," Remi said. "In a few minutes we'll take him to get an MRI. We should know more when we get the results back."

———

While Zack was gone for his MRI, I ducked into the restroom. I caught a glimpse of my reflection in the mirror—wrinkled uniform, tearstained face, bags under my eyes. I looked awful, but I didn't really care. I just prayed we'd get some answers soon so Zack could get better and we could all go home.

On the way back to the pediatric ward, I grabbed a couple of snacks from the vending machine to share them with Neil. We didn't say much as we sat there waiting. There was no point. We were both thinking about Zack.

———

They rolled Zack's crib back in, and a few minutes later, a doctor appeared. Once again, he asked us what had happened, and once again, Neil answered.

"We're still not sure what's causing this," the doctor said, "but the MRI shows that his retinas have hemorrhaged, and that's usually caused by trauma."

"His retinas have hemorrhaged? What does that mean?" I knew the retina was part of the eye, but I didn't completely understand what he was saying.

"Well, at this point, he's completely blind."

"Blind? Are you sure?"

"We're still looking for answers. I'll let you know as soon as I hear something."

And then he was gone.

"Do you want to hold him?" Remi asked.

I nodded, unable to speak. Remi dragged a rocker over, then carefully placed Zack in my arms.

"Rock gently," she said.

I could feel the warmth of him in my arms and in my lap as I held him. At one point, I never thought I would feel that life again, so I appreciated the moment now. But as I looked at his closed eyes, I wondered what it all meant.

Neil sat next to me, crying again. "How could this have happened?"

I felt sorry for my husband. I knew that he, like I, had dreams for our little boy—dreams that had seemed to drain away with the doctor's words. I wanted to comfort Neil, but I was afraid to move with Zack in my arms. I didn't want to risk disturbing all the delicate tubes and wires that were still attached to him.

I called Mom to give her an update.

"They're letting me hold him for a few minutes at a time. And I can try to feed him, though he's getting most of his nutrition through an IV."

"That sounds good, Brenda. Things must be getting better."

"Yes, but . . ." I broke down and cried. I wasn't sure how to tell her.

"What is it, Brenda?" The concern in her voice was back.

I cried so hard that I couldn't speak for a few minutes. All I could think was, *What kind of a life is he going to have now?*

"Just tell me."

"He's blind. He's completely blind."

Mom let out a deep breath. "Oh, sweetheart, I am so sorry. I'm so, so sorry." I could hear the love in her voice. "But just remember, Zack may be blind, but he's still alive."

Her words took me back to Flash. I remembered how I'd been able to help my pony navigate through the fields, even though he was blind. It was the first thing that gave me hope. Although Flash's scars and blindness remained after her accident, she had still led a full and happy life while she was with me. I would make sure Zack had nothing less.

The spinal tap tests came back negative for meningitis. The MRI confirmed the swelling and the retinal hemorrhage. But the doctors still had no idea what was wrong. Between seizures, they let me get close to Zack. I would lean over his crib and caress his body, rub his little face, or kiss his cheeks. Neil would stand behind me and put one hand on my back and one hand on Zack's foot.

Neil's parents had arrived at the hospital within hours of Zack being placed into the pediatric ward. But visiting hours were limited, so they spent most of their time in the waiting room.

There wasn't a lot of privacy. Although they could pull the curtain around Zack's area, the nurses never seemed to leave us alone. At least one nurse always stood nearby, making observations or writing notes on a clipboard.

When the shift changed, each new nurse and doctor on duty would stop by to ask the same question: "What happened?"

Neil patiently retold the same story about the bath. "He just started breathing funny."

As the hours passed, I noticed that fewer nurses responded to Zack's seizures. No longer did the whole team run to his bedside. Instead just one or two nurses showed up. It slowly dawned on me that they *expected* Zack to keep having seizures.

And he did.

With each one, I prayed it would be his last.

———

Neil and I had been at the hospital for almost twenty-four hours. We hadn't slept, and we had only eaten a few things from the vending machine. The next time Mrs. Meoni came in, she tried to coax me into leaving Zack's bedside.

"You need to eat something," she said. She was a sweet woman, and I could tell she was concerned about me. But I had no intention of going anywhere.

"Why don't you take Neil?" I said. "I'll wait here, and maybe I can go when he gets back."

They were gone maybe an hour. When Neil came back, Remi was changing out one of Zack's tubes.

"Can you come with me for a minute?" he asked. "Mom and Dad want to talk with us."

"You go ahead," Remi said. "I'll be busy here for a few minutes anyway."

"Are you sure?"

She smiled kindly at me. "I'm sure, honey."

The doctors and nurses had been telling us to take breaks, but I couldn't tear myself away from Zack. I trusted Remi, however.

"We'll just be in the waiting room if you need anything," I said.

"He'll be fine," she reassured me one last time.

I followed Neil out of the pediatric ward and into a small consultation room off of the main lobby. His parents were waiting for us there. Neil's dad had been a colonel in the army, which explained why he always looked so formal—and this day was no exception. Though they'd been there for hours, Mr. Meoni wore a suit, and Mrs. Meoni was fashionably dressed in a sweater and pants. As usual, her makeup looked impeccable and her jewelry coordinated with her outfit. When I was first getting to know Neil's parents, I had always thought they were on their way out to dinner or an important meeting. But eventually I realized that was just how they always dressed. They were always very polished, but they were also kind and good people.

I sat down next to Mrs. Meoni. She grabbed my right hand in both of hers and nervously caressed the top of it with her thumbs. Neil's dad was the first to speak.

"Something's happened, and Neil needs to talk to you," Mr. Meoni said. "Let him say what he needs to say, and then we'll deal with it."

Neil sat directly in front of me with his head down. "Something happened," he said. "I was scared." He started crying once again. "I'm so sorry."

"What are you talking about?" I asked. I was thinking, *Just hurry up. We've got stuff to do, and I want to see Zack!* I was already irritated with Neil for all his useless crying. "Just say it. What's going on?"

Neil just cried harder. "I dropped him," he said through his sobs. "I accidentally dropped him."

9

Accident Investigation

Neil's words didn't make sense to me. "How could you drop him?"

"I was giving him a bath, and when I picked him up, I . . . uh . . . I accidentally dropped him. I'm sorry. I am so, so sorry."

"Why didn't you tell me?" It felt like the room was getting smaller and the air was getting harder to breathe. "Why didn't you say something?"

"I was scared. I was so scared."

"Neil, they've been trying to figure out what's wrong with Zack, and you knew." My mind raced. In addition to the breathing problems, we knew Zack had seizures, brain swelling, and retinas that had hemorrhaged, but we didn't know *why* all this was happening. Could this be the reason?

"We need to tell them," I said. "If they'd known this had happened, maybe they could've made him better by now."

Neil was sobbing so hard now that he couldn't answer.

"I still don't understand why you didn't say something."

Mr. Meoni spoke up. "Let's all calm down. We can handle this."

"You need to tell them," I told Neil, getting to my feet. I was in shock. I needed to get out of the little room before it closed in on me further.

"It's going to be okay, sweetie." Mrs. Meoni reached over to pat my arm. I barely felt her hand.

"I've got to get back to Zack, and you've got to tell them." As I made my way back to Zack's bedside, I was numb with shock. I tried to figure out what it all meant, but my brain couldn't make sense of any of it.

75

Mr. Meoni entered the pediatric ward a few moments later, and he motioned to one of the nurses. After their brief conversation, I saw a doctor and at least one nurse with a clipboard follow him back to the lobby. I looked down at Zack, lying in his crib, wearing only a diaper, still moaning. I wiped away my own tears as I thought about what my poor baby must be going through. Then I prayed out loud, "God, you need to heal this child. Please, in the name of Jesus, I beg you to heal this baby . . ."

Someone closed the curtains around the bed.

———————

Neil showed up about an hour later, his eyes red and swollen. He sat in the chair next to me. "I am so sorry. I don't know how this happened."

I reached out and put my hand on his knee. "It was an accident."

I didn't ask any more questions about how it happened. Those details wouldn't help Zack get better. But I still couldn't understand why it had taken Neil so long to say something. It had been twenty-four hours since the accident. As I listened to Zack continue to moan, I thought about all the tests he'd undergone. How many of them had been unnecessary?

They did a spinal tap. They stuck a needle in my baby's spine and removed fluid because you didn't say anything. I removed my hand from Neil's knee and put it back in my own lap.

———————

"We're going to move you to a private room." The nurse began rearranging Zack's IVs and the cords that were plugged into the wall.

The private rooms were located near the entrance to the ward. They were surrounded by glass, so everyone in the ward had a full view unless the curtain was pulled. But the walls and door still provided more privacy than the thin curtains that separated the bays in the ward. I was grateful for the change but a little worried about what it might mean. Was Zack getting worse?

We'd been in the new room less than an hour when two women we'd never seen before walked in. Each wore a cardigan over a high-necked blouse. The short one reminded me of a librarian, and the tall one looked like the schoolteacher from *Little House on the Prairie*.

"We're from Child Protective Services, and we need to ask you some questions," said the librarian-looking one.

I tried to make eye contact with them, but their professional look and demeanor intimidated me. I stood over Zack, rubbing his foot, and Neil sat in the chair next to the bed. "Okay, shoot," I said. If it would help Zack, I'd answer anything.

"We can resolve this faster if we ask you questions separately." The tall woman motioned toward the door. "Mr. Meoni, would you mind coming with me?"

Neil looked at me, and I shrugged. He got up and left with her, and the librarian-looking woman sat down in his chair and put on her reading glasses. I remained next to Zack's bed, my eyes on him while I slowly caressed his arm.

"Will you please come sit down?" she said.

I was more worried about Zack than anything she had to say, but I was twenty-two and she was the authority, so I did as I was told and sat in the rocker next to his bed.

"Tell me what happened yesterday morning when you got up."

That seemed like a ridiculous question, and I couldn't see what it had to do with Zack, but I answered. She quickly followed up with more inquiries—lots of them. "How long were you at work? . . . What time did Neil call you at work? . . . What did he say? . . . When you got home, what did Zack look like? . . . What did Neil do? . . . Where was he in the room? . . . Where was Zack? . . . What position was he in? . . . Was there anything in the room that was out of place?"

I rocked in the chair—that's what mothers do even when they're not holding their babies—and answered each question, but I didn't really understand why she asked them. I thought, *Maybe knowing what happened will help them know what's wrong with Zack.* But I was in a hurry to finish so I could get back to Zack.

She could sense my impatience. More than once, she said, "I know this is hard, but it's very important. We just need to get through this."

At one point she asked, "Do you remember seeing any bruises on Zack's body?"

"No."

"The intake nurse reported that your son came in with small bruises on his face by his right ear."

I stood up and looked at Zack, lying in his metal crib. "I don't see anything."

"Well, they wrote in his chart that they saw some bruises. Do you know what those would be from?"

I looked closer and thought I saw some very faint marks. I hadn't noticed them at all until she pointed them out, and I had no idea what had caused them, but to help her out, I guessed. "Maybe it's from his swing. Sometimes when he falls asleep, he leans against the poles of his swing."

Each time the woman asked me a question, she'd take off her glasses, and when I answered, she'd put them back on to write down what I said. Then she would remove them again before asking the next question. With each one, I grew more impatient.

"Can you tell me what kind of a dad Neil is?"

"He's loving. He takes care of Zack. I guess he's just a normal dad."

What does this have to do with anything?

"Have you ever seen Neil get mad?"

"Well, yeah." *He gets angry, and I get angry, so what?*

"What does he do?"

"Well, we yell. He's moody. I don't know . . ."

How's this helping Zack? Let's move on to something that helps Zack.

"Have you ever seen Neil hit Zack?"

"No, of course not."

"Has he ever hit you?"

That's when I realized what was happening. They had separated us because they thought Neil had purposely done something to Zack, and they thought I was lying about it to protect him because I was in an abusive relationship. "It's not what you think . . ." I realized how stupid my answers must have sounded, and I wanted to explain.

"That will be all for now." The woman put her pen away in her purse.

A nurse appeared in the doorway. "We need to take Zack downstairs for more tests. I'll bring him right back." She rearranged his IVs, released the brakes on his crib, and rolled him out the door.

The CPS woman stood up. "I need to talk to my colleague. I'll be back before we leave the hospital."

———————

Neil returned first. His face was ashen. "They don't believe me. They don't think it was an accident."

His words confirmed my thoughts.

"Do you believe me?" he asked, desperate for my approval. "You believe me, don't you?"

"Well, yeah, I believe you. It was an accident."

But I also realized I didn't have all of the details. I didn't know what caused Neil to drop Zack or how it actually happened.

"I'm sorry," Neil said yet again. "I am so sorry."

"It's not your fault, Neil. It's not your fault, so don't take the blame." I didn't view his apology as an admission of guilt, but rather as a sign of his regret that this terrible thing had happened on his watch. "I'm still not sure how you dropped him, though."

"When I picked him up, he slipped out of my hands and hit his head against the inside of the tub."

The thought made me sick to my stomach. I wanted to ask more questions, but I wasn't sure I wanted to picture it anymore. It didn't matter, because just then, the two women returned together.

"We have enough concerns that we're placing you on the watch list," said the librarian-looking woman. "From now on, your visits must be supervised."

"What does that mean?" I asked.

"A social worker from either CPS or the hospital must be in the room with you at all times," she said. "And from now on, you'll have to leave the curtain open so the nurses have a full view of everything that happens in here."

She motioned to someone in the hall, and another woman came into our room. She didn't say anything, but just took a seat and started watching us.

The next twenty-four hours were a blur. Zack continued to have seizures, and I continued to pray out loud. As soon as his pinkie began to twitch, I'd say, "God, I claim this as the last seizure Zack will ever have." But there always seemed to be another seizure.

They continued to do tests, and I asked a lot of questions. "What's this medication for? Where are you taking him now? What will the results of that test tell us? Can I hold him again? Is he eating enough? Can I try to feed him?"

Then I realized the seizures seemed to be happening less frequently, and their duration wasn't as long. And finally, after three days, they stopped. The doctors had finally figured out how to regulate Zack's medicine. I was thrilled that he no longer experienced the seizures, though I worried that he would be on antiseizure medicine for the rest of his life—like his father.

Since Zack was now stable, Neil's parents coaxed us to go home, change clothes, and shower. Remi agreed. "If you want to leave, now would be a good time," she said. I trusted her to watch over Zack while I was gone. Besides, we were beginning to stink.

Driving home, I finally had the privacy to ask Neil more questions. "Tell me exactly how you dropped him."

"I was bent over the tub, washing him, and one hand was on his head and one was on his behind. When I lifted him up, his head slipped and bumped against the inside of the tub."

"You weren't kneeling down next to him?"

"No, I was standing. Why? There's nothing wrong with that."

I was just trying to picture in my mind what happened, but I didn't want to start a fight, so I let it drop.

With each shift, the new social worker on duty asked Neil and I the same, already-answered questions. I realize now they were trying to see if our stories were consistent, but at the time, we just found the investigation frustrating. Neil began to get defensive.

"I've already answered their questions," he said to me. "I've told them so many times, and yet they keep thinking I've been abusive. You know I haven't been, right?"

"It was an accident, Neil," I said for the umpteenth time.

"I don't understand why they have to keep asking the same questions."

"I don't know either."

But each time the CPS workers repeated their questions to Neil, new questions rose in my mind. I didn't doubt Neil's answers, but I was curious about what exactly had happened. How had he been holding Zack? How had Zack slipped? Where had Zack's head hit the tub? What had Neil done next?

When I asked Neil some of these questions, he just got upset. "You're sounding like one of the CPS workers."

Several days passed, each like the one before it. Zack hadn't improved since the seizures stopped, and Neil was growing more impatient with the social workers. We decided it would be best to take turns going home and getting some rest.

As we entered week two in the hospital, not much changed. Zack's head continued to swell. His soft spot bulged a little more each day until there wasn't enough room to contain all the fluid that had built up. The juncture points of his skull began to expand, making his head grow even larger.

By week three, the doctors knew they had to do something or Zack would die.

10

Release

Due to the hydrocephalus and the progressive enlargement of his head, we'll have to take aggressive action," the doctor said. "It's likely we'll have to insert a cerebral shunt to drain the cerebrospinal fluid from his brain."

"Huh?" I had no idea what he was saying. Fortunately, Remi was there.

"Zack has so much fluid on his brain," she said, "that it isn't draining properly. There's no more room in his skull for it to expand, so we have to get the fluid out. A shunt is a tube we can insert to allow the fluid in his brain to drain."

"How do you get the shunt in there?" I asked, trying not to freak out.

"It's major surgery," said the doctor, "which is why I'd like to try something else first. I'd like to go through his soft spot and aspirate it."

I looked at Remi.

"He wants to shave his head and then stick a needle into his soft spot and use that to draw out some of the fluid. If that works, Zack won't need a shunt."

Although a needle in my baby's soft spot didn't sound good, it sounded better than brain surgery. "Do it," I said.

The doctor picked up my beautiful, chubby, four-month-old boy, and Remi followed, carrying his IV bags. "You might want to go down and get a soda or something," she told me.

"No, thanks. I'll stay with Zack." I followed them to the adjacent treatment room, but when I got to the door, she told me I'd have to stay outside. Several other nurses came over and encouraged me to leave, but I refused. I stood outside the treatment room, praying, believing that God was going to heal my baby.

Then Zack started screaming.

Because he'd been lightly sedated ever since arriving at the hospital, I hadn't heard Zack make a noise other than that horrible moaning sound. But this was different. It sounded like he was in complete agony. Zack had cried out in pain before—when he had gas, for instance—but this piercing scream was unlike anything I'd ever heard. It sounded as if they were killing him.

"They're doing something wrong," I said to Neil, who had joined me outside the room. "They messed up!" I was getting ready to burst through the door when suddenly the screaming stopped. It just stopped. I stood there, muscles tensed and waiting for the door to open. There was nothing but silence—no moaning, no doctors talking, nothing. How could Zack go from screaming like that to silence? Had he died? I looked at Neil and knew he was thinking the same thing.

Remi was in there. She was the most loving nurse we had, and I knew she understood how much I was suffering. *She'll come out as quickly as she can.* But as time passed, I became less and less sure. *He's dead. He has to be dead,* I thought. My body went numb.

Finally, the door opened and I saw Remi's face. "He did great! You can come in now." Her words broke through the silence, and my numbness thawed as relief rushed through me. I walked over to Zack lying on the table, and immediately I could see that his head looked less swollen.

"It went great. It really did," Remi said. "We relieved the pressure, so for the first time in weeks, he probably doesn't have a headache. We can take him back to his room, and you can hold him if you want. He should be feeling much better."

He did seem more content, and he wasn't moaning anymore. I was so happy to have him back in my arms, so I could love on him. Finally, it seemed, we had turned a corner.

Twenty-four hours later, Zack's soft spot was bulging again. His moaning was back.

"There's too much pressure on the ventricles in his brain," the doctor said. "We're going to try aspirating again, but we can only do it three times. If it doesn't start draining on its own after the third time, we'll have to put in a shunt."

So now I had a short-term prayer goal. When they took Zack to the treatment room, I stood outside, praying for the procedure to work and for Zack to start draining on his own. This time when I heard the scream, I welcomed it because I knew it meant Zack would feel better. I prayed that it would be over soon and that Zack would be comforted. When they opened the door, I went in and grabbed my son. Once again he looked better.

———————

Twenty-four hours later we were in the same situation. Swelling. Moaning. Not draining on his own.

For a third time in three days, I stood outside the treatment room. But this time I kept wondering, *Who makes the rules? Who says we can't do this more than three times? Why not four?* I prayed on autopilot, repeating words and phrases over and over again, out loud and in my head. I hadn't realized other people were watching, but several nurses came by and commented, "You're doing great." "You're being very brave." "You're so strong." I appreciated their affirmations.

Again, the procedure worked. And again, I prayed and believed it would be the last time Zack would have to endure that kind of pain.

———————

The next day Zack's head was still swollen, but not as enlarged as it had been. "We're hopeful," the doctor said. "But we'll need more time before we know whether or not he needs a shunt."

What I heard was, "He's getting healed."

I believed God had heard my prayers and that my faith was affecting Zack's health. *Don't let up now*, I told myself. *You have to keep praying!*

It was unnecessary pressure, and even then I knew God doesn't work that way. At some level I was aware I couldn't earn Zack's health by praying more loudly or more consistently. But I didn't care. Praying was something I could *do*. So I kept on praying—hard.

Over the next few days, the fluid in Zack's head receded. He was draining and wouldn't need a shunt. It was good news and it gave me hope, but Zack's prospects were still uncertain. Every day I stood by his bedside, doing what I could to help him, by holding him and loving on him. That, as I saw it, was my first and my most important job.

My second job was to help Neil. He wrestled with a lot of guilt and needed constant reassurance.

The social workers kept a continual eye on us, and their questions persisted. They were never satisfied with the answers, so an official hearing was scheduled. We would have to appear before a judge, who would determine if there was enough evidence for a trial.

I called Mom almost every day to update her on what was happening. One day I was overwhelmed and tired of being the strong one. "I'm so exhausted," I told her. "Good things are happening for Zack, but I thought he'd be completely healed by now. And I'm so tired of having to comfort Neil. And now the hearing is coming up. I can't stand the thought of leaving Zack all alone, but they say I have to go."

"Brenda, I am flying out there so I can be with you next week. I'll stay with Zack while you're at the hearing."

We hadn't discussed her coming, so her words were a huge relief to me. *My momma is coming to help hold me up.*

Having Mom with me made all the difference. She just stepped in and seemed to know what to do. She would cuddle Zack, talk to him, and even change his diapers. I had never been brave enough to do that with all the tubes that covered him, but she just went ahead and did it. I learned so much about taking care of Zack from watching her. Without knowing it, she was teaching me how to be a mother to a child with special needs.

Her presence comforted me. When she left to take a smoke break, her familiar scent of perfume and cigarettes lingered. Just having her sit next to me gave me peace. It was nice to have someone to support me the way I'd been supporting Neil.

When I left Zack's room for the hearing, I felt good. Mom would take care of my son while I was gone, and she would be praying. When I returned, this would all be over.

Neil and I, along with the senior Meonis, walked into the courtroom. It looked like the courtrooms I'd seen on television. There was a judge behind a large wooden desk and a stenographer ready to take notes. There were no jurors, but there was a bailiff, who stood next to an empty chair.

Neil had brought one of my church dresses to the hospital, and I had changed into it before we left. He wore a long-sleeved shirt and a tie with a jacket. Neil's dad wore his military uniform, and Mrs. Meoni looked as put-together as always. Neil's parents had hired a lawyer, who was there to represent us. The room was filled with people we knew: my boss, our neighbor from across the hall, Remi, the intake nurse from the emergency room, and the social workers from CPS, who were there with some lawyers.

The lawyer directed us to sit down behind a table, and he joined us there. After some initial legal talk, the judge looked at Neil and me. "We're here because we want to hear your side of the story. This is just to talk about what happened, so we can see if there is any evidence of abuse. If we don't find anything, this will be the end of the investigations and you'll be done."

A lawyer from Child Protective Services questioned the social workers first. They told the judge what we had said during our interviews. I felt that they put a negative spin on our answers.

"It was twenty-four hours before he told anyone he'd dropped the baby," said the tall social worker. "Why did he wait so long?"

"He was afraid!" I wanted to yell, but I held my tongue.

"For the past four weeks, we've observed Neil cry and apologize at least once a day like he's guilty."

Our lawyer interrupted. "Could it be that, instead of feeling guilty for abuse, he's just sorry this happened to his son while he was in charge of him?"

"I guess so," she conceded.

The CPS lawyer questioned my boss about my qualities as an employee. He responded with extremely positive comments about my work ethic and character. Next the lawyer asked my neighbor if he'd ever heard us fight. The neighbor said no. The lawyer asked a friend of ours how we acted toward Zack. She told him we were very loving parents.

The hearing seemed to drag on and on. It was like a never-ending drama.

The admitting nurse got on the stand and talked about the bruises she had seen on Zack's cheek. Their lawyer asked if the bruises could have resulted from Zack falling asleep in the swing. "I doubt the poles on the swing could've caused them. It would take trauma to break the blood vessels, and I don't think falling asleep against a pole would cause that."

Remi took the stand next, and the lawyers peppered her with questions.

"What is your relationship to the couple?"

"For how long each day have you observed them?"

"Do you see any signs of abuse?"

"Have you seen anything that would make you think either one of them is unfit to be a parent?"

Remi was consistent in her answer to all of their questions. "These are very loving parents. They ask a lot of questions. They're involved in their son's care, and I haven't seen anything that would make me think they are unfit."

Then Neil was on the stand. He told the same story about dropping Zack while getting him out of the tub, but this time he added information I hadn't heard before: "He didn't breathe right, so I shook him."

That comment brought on a barrage of new questions.

"How hard did you shake him?"

"Did you shake him violently?"

"When you shook him, did you hit his head against the wall?"

"Did you throw him on the bed?"

"No, I just shook him like, you know, 'Are you breathing? Are you breathing?'" Neil's voice trembled. I could tell he felt terrible.

A doctor we'd never met took the stand next. She told the judge that when a brain has been injured, even a little shaking can result in more damage.

Then it was over.

Our lawyer told us there were several possible outcomes. The first and best was that we'd be cleared completely. The second was that the judge could find cause for concern but not enough to send it on to the district attorney for charges to be pressed. In that case, our name would go on a probationary list, meaning we'd be immediately investigated if anything else happened. The third and worst outcome was that he'd find enough evidence to press charges against one or both of us.

The next day, Mom was sitting in the rocking chair, holding Zack, and I was helping the nurse change his sheets, while Neil watched. Another nurse appeared in the doorway and motioned to our social worker, "You've got a phone call."

Just as the CPS worker stepped out, Mr. Meoni appeared at the door.

"I just talked to the lawyer," he said. "The judge ruled that the allegations were unfounded,"

"What does that mean?" I asked.

"It means *she* won't be back," he said, pointing at the social worker's chair. "There wasn't enough evidence."

"What about the list?" Neil asked.

"The allegations were unfounded. Your name won't be on the list."

It was exactly what I'd expected. While I was glad to be done with it all, it still made me angry that they had put us through all of that for nothing!

After the fourth week in the hospital, Zack was no longer on IVs. He hadn't needed oxygen in a while, and he was eating on his own. And with each step Zack took forward, the nurses seemed to take one back. They rarely hurried anymore when it came to Zack. They would check his vital signs and record the numbers in his chart and give him his seizure medication. But beyond that, there didn't seem to be much they could do. They seemed to be done treating Zack, but the doctors weren't comfortable releasing him yet. They probably knew what a challenge he would be for a twenty-two-year-old mother with a full-time job.

Although the timing of Zack's release wasn't critical for the medical staff, it was getting increasingly important for us because my sister, Kim, was getting married. The wedding was in less than two weeks, and we were all concerned about what would happen. I was supposed to be her matron of honor, Neil was to be an usher, and of course, Mom was the mother of the bride. Neil and I had booked our flights months ago, and Mom was scheduled to return soon. So now that Zack didn't seem to be getting any new treatments, we felt it was time for him to be discharged. I hoped Mom would help me convince the doctors that I could handle taking care of my son.

———————

Mom and I sat side by side, listening to the doctor describe Zack's condition. He pointed to the images of his brain. "Zack has brain damage in the occipital lobe from where his head hit the tub, and there are other pockets of damage from the shaking. There is blood in front of his retina, and with no way for light to get in, no signals are going to the back of the brain. There's a chance his body could reabsorb the blood and some light could get through, but we won't know that for months."

I almost gasped when I heard that. There was still a chance that my son would see again. Silently I started praying and believing for that.

The doctor agreed that we could take Zack home. "He'll still need a lot of ongoing therapy and care. Here's a list of agencies that can help. Make his life what you can."

"What will he be able to do?" I asked. "Will he ever be able to go to school? Will he learn to walk?"

Mom reached over and with her palm began making small circles on my back.

"You'll be lucky if he ever sits up," said the doctor.

"And that's as good as it gets?"

"Hear me clearly," the doctor said. "His brain looks like Swiss cheese, with large pockets of damage. You'll be *lucky* if he ever sits up."

"But he's going to survive?" Mom asked.

"He's going to live. Now you make the best of it." As I watched the doctor walk out of the room. I looked over at Neil, who sat quietly lost in his own guilt.

Saying nothing.

Doing nothing to support me.

And I thought, *Now I will take care of everyone.*

11

Going Back Home

As soon as we got home, I wanted all traces of the hospital off of Zack. I bathed him to get rid of the hospital smell and then took him to his room so I could change his diaper. It was a wonderful feeling to have my baby back where the comforter and wallpaper matched, everything was pretty, and he smelled normal again.

Zack's "Baby's First Calendar" still hung on the wall. I looked at the stickers I'd placed on the dates marking his first smile, the first time he'd held his head up, and the first time he'd rolled over. The past six weeks were blank while he'd been in the hospital. Was I supposed to add new stickers when he reached these milestones again, or should I take the old stickers off and reapply them on the new dates? Would I ever be able to add a sticker for the first time he sat up? I had no idea what the future held, so I took the calendar off the wall and hid it in the bottom drawer of Zack's dresser. While I was at it, I grabbed his baby book and put it in there too. Although I would bear six more children, I never kept another calendar or baby book for any of them.

We took lots of pictures of Zack over those next few days. I would prop him up on the couch, and Mom would snap a few shots. Then Neil would hold him up by his jumper so it looked like he was standing, and Mom snapped more. Neil and I watched as Mom tickled him just so we could see those big dimples when he smiled.

The three of us didn't want to ever put him down. We fought over who got to hold him next. We were so thrilled that Zack was alive that he was all we focused on those first few days. I lived in the moment as I never had before and maybe haven't since. A sense of relief enveloped me—it was all over, and we were going to be okay. Mom and Neil were still uncomfortable with each other, and we knew Zack still had a long way to go, but for the time being we were determined just to enjoy our baby.

Life seemed almost normal—like we had a do-over.

———————

Before we left the hospital, Mom had asked the doctor if it would be okay for us to fly to Iowa with Zack for Kim's wedding.

"As long as you're aware of the situation and the risks, you should be fine," he'd said. "If anything happens, take him directly to the hospital." He told us to watch for signs of vomiting, seizures, or swelling. So once we got Zack settled at our apartment, we all got ready to go to Iowa.

Mom left earlier than we did so she could get home to help Kim. Zack, Neil, and I followed a few days later. When we arrived at the airport, my whole family was there to greet us. It was the first time most of them had seen Zack. When they looked at him, I could tell they wanted to say something, but they weren't sure what. "Ohhh" was about the best they could offer.

I knew Zack looked a little odd. His head was still huge, and it had been shaved around the soft spot. But my baby was alive, and that was all that mattered to me.

Dad held out his weathered hands to take Zack. I gently placed him in Dad's arms. He pulled Zack to his chest, his tanned arms tightly wrapping around my baby's tiny body. And then my dad started crying—big, manly tears. I wasn't sure what to do. I had never seen Dad cry like this before. I looked at Mom. She put her hand on his shoulder and whispered in his ear.

I'm sure Dad had wondered if he would ever see his grandson again. Zack's condition was overwhelming and scary—no one knew what to expect. So Dad was crying happy tears just to hold Zack again. But I could tell that

Dad was sad too. Zack looked so different from other babies, different from when Dad saw him after he was born. As the first grandson, Zack held a special place in his grand-father's heart. Dad had to be wondering if he'd ever be able to take Zack fishing or teach him how to ride a horse. It was something I wondered too.

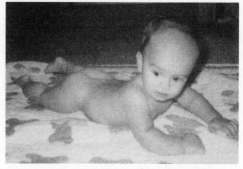

My baby boy Zack lying on the quilt my mom made for him just weeks after his injury, late October 1989

On the morning of Kim's wedding, we were all dressed up, even Zack. Kim had ordered a six-months-size tux for Zack to wear. Everyone said how cute he looked in that little tux. But there were a lot of double takes, too, when people first saw him. I began to realize that this would just be a fact of life for us. Sometimes it would take people a little longer to see what I saw—an adorable little boy with dimples that lit up his chubby face. But eventually, I saw, they came around.

I enjoyed the rest of my day with my family. I was proud to stand by Kim and John as they committed their lives to each other, just as Neil and I had done more than a year earlier. But most of all, I loved watching family and friends coo over my baby in his tiny tux.

We stayed a few more days in Iowa before flying back to Virginia. It was hard to say good-bye to Mom and Dad because we weren't sure when we would see them again. We hoped it would be Christmas, but we didn't know if we could afford another flight so soon. We also knew I wouldn't have a lot of time off. I hadn't been back to the office since I got the phone call from Neil. My staff sergeant had been tremendously supportive during my long leave of absence, but I needed to get back to work.

Back in Virginia, Neil and I discussed child-care arrangements. Our lawyer had suggested that to protect ourselves, we should find someone other than Neil to watch Zack. If Zack ever turned up with another bruise after Neil had watched him, the suspicion could start all over again.

But we didn't have many options. Day care wasn't affordable with only one of us working, and I was still the only one with a job. In addition, we were limited by having only one car. So we decided to just make the best of it. I went back to work, and Neil resumed care of Zack.

But after a few weeks into our new life, I knew things would never be the same. Alone with Zack all day, Neil was filled with guilt. By the time I got home every evening, he was in need of a therapist. And that therapist was me.

"I can't believe this happened," Neil would say. "I am so sorry."

Or I'd catch him staring at Zack. "Look what I've done."

"It's not your fault," I'd remind him. "It was an accident. You love him, and that's all that matters."

But the situation took a toll on me. I couldn't sleep well at night because I wanted to take care of Zack. I then worked all day, but my mind was constantly thinking of my son. In the evening, Neil drained whatever emotional energy I had left. I never had a break.

We decided to spend a weekend at Neil's parents' house. They could help with Zack, and the change of scenery would do us all good. But while we were there, Zack started vomiting. We all went on high alert and rushed him to the closest emergency room. Vomiting was one of the symptoms the doctor had warned us about.

As soon as the intake nurse heard Zack's medical history, however, she told us she had to call Child Protective Services.

"Why are they calling them?" I asked Neil. "Weren't we cleared?"

I didn't understand; we weren't on the watch list. But with our recent history, and with Zack still under Neil's care, apparently we were going to be watched anyway.

Suddenly we were back in the worst of it. Nurses whisking Zack away. Doctors ordering tests. Everyone waiting on the results.

I called Mom and told her what was happening, but not for a minute did I think Neil had anything to do with it.

Finally, the results came in.

Zack's brain scans showed no change, but he had tested positive for the flu. After giving him fluids, the doctor said we were free to take him home.

I couldn't take the stress any longer. I wanted to be home with Zack. I wanted people to trust my husband the way I did. I wanted Zack to have the flu without it being a big deal. And I wanted to move back to Iowa, where my family would be closer and they could help us start fresh.

But I couldn't do any of that because I was still a marine. After giving birth to Zack, I had reenlisted for four more years. In fact, I had planned to be a lifer. But now something had to change.

The next day I had a meeting with my commanding officer.

"I can't do this anymore," I said. Though I wasn't a crier, I cried then. "So much has happened. I need to be home with Zack."

He was very kind. "There's this thing called a hardship discharge, and you can apply for it. You'll be able to leave immediately upon approval, and you'll still have an honorable discharge. I'll get you the paperwork."

There was a stack of forms, and it took several weeks to fill them all out and gather the necessary supporting documents. Zack's doctor wrote a letter saying it would be in Zack's best interest for me to be at home. Mom wrote a letter describing our situation and explaining how our moving back to Iowa would allow my parents to help. I had to write an essay, and it was important that I said everything that needed to be said. Both Mom and Neil proofread the final copy before I turned it in.

So I was petitioning the Marine Corps to release me from my obligation. I would never have left the marines otherwise. Despite the paperwork, ours was an easy case to make. Because my life had become so difficult, I could no longer be the marine I longed to be.

In mid-December, I met with the commanding officer of the entire base regarding my application. I was nervous, but he tried to make it easier.

"Tell me what happened," he said.

And I did.

"I know you've been through a lot," he said, looking like a kindly grand-father. "I don't think you'll have any trouble with this. The ruling will happen in January, but until then, you can go ahead and plan as if you won't be returning." I left his office with a mixture of relief and profound sadness. I was leaving the Marine Corps I loved. Both my income and my identity were tied up in being a marine. It had been my dream for so many years.

And now the dream had ended.

———————

While waiting for my discharge to come through, Neil and I came up with a plan. The three of us would move to Cedar Falls and live with my parents until Neil could get a job. We hoped he could find a job at the post office, because they hired a lot of vets, paid well, and offered good benefits. If that didn't work out, we were confident he could find something.

Mom flew out to Virginia shortly before Christmas. We packed up a few of Zack's things, and she took him with her back to Cedar Falls. Neil and I stayed to clean out the apartment, sell our furniture, and pack our belongings. As soon as we got the official approval from the marines, we would make the drive back to Iowa.

I spent my baby's first Christmas without him in my arms. I don't remember what we did that day, but I remember that I spent it thinking about that dark hair, those chubby cheeks. And those dimples—those irre-sistible dimples. My arms felt empty and my whole life off-center, as though a part of me were missing.

Though it was my baby's first Christmas, it was not the silent night I'd dreamed about.

12

Moving On

I unloaded a few boxes and carried them down the hall to my old country-themed bedroom. My bulletin board was still on the wall, covered with the senior pictures of friends I hadn't talked to since graduation. My cheerleading medal hung on the corner of the board. One of Mom's cotton quilts covered the double bed I would now share with Neil. I could smell the freshly laundered sheets. Almost five years had passed since I had called this place home. Now, at age twenty-two, I was moving back in.

Mom had cleared out space for Zack in her sewing room. She had found a crib and bedding at a garage sale and had done her best to make the space comfortable for him. Now she was unpacking boxes in my room.

"Larry," she called out to my dad, "get a hammer and a nail and come here." She had opened a box of framed pictures and wanted to hang them on the wall in Zack's room.

Dad showed up a minute later. She handed him one of many pictures of Zack, and he held it up against the wall.

"No, a little to the left," Mom said as she directed Dad. "Now back just a smidge to the right. There!" Dad pounded the nail into the Sheetrock and hung the picture. Mom stepped up to straighten it. Then they both stood back to admire their work.

I couldn't help but smile. Even if the circumstances weren't ideal, I knew Mom and Dad would do whatever it took to help us. And though I already missed being a marine, I believed all would be well with us as long as we were together.

That's when that old saying, "Home is where the heart is," took on new meaning to me. Zack was my heart. Wherever he was would always be home for me.

After we got settled, finding specialists for Zack was my first task. The list was daunting. Zack needed physical therapy, speech therapy, and occupational therapy. He saw a pediatrician, a neurologist, and an ophthalmologist on a regular basis, and other doctors as necessary. He also saw an early developmental intervention specialist. I had to find all those people and set up the appointments.

The good news was I was able to locate excellent specialists. The bad news was that most of them practiced at the University of Iowa Hospitals and Clinics in Iowa City, seventy-five miles away. The drive from Cedar Falls took us ninety minutes one way—two hours if construction or poor weather slowed things down—so a single appointment ate up the whole day. Neil joined me for those trips. The local appointments in Cedar Falls I handled myself.

On the days he wasn't helping out with Zack, Neil worked to qualify for his driver's license. But to be licensed in the state of Iowa, he needed a full medical evaluation from the Veteran's Hospital, which of course was also located in Iowa City. He also had to go there for checkups and adjustments to his medicines. So until he was cleared to drive, I had to take him there.

We had a little money saved, but we mostly used it to buy gas to get back and forth to the doctor appointments in Iowa City. We also tried to help my parents with expenses, such as groceries. But after three or four weeks, there wasn't much left, and Dad had to take a second shift at John Deere to help pay the bills. I could tell Mom was worried about his working so much. We had only lived there a few weeks when she began to hint that Neil needed to be working.

"He's helping me with Zack," I told her after an especially strong hint.

"He needs to get a job, Brenda. Now." She was no longer mincing words.

"It's not that easy, Mom, especially with his medical history."

"He can go down the road to McDonald's."

Neil started his job search, but he didn't have much luck. "No one wants to hire me."

I decided to pass along Mom's idea. "Maybe you could get a job at McDonald's," I said. "Just for a little while."

He shook his head. "There's no way I'm working at McDonald's."

"Well, I just thought maybe it would be a way to—"

"Are you crazy? I am not working at McDonald's!"

I was rocking Zack when Mom came in and switched off the TV so she'd have my full attention. "Did you talk to Neil about getting a job?"

"Mom, he's not going to work at McDonald's."

"Why not? Your dad's the kind of man who does whatever it takes. When he didn't have a job, he went door to door just asking for anything he could do to make some money."

"Neil's trying. Would you just cut him a little slack?"

"I will when he gets a job to support his family."

"Mom, he's on medication for seizures." I had hoped she'd be more understanding.

"Which is why he needs a job with medical benefits."

Just then, Neil walked in. Mom turned the TV back on and left the room without saying another word. It seemed she just couldn't understand how hard he was trying.

Later that week, while Neil and I were driving to one of Zack's doctor appointments, we passed a set of golden arches. I decided to try again.

"I know you don't want to work at McDonald's, but my dad worked whatever job he could to make ends meet. He even went door to door looking for work."

"Something will come up," Neil said. "I'm working on my résumé, and I'll take it to the post office as soon as I finish."

"Let me know when you're ready, and I'll drive you." I prayed that the post office would offer him a job.

The following week, Neil and I took his résumé to our local branch of the post office. The first one we stopped at wasn't hiring.

"Let's try another one," I suggested. I couldn't stand the thought of telling Mom he'd been unsuccessful.

But it was the same story wherever we tried. He would go in with high hopes and high spirits but return to the car dejected.

"They're not hiring either."

Over the next few weeks, whenever we didn't have medical appointments, we visited the post offices in every small town around the Cedar Falls area. The answer was always the same: "We're not hiring."

Our lack of progress frustrated Mom. "Tell him to send his résumé to every post office in Iowa if he has to! Somebody's got to be hiring!"

I suggested that idea to Neil, but I didn't tell him it was from Mom. There was enough tension between them already.

I had to do something to help out, but with Zack's needs, I obviously couldn't get a full-time job. When I heard that a friend of Mom's sold Mary Kay cosmetics, I wanted to know more. When Kim and I were sixteen and fourteen, Mom had bought each of us a starter kit of Mary Kay makeup from a friend of hers. I was thrilled! I'd studied all the tips and techniques until I got really good at applying it, and I'd had a lot of fun experimenting with colors and styles. Now I wondered if selling Mary Kay would be a good job opportunity for me.

Mom's friend, Janet, came over one evening with her makeup kit and showed me what she did. I knew it was something I could do too. She loaned me the money to get my first kit, and I started holding Mary Kay parties for all of Mom's friends. I was really good at it too. I suspected that some of my sales bordered on charity—Mom's friends wanting to help her daughter—but I didn't care. Money was money, and I knew they received a quality product. I quickly paid back what I owed on the kit and began making a profit. Soon I was booking parties outside of Mom's circle of friends.

But Neil wasn't always happy about it.

One night Kim came over to the house. "Hey, guess who I ran into yesterday." She mentioned a girl we both knew in high school. "I told her you were selling Mary Kay, and she said she'd love to have a party at her house." She dropped a piece of paper onto the table next to me. "Here's her number. You can give her a call."

I picked the paper up and looked at it. "This is great—thanks. That makes three parties this month." Then I looked at Neil and saw his frown of disapproval. "Well, maybe I should wait on this one," I said, tucking the phone number in my pocket.

Mom and Kim exchanged glances but didn't say anything.

Later I questioned Neil. "Why didn't you want me to take that party? I thought you liked my bringing in extra money."

"It's not the money," Neil said. "I just don't think you need to be hanging around with old friends from high school."

In days to come I would realize that Neil didn't like me hanging around anyone besides himself.

The tension at the house continued to build. I got tired of trying to defend Mom and Neil to one another. I was also getting very tired of Neil's moodiness and his resistance to my Mary Kay work. Then, just when I thought I couldn't take any of it any longer, Neil received a call from the post office in Cedar Rapids. They had an opening and wanted to hire my husband.

Cedar Rapids was the second-largest city in Iowa. With two hospitals, it offered many more doctors and therapists than my parents' town of Cedar Falls. Even better, Iowa City, where most of Zack's specialists practiced, was only half an hour south. And since Cedar Falls was only an hour north, we'd still be close to family. Cedar Rapids was the perfect location for us—right between my parents' home and Zack's medical services.

With the help of a VA loan, we bought a small three-bedroom house for fifty-two thousand dollars. It was located across the street from a Catholic high school. The neighborhood was quiet and safe, and there was a park nearby where we could take Zack and let him swing.

We still had only one car, but we made it work. Neil worked the night shift and slept during the day. I dropped him off at work and then picked him up the next morning, when his shift ended.

We quickly settled into routine. Neil would go to bed around seven in the morning. I'd feed Zack breakfast and play with him a little before heading off to his appointments. If we didn't have anything else to do, we'd go for a walk in the neighborhood or, when the weather turned colder, at the mall. At night, the three of us would have dinner together before it was time for Neil to go to work. It wasn't quite the life I'd planned, but it was a good life, and I was happy.

The day Neil got his driver's license was a big day for all of us. We even talked about getting a second car, but things were working well the way they were. Besides, with the mortgage and medical expenses, we really couldn't afford another vehicle.

Perhaps that's why I was so surprised when Neil took the car one day and returned with a request. "Can you drive me to the motorcycle dealership?"

"Why?"

"Because I just bought one, and I need to pick it up."

"You did what?" I couldn't believe what I was hearing.

"I bought a motorcycle."

"Neil, what if you have another seizure while driving? You could kill yourself!"

"Maybe so, but at least I wouldn't hurt anyone else."

That's your rationale? I wanted to ask him about the money—and the weather. A motorcycle didn't seem like a very practical idea in Iowa. But Neil was too impatient to have a discussion.

"Come on! Grab Zack and let's go!"

On the way over, I thought more about it. Perhaps if he bought a cheap used motorcycle, the expense wouldn't be as bad, and if he only rode it when the weather was nice, maybe having two vehicles would be a good thing. And of course, gas for a motorcycle would cost less. I'd nearly talked myself into the idea when Neil led me to the showroom floor.

"Here it is." Neil ran his hand over the black leather seat.

The oversized price tag still hung on the shiny metal handlebars. This wasn't a cheap used motorcycle. It was a brand-new, top-of-the-line motorcycle.

I had a choice to make at that moment. I could make a big deal out of Neil's choice—which I wasn't happy about—or I could make the best of it.

I chose the latter.

Only later would I wonder if that purchase was a sign of what was to come.

Zack's doctor appointments often frustrated me. We would buy gas to drive to Iowa City, pay to park the car, and then make our way through long corridors in tall buildings to get to each specialist's office. We'd sign in and wait until the doctor could see us.

Because most appointments were at the teaching hospital, we usually had to be checked by the medical students and residents before we could see the specialist. And that encounter almost always started the same way. A young medical professional in a white coat would say, "Can you tell me what happened?" Then we'd have to tell him or her the whole long story about Zack's accident, his time in the hospital, and all the treatments we'd tried since then.

The appointments at the pediatric ophthalmologist's office were the worst because the residents usually insisted on running a whole series of tests. Zack would sit on my lap while a resident held up a shiny object or a toy and say, "Look, Zack, what do you see?"

I would say, "He can't see anything."

"Here; grab this," she would say, ignoring me while she shook the toy in front of his face.

Zack would sit there motionless.

"Let's turn off the lights and try it," she'd say.

I'd think, *That's not going to work either.* But she'd repeat the same tests, this time using a flashlight.

I soon discovered that if I used medical terms, I could speed up the assessment and the resident would take me more seriously. So I began to say things like, "His occipital lobe is damaged," or, "His retinas hemorrhaged." This seemed to motivate her to finish the exam more quickly. Once she finally finished, we'd wait some more until the doctor came in.

The doctor would take a quick look at the resident's notes, ask a few more questions, and occasionally run a test or two. Then he'd say the same thing he said before: "We're hoping his body will reabsorb the blood on his retina. We'll see him back in six weeks to see if he's any better."

I would leave those appointments so frustrated! They seemed like such a waste of time and money. I knew everyone was just doing his or her job, but I didn't see a lot of progress. I wanted to say, "Hey, Doc, if you're such a big-shot specialist, can't you just touch him and fix him or something?"

I had the same frustrations with Zack's therapists. Appointment after appointment, I watched them lay Zack on his stomach, and I'd think, *Really? This is what I'm paying you for? You're putting a box in front of him and telling him to crawl to it.* And yet I took him again and again, hoping and praying the therapy would help him.

The therapists would give me homework to do too. I had to do exercises with him, like stretching his legs. Imagine taking a toddler and saying, "Okay, now, Mommy is going to stretch your hamstring." He hated it and he cried while I manipulated his muscles, but I prayed it would benefit him someday.

As a mom, all I wanted to do was hold my son and love on him, but I couldn't. I had to be the one who stretched his muscles and strapped him into the car seat for the long drive to see the doctors and the therapists. Some days I cried, too, because he couldn't understand what I was doing or why I was doing it.

Every time I looked at Zack, I felt so thankful he was alive. When I prayed for his complete healing, I believed it would happen. My faith was that strong. But now that it was obvious that Zack would never be completely healed, I wasn't angry at God and I didn't lose my faith; I was just disappointed. I still felt like God had heard my prayers and kept Zack alive when the odds had been stacked against him. Now it was my responsibility to help Zack reach his potential and do whatever it was God had planned for his life.

Although the doctor had said Zack would be lucky to just sit up, it never occurred to me to think that he wouldn't walk. Perhaps it was ignorance or denial, but in my heart and in my head, I knew that one day he would. I just thought it would take a little longer.

On Sundays, I went to church with Zack while Neil slept. After a particularly hard week, I remember praying, "I need you, God. I need your strength. I believe you are healing Zack even when I can't see it. I am not giving up. I am not backing down. I don't understand what's happening, but I don't have to. I know you love me. I know you love Zack. And I know that's enough."

I decided that come what may, I would make the best of Zack's situation. I was going to give him the best I had no matter what. What other choice did I have? I wasn't going to just sit at home and hope things got better. I was the type of woman who took action.

As a marine, I had been trained to serve.

Now, instead of serving my country, I would be serving my son.

13

Struggles at Home

When I looked at Zack, I saw a fat little bundle of joy. Oh, was he cute! But when Neil looked at Zack, what he saw was guilt staring back at him. As a result, he tended to obsess about our son's disabilities. And as hard as I tried not to let this difference in outlook affect our marriage, it took its toll.

When we were at the mall during Christmas, for instance, Neil kept dwelling on Zack's blindness. "Oh, I wish he could see this!" he said as we walked past the toy store. And when we passed the brightly lit Christmas trees, he said, "Zack would love these lights if he could only see them."

"He can see more than you think," I'd say. What I was really thinking was, *I wish he could see it too.* But of course, I would never say that out loud. It would only make Neil feel worse. I knew it was my job to build Neil up when he felt low, and he expected me to do it.

As time went on, Neil had other regrets. "I wish he could walk or come to me when I called him," Neil said one day while we sat on the couch, watching him play.

"Zack's doing great!" I said, trying to cheer up Neil.

"Yeah, but I wonder what he could've been."

"Don't ever say that. I love Zachary just the way he is."

But Zack was getting bigger, so his physical delays were more noticeable. Those became constant reminders to Neil about the accident. I think Neil also felt the judgment of friends and family in a way that I didn't. Whatever the reason, Neil's guilt increased instead of diminished, and so did his moodiness. And though I tried hard to be understanding, Neil's attitude bothered me. To me, it seemed dismissive of the progress Zack had made and also dismissive of the time, effort, and prayers that I poured into Zack each day.

Despite his challenges, Zack was a joyful child, loving and interactive. During our many doctor visits and therapy sessions, I met parents whose kids were incapable of even acknowledging them. I thought it was a blessing that at least Zack knew we loved him and was able to show that he loved us back. That was all I needed. I just wished Neil could see Zack the way I saw him.

The differences between Neil's outlook and mine meant I couldn't share everything with him. If Zack had a good day at therapy, I told Neil all about the improvements he was making. But if Zack had a bad day or a setback, I had to keep that to myself. If I didn't, I'd have to spend the rest of the evening trying to bring him out of a guilt-induced depression. It just seemed better for me to keep the problems to myself.

Even when Neil's attitude frustrated me, the idea of leaving him never crossed my mind. I believed that an affair was the only biblical reason to get a divorce, and that would never happen because I was committed to Neil. Of course we had arguments, but they were never huge, certainly not anything to separate us.

One of our recurring arguments happened whenever Neil got jealous. He would accuse me of being too friendly with a waiter or a store clerk. From my point of view, I wasn't flirting; I was just being nice. But it just seemed easier to apologize and move on than to argue about it. What choice did I have? I could live with someone in a bad mood or do what I could to make it better. I chose to make it better. Taking the blame for something I didn't do seemed a small price to pay.

Our other recurring fight had to do with money. I blamed Neil's motorcycle for making things tighter than they should be. He blamed me and my phone calls to Mom. After examining the phone bill, he'd ask, "Why do you need to talk to your mom that much?"

Phone calls to Cedar Falls were long-distance, and I knew they could add up. But I didn't feel I talked to her that much. In fact, I kept a lot to myself, not talking to anyone. I was determined to be the strong one, not showing any weakness. I did what I could to manage the negative information about Zack, to be mindful of anything that could make Neil angry or jealous, and to encourage him when he was down.

It was exhausting work.

———

Fortunately, we began to see progress with Zack. The therapists taught him how to sit. Then they taught him how to walk, which first involved developing the strength in his leg muscles so he'd have a base to stand on. Over and over again, both at therapy appointments and at home, we would spread out his fat little legs, stretching them a bit more each time to prepare his muscles for walking. He was outfitted with leg braces and a walker to help with balance. Three times a week the therapists would coax him into taking just one step. One therapist would stand behind him while the other would coax him to reach for things.

When the big day finally came and Zack took his first step in therapy with his walker, the therapists and I got so excited that we screamed, and that scared him so much that he fell down and cried! But I still couldn't wait to tell Neil what had happened. That step meant that soon Zack would be able to get around on his own.

There was other good news too. At one of the ophthalmologist appointments, the doctor noticed that Zack's body had indeed reabsorbed some of the blood on his retinas. That meant Zack might now regain some limited sight. At the next appointment, the doctor thought one of Zack's eyes did respond to light.

Over time, it became obvious that Zack had some sight, but we weren't sure how much. When the doctor discovered that one eye was stronger than the other, he asked me to patch the strong eye so the weak one would get more use. That made sense from a medical perspective, but it was a very difficult thing to try to put a patch on the good eye of a toddler who could barely see. He didn't understand I was helping him, and he would scream and fight me. It was hard, but I did it because I saw hope for Zack's future.

———

I met the few friends I had in Cedar Rapids through selling Mary Kay. I usually did shows in the evenings before Neil went to work or on his days off, and each week I attended evening sales meetings to learn about new products or techniques. But Neil wasn't happy about my part-time career. Every time I left to do a show, he'd get mad at me.

"Why do you have to wear so much makeup?" he'd ask.

"Because that's what I sell. I have to wear it so the women will want to buy it."

It didn't matter what time I got home. His question was always the same: "Why are you so late?"

I would try to explain that a lot of people had placed orders or that the hostess had wanted to place her order after the guests left. But no matter my reasoning, it wasn't good enough. Neil said he didn't like my selling Mary Kay, but I think what he really didn't like was my making friends and going places without him.

Overall, though, things were good. We lived week to week, paycheck to paycheck; but that didn't bother me. It was the way I'd grown up, and it felt comfortable and familiar. There was a rhythm and a flow to our lives that worked.

Now that Zack was two, I thought it was time to have a second child. I had always wanted more than one child, and I wanted Zack and his future sibling to be close in age, just as Kim and I had been. I also thought that having a happy, healthy baby in the house might give Neil something else to focus on and bring us closer together. We talked, Neil agreed, and I went off the pill that spring.

A few weeks later a test confirmed what I already suspected—I was pregnant! I bought a couple more tests just to be sure. They were all positive. I laid them out on the table for Neil to see when he got home from work.

When he came in, I held Zack in my arms and stood next to the table of tests. It took him a minute to understand what he was seeing, but then a big grin spread across his face. "Momma's having a baby!" he said, hugging us both.

Zack had no idea why everyone was happy, but he smiled too.

"I love you," Neil said, kissing me deeply. Then he glanced back at the table and the four very expensive tests. "How many of those are you going to buy?" he said. "We're pregnant! Quit buying tests."

———————

November was cold that year, and the snow came early even for Iowa. One morning, while Zack ate his breakfast in the kitchen, I gathered up the laundry and took it down to our unfinished basement. Our laundry room shared a wall with the garage, and as soon as my bare feet hit the cement floor, I knew I should have at least worn slippers. It was freezing cold and drafty downstairs, and I was only wearing an oversized maternity T-shirt and panties. I hurried to throw in the load and get back upstairs. Neil was due home any minute. As I added detergent, I made a mental note to ask him if we could insulate the basement better.

I ran back up the stairs as fast as my basketball-sized belly would let me. But when I got to the top, the door was closed. Had Zack shut the door, or had it shut by itself?

I tried to open the door, but it was locked. I pounded on it, calling out, "Zack! Zack! Come open the door."

Then I realized how stupid that sounded. Although Zack was somewhat mobile, he wouldn't be able to unlock the door. I pressed my ear against the wood and tried to listen to what was going on. I heard him in the kitchen, opening and closing cupboards and rummaging through their contents.

The knives! Our knives were kept in one of the kitchen drawers. All I could think about was Zack's pudgy little palm reaching into one of those drawers and cutting his hand, or worse, losing a finger.

I pounded again. *Maybe if he hears me, he'll come and stay by the door until I can figure out what to do.* "Zachary! Momma's right here, darlin'. Momma's right here." But it didn't work. I still heard him digging through the cupboards.

I ran down the stairs, out through the garage, and into the snow, not caring about the freezing cold on my bare feet. I ran to the backyard and tried to look through the kitchen windows, but the curtains were all pulled to keep out the cold. I tried the back door and then the front door, knowing they would both be locked, but praying they weren't.

They were locked.

I didn't know the neighbors, but that didn't matter; they weren't home anyway. It was probably a good thing, considering how crazy I must have looked, running around outside, seven months pregnant, in nothing but a T-shirt.

I ran back inside so I could hear what Zack was up to. I tried to be careful going up the stairs. The last thing I needed to do was to slip and fall because of my wet feet. At the top of the stairs, I pressed my ear against the door. Zack was playing with something, slamming it repeatedly on the floor.

Maybe I could remove the doorknob. I raced downstairs for the second time to see if I could find tools. But the longer I was away from Zack, the more I panicked. *Where are the tools? Where is Neil? He should be home by now!* At least when he got home, he would have a key to the front door.

Back at the top of the stairs, I was in full panic mode. I screamed uncontrollably and pounded on the door. "Zack! Zack, can you hear me? It's Momma, Zack!" When I stopped, I heard occasional movements from the kitchen. He was still there and still okay. Then the phone rang.

"Zack! Get the phone, Zack. Get the phone."

I knew Zack couldn't answer the phone. But if he pulled on the cord or knocked the receiver off the hook, whoever was calling would know something was wrong. They might call the police. Or if it was Neil, he'd know to come home immediately. But I didn't hear Zack move, and the phone stopped ringing.

I took one more look at the doorknob, and something in me snapped. I grabbed the railing, leaned back, lifted my leg, and kicked the door. After several kicks, the wood started to shatter. I didn't think about falling down the stairs. I didn't think about the baby or going into labor early. I didn't think about anything but Zack and the knives. I kept kicking until the metal lock plate on the doorjamb broke off.

The door swung open, and I saw Zack sitting on the floor, playing with the Tupperware and having the time of his life. I ran to him.

"Momma's here. Momma's here. I am so sorry. Momma's here." I hugged and loved on him until I calmed down and my breathing slowed. That's when I begin to think clearly and realized I could have done something to hurt the baby.

I panicked all over again. *Where is Neil?* I called the post office and asked if they could send Neil home immediately. It was past the end of his shift.

"I'm sorry," his supervisor said. "Neil isn't here."

He must be on his way home.

I cleaned up the mess I'd made, found Zack some appropriate toys, and put the Tupperware away. An hour passed. I dressed and got Zack dressed because I knew I'd likely need to see the ob-gyn for a checkup.

Another hour passed before Neil came home.

"Where have you been?" I asked before he even made it through the door.

"I was working," he said. "What happened here?" He began to examine the broken door as a way to avoid looking at me.

"You were working until when?"

"Until my shift got over."

"Your shift was over at seven. It's after nine now."

"Uh, I just decided to get a beer with some friends."

I didn't ask, "Why? You've never done that before," or, "What bar is open at seven in the morning?" I wanted to keep the peace, and those questions would have enraged him. But I knew he wasn't making sense.

"What are you so upset about?" Neil asked.

I explained what had happened.

"We'd better call the doctor and get you checked."

He waited while I made the call and then rode with me to the office. The doctor examined me and said I was fine. Nothing was wrong.

On the way home, I tried to ask Neil more about what happened.

"Why are you asking so many questions?" he snapped. "What do you think I'm doing?"

"I don't know. Something just seems . . . different."

"I go to work to support you and Zack. That's what I do. Why would you think today would be any different?"

I stopped asking questions. It had been a terrible, stress-filled day, and I didn't want a fight. But something about Neil's story didn't add up. Something just didn't seem right.

Two weeks later, I got another call.

And things got worse.

14

Saying Good-bye

On a cold day in November, Mom called to tell me that Grandpa Woodyard had passed away. His death wasn't unexpected, but I was stunned when Mom told me the news. No one close to me had ever died.

Grandpa and Chach had lived in Arkansas for years after he retired. But when Grandpa got ill, they moved back to Iowa, and eventually Chach had to put him into a nursing home in Cedar Falls.

Although his health had deteriorated, the affection he and I shared for each other had never changed. When I was a child, my cousins had often teased me with, "You're Grandpa's favorite," or, "He spoils you!" And as I grew older, I'd realized we did have a special bond. He called me "Baby Who," and every time I went to Cedar Falls to see Mom and Dad, I would stop by the nursing home and spend time with him. Now, just like that, he was gone.

My oldest cousin, Chris, called me the next morning. She was handling the arrangements. "Brenda, would you please give the eulogy?"

I hesitated. "I've never done anything like that."

"You can do it—I know you can. All you need to do is say a few words about Grandpa's life and what he meant to all of us."

She kept on urging, and I finally agreed. It was the least I could do to honor my grandfather.

I was nervous as I walked to the podium at the funeral, but I decided I'd just do the best I could. I shared a few stories about Grandpa and talked about how he had nicknames for each of his grandkids. And I thought I must be doing all right, because when I told funny stories, people laughed. On what was otherwise a sad day, it felt good to share some laughs together. Grandpa would have liked that.

I also enjoyed spending the day with my extended family—something I rarely managed to do anymore. Although Cedar Rapids wasn't that far away, it was hard to find a time to get together, especially now that Kim and John were living in Davenport. But mostly it was hard because Neil didn't really like hanging out with my family. Some of them didn't like him much either, so I would try to compliment or defend him whenever someone spoke ill of him. Today, though, I barely even saw him.

On the drive back to Cedar Rapids, my belly felt even larger than it had on the way up. I couldn't sit up comfortably, so I leaned the seat back, careful not to get too close to Zack's car seat. Maybe it was nervous energy because of the baby, or maybe it was relief that the funeral was over, but I found myself babbling the whole way back, telling Neil about what it was like to speak in front of all those people and the nice things they had said afterward.

About halfway home, it occurred to me that Neil hadn't said much.

"Well, how do you think I did?" I asked, hoping for a compliment.

There was no reply.

"Are you mad about something?"

Again, nothing. He stared straight ahead, a coldness in his eyes.

"You're so quiet. You've been quiet for two days."

"Yep," he said.

I figured someone had said something to him that he didn't like or I'd done something to make him mad. Now I would have to figure out what had happened so I could apologize. But honestly, I couldn't think of anything. "Just tell me what's wrong. Did Mom say something?"

"Nope, I'm fine."

"You sure?"

"Yep, I'm sure."

"Because whenever you act like this, it doesn't seem like you even like me."

Nothing.

"And you've been acting like this a lot lately."

Nothing.

"Neil, do you still love me?"

"Um, yep. I still love you."

His words felt as cold and wet as the November snow. "Then why are we having this argument?"

"We're not having an argument."

"Yes, we are."

"No, it's just your hormones from being pregnant."

Maybe he was right. It had been an emotional week with Grandpa's death. Neil had felt a lot of stress from having to spend so much time around my family. Maybe I was just making a big deal out of nothing. There was no point in arguing further. I let it go.

That night, after I changed into my T-shirt and put Zack to bed, I knew what I needed to do. *He'll say yes to sex.* Although it wouldn't be much fun for me at this stage of my pregnancy, it would put him in a good mood. I took off my T-shirt and slipped underneath the covers. Neil was turned away from me, so I started rubbing his back. He didn't get the message, so I snuggled next to him until we were spooning—as much as was possible with a belly full of baby—and caressed his arms and then his legs.

The baby started to get excited.

At least someone was.

"Can you feel the baby kicking?" I asked.

"Yep."

I could tell by his tone that nothing was going to happen. I waited a few minutes—still nothing—and then rolled over to my side of the bed. I wasn't used to getting nothing.

"This isn't working. You don't talk to me, and you don't want sex. You might as well tell me what's making you so mad."

I stared down the hall to Zack's room while I waited for Neil's reply. After a pause, he turned onto his back.

"I'm attracted to another woman."

I threw off the covers and heaved my pregnant self out of the bed. "What did you just say?"

"I'm attracted to another woman," he said, staring at the ceiling. "I'm sorry."

He didn't need to say more or explain the details; what he said was enough for me to make up my mind about what I was going to do. "I'm outta here!" I grabbed my T-shirt from the floor and pulled it on. "How could you do this?" I flipped on the bedroom light, opened the closet door, and found my suitcase. As I threw clothes into it, I thought through all the things I had done alone.

I prayed for Zack alone. I attended church alone. I went to so many of Zack's appointments alone. For years, I alone had provided our income. I had longed for Neil to get more involved. Now I couldn't wait to get away from him.

I hurried down the hall and grabbed the phone.

Neil yelled, "What are you doing?"

"I already told you," I said, dialing Mom's number. "I'm outta here!"

Mom answered.

"Neil has a girlfriend. Can you come pick up Zack and me?"

I heard Neil jump out of bed and pull on his pants.

Mom said, "Oh, Brenda, sweetheart. I am so sorry! I was always afraid something like this would happen."

I could hear her telling Dad, "Neil's cheated, just like we thought. We need to go get her." Then back to me, "Sweetheart, we're leaving now. One of us will be there as soon as we can."

I was so intent on getting out of the house that what she said wouldn't sink in until days later. *They expected this!* I hung up the phone and started packing my prenatal vitamins and other things I needed from the kitchen.

"Brenda, stop. Don't do this." Neil was following me around the house now.

"I can't believe you cheated on me!" I grabbed another bag and filled it. "Who is she?"

"That's not important."

It would take Mom and Dad an hour to drive from Cedar Falls, and I wanted to be ready when they arrived. I ran around the house—half-frantic, half-stunned—gathering up the things Zack and I needed most. We could come back later and get the rest of it.

Neil continued to follow me from room to room. "Let's talk about this."

Now he wants to talk?

I returned to the bedroom, got dressed, and put more clothes in the suitcase. I went to the bathroom and collected a few items and returned to put them in my bag. Neil kept following me, trying to get me to look him in the eye. But I wouldn't. The more he tried to slow me down, the faster I moved.

Finally he grabbed my face and turned it so I'd have to look him in the eye.

So I did. I stared right at him. Through clenched teeth, I said, "Don't touch me! Get away from me."

He dropped his hands.

I had never been cheated on, and I'd never known anyone who was. I didn't know how to act or what to do. All I could think about was getting out of there. I was furious about all those times I had taken the blame for his bad behavior. But most of all, I felt hurt and betrayed.

I didn't want to hear his reasons, his excuses. I was sick of his excuses. I had already repeated enough of them to my family. I had nothing left for him. Getting Zack and myself out of there was all I cared about.

Neil grew more agitated as I carried the bags to the front door. "Stop! We need to talk!" But I had nothing to say.

I went into Zack's room and flipped on the light. Amazingly, he was still sleeping soundly. I carefully reached under him and tried to pick him up without waking him.

"You're not taking Zack," Neil said, suddenly lowering his voice. He stood in Zack's doorway, blocking me from leaving.

For the second time, I turned and looked him directly in the eye. "I am taking Zack. We are going to my mom's, and you are not going to stop us. Now, get away from me."

Neil finally got the picture. He dropped his arms and stepped aside to let me pass.

I held Zack tightly against my chest as I walked to the living room and sat in the chair closest to the window. It was late, and few cars were on the street.

As I waited, in some small way, I felt a release. Lately, nothing I did had broken Neil out of his bad attitude, and the years of dealing with his moods had taken their toll. But now that I was leaving, the responsibility was no longer mine. I had been trying to protect Neil from Mom and Mom from Neil. But now everyone knew the truth. Neil was exactly who they'd always said he was.

––––––––

Kim arrived in less than an hour. She had just walked into Mom's house when I called, and she wanted to be the one to come and get me. She and John were still in Cedar Falls for the funeral and had planned to drive back to Davenport the next day. She helped me load the bags and Zack's car seat into her car. Neil stayed in the bedroom, and we took off without saying a word to him.

I had felt the tears building as I'd gathered my things and waited for Kim to arrive, but I hadn't wanted to give Neil the satisfaction of seeing me cry. Once in the car, however, I let loose. By the time we were on the highway, I was choking on my own sobs.

"Oh, honey." Kim reached over to rub my belly as she drove. "Calm down. Please just calm down. You can't do this to your baby."

She was right. I did my best to gain control and stop the intense sobbing, but the tears still flowed.

––––––––

When we got to the house, Mom and Dad were watching through the window. I ran inside and straight into their arms. Zack had fallen asleep in the car, and Kim brought him inside and tucked him into his old crib in the sewing room. I could feel hands rubbing my back and see the concerned looks on my family's faces. Despite my pain, I felt very loved. I tried to talk, but I'm sure I didn't make much sense.

"Let's get you to bed," someone said. "You're exhausted. We can talk in the morning."

Mom ushered me back to my old mauve and dusty-blue room. Kim grabbed a T-shirt out of one of my bags and helped me undress. I had slept in this room the night before the funeral, just twenty-four hours earlier, but it had been with Neil. Now I would be sleeping there alone.

In the dark, as the baby kicked, I called out to God. *How could this happen to me? How could this happen after all I've done for him? I've worked so hard to do everything right.*

In the darkness of my high school bedroom, eight months pregnant, I knew I had every reason to fall apart, to give in to whatever emotions swept over me. But feeling my baby kick, I made a decision to be strong. I had six weeks until my due date. I could be strong for six weeks. I would set aside the tears and do whatever I needed to take care of the growing life inside of me. Then I'd worry about the future.

———————

Neil called the next morning. "If you're not coming home, I want to at least see Zack."

"Fine, but you're not taking him anywhere. You can come to Mom and Dad's and see him here."

Neil wasn't happy with that ultimatum, but he wasn't in a position to argue.

I asked a few more questions and got a few answers. The woman he was cheating with was just a girl—a nineteen-year-old girl. He had met her at work on the night shift.

"Why'd you do it?" I asked. "Just tell me why."

His answer was incomprehensible to me. "She doesn't tell me to take the garbage out. And we don't fight about money."

All I could think was, *Are you kidding me?*

"I'm done!" I said and hung up the phone. He called back several times over the next few days, and I refused to talk to him.

Thanksgiving was only a few days away, so people were in and out of the house, bringing food for the annual Woodyard family Thanksgiving dinner. Everyone expressed their concern and wanted to make sure I was taking care of myself and the baby. They said that Neil's behavior had only confirmed who they thought he was.

"He's emotionally manipulated you," one cousin said.

Aunt Helen said, "I remember when he wouldn't let you order a Pepsi when you were eating out because he said you couldn't afford it. But you were the one with the job—he wasn't even working. It made me so mad that he could control you that way."

Someone else brought up Zack's accident. "I still can't believe he didn't tell you what happened for twenty-four hours!"

Although what they said was true, I still tried to defend him. "It was so hard for him. He was on medication and having seizures." Or, "Of course I had to be the one who worked. He was too sick."

"I don't believe it," someone muttered under his breath.

"I remember when you and Neil were living here and you would go to your Mary Kay shows," Kim said. "You'd be all dolled up and looking amazing, but he always had to say something just to knock you down."

"Well, he just didn't have a lot of friends, so he didn't like it when I was gone too much," I said.

"I just got tired of seeing my beautiful, strong sister treated that way," said Kim. Her words were kind and spoken with tenderness. "I saw you go from this strong, independent United States Marine to a woman who was beaten down. It bothers me. You have such low self-esteem, and you never used to be that way. He blames you for everything, and you apologize whether you did it or not."

I thought about all the times I'd said, "I'm sorry," promising never to do it again but not even sure what I'd done.

Kim was right. I *had* been beaten down.

I couldn't believe I'd let that happen.

——————

On Thanksgiving, family members greeted each other with hugs and "Happy Thanksgiving!" They greeted me with loving and concerned looks, saying, "You can't go back there!"

And I agreed.

For the past three days I had listened to them tell me how horrible Neil was. Their words were true, and I had no way to defend against them. I also knew that if I chose Neil, I risked disappointing my family.

I finally decided he wasn't worth it.

15

Moving Out

Over turkey and banana pudding, the entire Woodyard family decided I would move out of Neil's house the next day. Aunt Helen offered to watch Zack. Dad said he would rent a U-Haul truck. Cousins and their spouses agreed to help unload the house and load the truck. No one wanted me to go, but I had an ob-gyn appointment back in Cedar Rapids. Kim offered to take me to the doctor while everyone else went to the house. I figured I could swing by the house after the appointment and show them what to pack.

I called Neil to warn him we'd be coming. "I'll be there tomorrow to get a few things," I said. "You need to be gone so I won't see you when I get there."

"What time will you be here?"

"I'll be there at nine."

At eight the next morning, a convoy of five cars and a U-Haul truck gathered at my parents' place and prepared to head out to Cedar Rapids. It looked as if a military operation had convened to invade my old house. "We need to be careful," one of my cousins said to another. "He may be watching the house, and we don't want anything to happen to Brenda."

We caravaned down the highway, and once we reached Cedar Rapids, the truck and four cars turned off toward my house. I'd already given my keys to Mom and Dad.

Kim and I headed straight to my doctor's office. Once I was there, the doctor did his usual workup, but he looked worried after listening to my heart. He listened to it several times to make sure it wasn't a fluke. Finally, he put down his stethoscope. "I am hearing palpitations that concern me. I think maybe we should put you on a monitor."

I looked at Kim, who sighed heavily. The doctor heard the sigh. "What's going on in your life?" he asked. "Is there any possibility this could be stress related?"

How do I even begin to tell him what's going on?

"Well, earlier this week my husband admitted he was having an affair. I have a son who's brain-damaged and mostly blind, and I'm nearly eight months pregnant and moving back into the house with my parents. Oh, and my grandpa died."

The doctor, looking stunned, started to tear up.

"It's okay. Really, it's okay," I said, trying to reassure him. "But I'll need to take my records with me today since I'll have to find a new doctor in Cedar Falls."

He nodded, dabbed his eyes with a tissue, and then finished my exam. After we received my records, we left. Kim wanted to go straight back to Cedar Falls, but I insisted on going to the house. Ten people were there, loading things up, and they had no idea what to get. I wanted to make sure they got everything of mine.

During the drive over, I thought about how divorce had never been an option for me. When I promised to stay married, I meant it. Even during our worst arguments over money or Neil's jealousy, he had never mentioned the D-word, and I had never even *thought* it.

I wasn't even sure what being divorced looked like.

When we got to the house, Mom said they hadn't seen Neil all day. She asked how my appointment had gone.

"You won't believe this," Kim said, "but when the doctor heard Brenda's story, she had to console *him*."

They both smiled a little. I could tell they were proud of me for being strong. Mom led me into the house, where I could see they were clearing out everything—furniture, dishes, clothes, pictures from the walls. Everything was going.

"Take that too!" Mom said, pointing to a lamp.

"We can't take everything," I said. We didn't have overhead lights in the living room; we had to use lamps. If they took the last lamp, they'd be taking the only light source. "How's Neil going to see anything?"

"We're taking it all," Mom said. "You're the one who worked for years to pay for it, and it was your credit history, not his, that let you charge it."

My uncle Rick picked up the lamp and took it out to the truck. The only thing left in the living room was an oversized painting hanging on the wall. Neil had painted it, so they left it for him.

As we walked to the kitchen, I noticed that the table and chairs were gone and the cupboard doors were open. The insides were bare. *At least there's an overhead light in the kitchen*, I thought.

Then someone walked over to the overhead light and unscrewed the bulbs.

"You're taking the lightbulbs?"

"We'll leave the appliances. You said you still owe money on them anyway."

"At least leave him a fork," I said.

"We've packed the forks," Mom said. "We're not leaving him a fork."

I wandered through the rest of the house. Zack's room was completely cleared out—bed, dresser, clothes, everything. I couldn't believe how quickly my family had worked. The only thing left was the wallpaper border I'd hung just a few weeks earlier for the new baby.

A wave of emotion suddenly washed over me. I fell back against the wall and cried so hard I couldn't hold myself up. I slid down the wall until I was in a squatting position, put my face into my knees, and sobbed.

Family members immediately surrounded me, talking softly. "It's going to be okay," they said. "Don't cry, Brenda." Kim wrapped her arm around my neck to comfort me.

"This was my baby's room. This was my baby's room," I repeated through my tears.

I squatted there, my back pressed against the wall, until the tears stopped. Once I had calmed down, Kim got her arm around me and helped me stand. She led me down the hall to the living room, where someone produced a chair, and I sat down. Mom handed me a Kleenex and wiped my hair—matted with sweat and tears—out of my face. Meanwhile, others kept carrying things out of the house.

They loaded the last box, and it was time to go. I stood up, and they took the chair I'd been sitting on and put it in the truck. We were almost to the door when Mom said, "Ice trays!"

Mom returned to the kitchen, opened the freezer, got out the ice cube trays, and dumped the ice in the sink. She tucked the trays under her arm and said, "We can go now."

I couldn't help but laugh as Mom strode victoriously to the passenger side of the U-Haul with those stupid ice cube trays stuck under her arm.

———

When the phone rang that evening, I knew it was Neil. Although I had refused all of his calls up until now, I said, "I want to take this one."

"What do you think you're doing? You took everything! You can't do that!"

"Yes, I can. In fact, I already did."

He screamed and swore.

I hung up the phone.

When he called back, I didn't wait for him to say anything. "I am not going to talk with you if you're going to scream like that." Something inside of me had snapped. "You're not treating me like this anymore," I said. "Call back when you want to come visit Zack."

I hung up the phone. I was determined to never let a man mistreat me again.

But as tough as I sounded on the phone, inside I was still a mess. In bed that night, I cried out to God, *Where are you? Why is this happening to me? If you truly have a purpose for my life, how can this be my purpose?*

I felt so rejected. I had wanted Neil to love me the way I had loved him. For better. For worse. For*ever.*

Mom must have heard my crying because my door creaked open. "Can I come in?"

"Mom, who's ever going to want me?" I asked through my cries. "I'll soon be a divorced mother of two—with a special-needs child!"

"Next time you'll wait for a man who deserves you." She sat next to me on the bed and let her words sink in. Then she rubbed my belly. "I think it's going to be a girl."

"I can't imagine having a girl after having Zack," I said, sniffling.

"She's going to be wonderful," Mom said. "And beautiful. This baby girl's going to look just like you."

She sat there for a long time, making up stories about what this girl would grow up to do and who she would turn out to be. When I got really quiet, she said, "Now I need *my* baby girl to get some rest."

I smiled. I liked having my mom take care of me. And for a moment, I actually believed things would be okay.

———

My moving in with Mom and Dad had to create hardships for them, but they didn't complain, and they helped the best they could. Neil and I didn't have a lot of furniture, but I sold what I could to get some money to help with expenses. Mom went to garage sales to pick up little things to turn her sewing room into a sweet little room for a boy and to pick up things we needed for the new baby. Dad helped me find a lawyer. The lawyer advised me not to file for divorce until after I had the baby so Neil's insurance would pick up the costs. Neil and I had argued about visitation details, so he hadn't seen Zack since the night I left. That was fine with me. Things were moving fast, and we hadn't talked a lot.

I had just entered my ninth month when I saw my new ob-gyn for the first time. I gave him my records and explained my situation. I had been crying a lot, and I was terribly worried that my out-of-control emotions could harm the baby.

"You're doing fine," the doctor said. "A little crying won't hurt anything."

If he only knew. It was anything but a *little* crying.

"But you're under a lot of stress," he added, "and the baby is healthy, so

131

let's just go ahead and early induce this baby next week while I'm on call."

Having an exact date to deliver helped me prepare for my baby's birth. Dad agreed to watch Zack. On the scheduled day, Kim drove up from Davenport, and she and Mom took me to the hospital. As for Neil, I wasn't going to even give him the honor of being there; I'd rather give birth alone. I filled out the paperwork while Mom watched *Live with Regis and Kathie Lee* on television in the lobby. Kim had brought her video camera and was determined to document every moment. She even filmed while I filled out the hospital forms. When I got to the question, "Doctor's first and last name?" I had to laugh. I didn't know his first name, and I wasn't sure how to spell his last name.

The nurse reviewed the form and saw that I'd filled in Neil's information. "Is the father on the way?"

Kim immediately said, "No."

But that wasn't the only time we were asked. Several times that day, a nurse or other medical professional asked, "Is the dad coming?"

Each time, Kim would make light of it. "Nope, it's just us girls," she'd say, or, "We're making this a girls' day." She did her best to keep things light and happy for my baby's arrival.

They gave me the medication to bring on the contractions, and soon the labor started. Kim kept videotaping, narrating what she filmed. "There's Grandma Jenny Jo. She's so excited for her new grandbaby. And Zack and Papa are at home, just waiting to hear from us."

As the contractions grew, I squeezed Mom's hand, but I didn't make a sound. I didn't moan, and I didn't scream. Not a noise. Between contractions Kim would pick up the camera and tape. "She's so quiet—my strong, strong sister."

I liked being strong and in control. I hadn't felt that way in a long time.

Mom stroked my hair and whispered in my ear. When a nurse asked if some nursing students could come in and watch, I said yes. Between contractions, I grew sleepy and maybe even a little loopy from the medication. As the birth got closer and the room got fuller, I heard Kim ask me if she should continue taping. I mumbled something in response, but she couldn't understand me.

"Well, we can't go back and do it over, so I'm just going to continue taping. If you want to delete it later, you can."

I nodded.

The baby began crowning, and from behind the camera I heard Kim say, "Oh my goodness, she has so much hair."

Mom had already guessed the baby was a girl. Now Kim was assuming the same thing. After the last push, the doctor proudly held up my precious new baby and said, "It's a girl! Good job, Mom."

I lay back in the bed and watched Kim follow the nurses with her camera. They carried my baby girl over to the heat lamps so they could clean her off. "Look at her big, black curls. And she has dimples, dimples just like Zack."

The whole mood in the room changed. Joy in the form of a person had entered. I thought back to the night Neil and I discussed having a second child and how we both thought that a new baby would bring us more joy. Now I needed that joy more than ever, and already she was making the world—at least my world—a better place.

I named the baby Jesse Jo. And she did look just like her brother. She even had cute, little-girl dimples.

"I told you she'd be beautiful," Mom said. "Just like you."

It was a happy moment. The road ahead wouldn't be easy, but in that moment, I wanted to prolong the good feeling this little girl had brought to all of us.

After Zack and I moved into my parents' house, Zack and his grandpa had become quite the pair. When Dad went to the basement to shower, he liked to take Zack with him. We'd hear them both singing songs through the vents in the floor. They'd emerge later wearing pj's and matching robes. Mom would make them popcorn, and Zack would sit in the chair with Grandpa while they ate from the same bowl. Mom always put a toothpick in the bottom of the bowl for Dad to pick clean his false teeth. When Zack found the toothpick, he'd triumphantly hand it to his grandpa. Dad was becoming a father figure to Zack.

A couple of hours after Jesse Jo was born, Dad brought Zack to the hospital. "Here comes two peas in a pod," Kim joked. Zack walked in with a candy bar in one chubby fist and a Pepsi in the other.

Dad picked up Jesse Jo and then bent down so Zack could meet her too. Zack leaned over and smelled her hair.

Then he smiled with those big dimples.

———————

In Mom's converted sewing room, I held both my children in my lap and rocked them. A broken family wasn't what I wanted for my kids. I felt I had failed to pick someone worthy of them. Worthy of me. I knew they wouldn't even exist if not for Neil. But they'd still pay the price for my picking the wrong guy—for not waiting, as Mom put it, for someone who deserved me. Someone who deserved *them*. I felt sad for everything that had been lost.

As a girl, I had dreamed of becoming a marine. Of marrying a marine and raising a perfect family in our perfect, picket-fenced home. But reality had shattered all my dreams of perfection. Life wasn't at all what I had planned. But I still knew that I had a choice—the choice to make the best of what I had. The life I'd expected had died. But my unexpected life was there for the taking.

Jesse Jo's pudgy fist and tiny fingers were wrapped around my finger. I smiled as Zack smelled her hair. I looked at my two beautiful children and thanked God. Then I made him and them a promise:

I'm so lucky to have these kids. I'll do whatever it takes to give them a good life.

Part Two

THE MAN I WANTED

1992–1998

16

Decisions

The courtroom reminded me of the one from the Child Protective Services hearing. I stood before the judge, watching him carefully read through each paper. *Couldn't you have read these before? I want to get home to my baby.* I glanced at my blouse and prayed my breasts wouldn't leak. He read through all the witness statements—letters of support from my friends and family. Neil wasn't required to show, and he hadn't.

The judge slid his thick, black-rimmed glasses down his nose and looked at me over the top of the heavy frames. "Is this really what you want?"

"Yes sir."

"Are you sure?" He glanced at my lawyer.

The courtroom was completely silent. The lawyer gave me a reassuring smile. A rush of milk released from my breasts. "Absolutely," I said, praying the breast pads would do their job.

After I had told the lawyer about Zack's accident, he had obtained a waiver so I wouldn't have to wait the usual six months to finalize my divorce. Although I'd never felt like Neil dropping Zack was anything other than an accident, the lawyer advised me to err on the side of caution. He included language in the divorce agreement that required Neil's visits to be supervised by me at my house. "We might not get this passed. But if we do, you won't have to worry about meeting to drop off the children or about not knowing what's really going on. If there's ever a little scratch on

Zack's head or on your daughter, you know it'll trigger the Child Protective Services stuff to come up again. If this is granted, it will prevent that."

It was nice to have someone protecting my interests.

"I'll grant this," the judge said as he inked his name on the paper. He also ordered Neil to pay regular child support, but on his salary it wasn't much. "I wish you the best of luck." He was probably thinking, *Glad she's not my daughter!*

And that was it. I was divorced.

Jesse Jo had been born in January, I got divorced in February, and in March, Neil and I would have celebrated our four-year anniversary. Though I felt sad, mostly I felt relieved not to have to take care of him and his moods any longer. But I didn't want anyone to know I felt that way. Somehow it cheapened our marriage if people thought I was happy to be out of it.

When I got home, I walked into the kitchen. Mom was there, holding Jesse Jo. I looked at Mom from the other end of the long kitchen table. "It's done," I said, searching her eyes.

She looked relieved. Relieved, but also sad. Her eyes were a mirror to my soul. "Oh, sweetheart, it's going to be all right."

As with so many other events in my life, I didn't have time to hang out in the kitchen and think about what it all meant. Jesse Jo was hungry, and Zack needed me to be his mom. There was no point in crying when diapers need to be changed.

––––––––––

Neil had seen Jesse Jo for the first time when I was still in the hospital. He tentatively entered the room and said, "How're you doing?"—just like nothing had happened.

I didn't say anything.

"Can I hold her?" he asked. Mom probably wouldn't have let him, but she wasn't there. I handed the pink bundle to him and watched as he opened up the blanket and checked her out. "She's so beautiful!" he said with tenderness in his voice. "She looks just like Zack!"

I was tired, so I kept dozing off, but every time I awakened, he was still holding her, just staring at her.

An hour later he said, "Well, I'd better get back. It's a long drive home." He took one long look at me. "I miss you guys."

I didn't say anything.

———————

After the divorce was finalized, Neil could see the kids for four hours every other week. He would drive to Mom's house on a Saturday or Sunday and play with the kids for a few hours. I'd start out watching them play in the living room but eventually move around the house, throwing in laundry, making snacks, or doing other chores while he occupied the kids. So one Saturday when I heard his knock on the door, I expected the visit to be just like the others.

But before I opened the door, I knew this one would be different. Through the glass I saw he'd brought *her* with him. He hadn't called. He hadn't asked. He had just shown up with her. I was stunned that he thought it was okay to bring his girlfriend. But I was even more appalled that she would *want* to come.

With my hand frozen on the doorknob, I knew I had a decision to make. I could get ugly and yell at them both. Or I could let her in and just take the high road.

Zack walked over to see what was going on. I glanced down at him and decided to do what was right, even if it didn't feel right.

I opened the door, and without saying a word, I motioned for them to come in.

I didn't introduce myself to the girl, and Neil didn't bother to make any introductions. But I knew who she was. One of my Mary Kay friends had seen her on the back of his bike and had described her as "young and pretty, with long, dark hair." During one of our conversations before the divorce, Neil had told me her name was Sharon. She worked as seasonal help on the night shift at the post office. There was no doubt this was her.

"This is Zack," Neil told her, ruffling Zack's hair. "And this is Jesse Jo." He picked her up out of the swing and placed my baby girl in his girlfriend's arms. I bit my tongue and sat down where I could still see everything without being close enough to be a part of their conversation.

It was hard to watch them. No one had ever rejected me before. I'd been the one everybody picked. Now I was in the same room with the person my husband had cheated on me with. And she was playing with *my* kids.

They had brought gifts for Zack and Jesse Jo—trinkets, really, but they were still more than I could afford. It made me sad that Neil could give them things I couldn't because I was buying their food, clothing, and diapers.

I tried to take an inventory of Sharon's assets. She was younger than me. *There's no way I can fight that.* She was obviously very pretty. *But prettier than me? Does he really find her more attractive?* He'd already told me he liked her because she didn't tell him to take out the trash. So maybe she was nicer than me. *Just wait until you live together and she needs the trash taken out.*

With her in my living room, it was easy to make comparisons. But the more questions I asked myself—Did we not have sex enough? Was I too fat during pregnancy? What was it about me that made him choose someone else?—the more I realized there were no easy answers. Even if I asked Neil those questions, I knew I wouldn't get a straight answer. Maybe he didn't even know the answers.

Rejection from a husband rocks you to the core of your identity. You have to reconsider everything about yourself, everything about your partner, and everything you believed about your relationship. Once trust is destroyed, you become distrustful. It's hard to know what's true and what isn't.

But in that moment, I realized the truth: I was still the strong, capable, and, yes, pretty woman I had always been. I was also a dedicated mother, doing what I could to serve my children and provide them the best life possible. I didn't need to compare myself to a nineteen-year-old to know that. Nor did I need a man to tell me that. I was fully capable of knowing it on my own.

I was brave enough to walk away from Neil and into a future that would include food stamps and low-income housing. And I was brave enough not to live my life with someone who didn't deserve me or my children. Although Neil's visit shook the very core of my identity, by the time he and his girlfriend left, I had no doubts about who I was.

He didn't hold any of the answers I needed.

They were all inside of me.

I still had doctor appointments for Zack and now for Jesse Jo too. We were eligible for Medicaid, and that helped to cover most of our medical costs, but other expenses remained. So one of my first jobs as a newly single mom was learning to navigate the many government services that were available to us.

Through a little research and a few tips from friends, I learned we were eligible for food stamps, Supplemental Security Income (SSI), government or Section 8 housing, and WIC vouchers—from a federal supplemental nutrition program for women, infants, and children. Each of the government programs required that I fill out paperwork and demonstrate proof of eligibility. Once we were granted the benefits, they only lasted for a specific period of time, and then I would have to reapply. Getting the assistance I needed was a full-time job that summer.

Of course, I already had a full-time job taking Zack to his doctor and therapist appointments—and now that we were back in Cedar Falls, the round-trip drive took at least two hours longer and required a lot more gas. I needed to develop a better plan to make money and take care of my family.

One day Mom and I were talking about that in the kitchen and she asked, "What do you want to be?"

"I don't know," I said. "All I ever wanted to be was a drill instructor."

"You're so good with Zachary. I wonder if there's anything you could do with the skills you've developed while taking care of him."

She was right. Just being around the medical community, having a child in the hospital, and assisting with years of therapy teaches you vocabulary and skills you wouldn't otherwise have.

"Have you ever thought about nursing?" Mom asked.

I had never thought about that. Nursing seemed a pretty big leap from being a drill instructor.

"I've heard the pay isn't bad," Mom said, "and the hours are flexible. Besides, if you were a nurse, you could always take care of Zack."

"That's a great idea." I said. "Zack would have care for the rest of his life, regardless of what I could afford."

But I would have to go to school to be a nurse, and I knew that would cost money. I was barely getting by as it was, and I wasn't sure if I could swing it financially. I didn't even have a car. Ours had been sold because neither Neil nor I could afford the payments.

Still, Mom's idea was a good one. I told Mom I'd look into it.

———————

Hawkeye Institute of Technology (now Hawkeye Community College) was located just across the river from Cedar Falls in the little community of Waterloo. It's one of two colleges in the Cedar Falls area. The other is the University of Northern Iowa. But everyone I talked to told me that Hawkeye Tech was the place I should look into for a nursing degree.

As I walked onto the campus, I told myself not to get my hopes up. Nursing school might cost too much, or I might not qualify for the program.

But my worries proved unfounded. An adviser told me I would move to the top of the admissions list because I had been a marine. I would also be eligible for special grants and loans. She gave me detailed information about the nursing program and the prerequisite classes I'd have to take in the fall before the program started in January.

She ordered a copy of my high school transcript and my discharge papers from the marines and said she'd let me know when they arrived. Meanwhile, I worked on other arrangements. I asked Mom about watching the kids while I was at school. She agreed. She had my back. So did Dad, who agreed to pick up some additional shifts at John Deere.

With my parents' help plus a combination of grants and loans, I found I could just barely afford nursing school. The grants helped me buy a cheap, little beater car, which I would drive until it was no longer fixable. During my entire time in the nursing program, I took out the maximum amount of loans that I qualified for. That, of course, put me into debt. But it also got me through school.

On the first night of my first prerequisite class, I walked into the classroom and immediately felt out of my comfort zone. Everyone seemed younger than me. No one else had been in the military, and I was pretty sure I was the only single mother. I obviously did not fit the demographics. But that class lifted my confidence anyway. I met new friends, and after doing well on several tests, I thought, *I might even be kind of smart.*

―――――――

When Jesse Jo was a couple of months old, I had started attending a singles' group at a local church. I saw it as another step toward rebuilding my life. But when it came to men, things were different now. I was no longer flattered every time a man showed interest or thought I was attractive. I no longer believed I *needed* a man to be happy. I was happy alone.

But as soon as I started dating, once again, the unexpected came dancing into my life.

17

Wanted

Some of my classmates asked me to join them at the opening of a new country bar, Wild E. Coyote's. I agreed to go with them. Mom and I had been taking line-dancing classes with some of her church friends, and this would be an opportunity to try out my new dance moves. Little did I know how that one decision would change my life.

Mom and I went on ladies' night. We could get in without paying a cover charge, so it was a cheap night out, especially since I didn't drink alcohol and Dad was happy to watch the kids. We took separate cars, and after Mom left I hung out with my friends.

The night was so much fun that Mom and I made ladies' night a habit. I had a simple rule. If you were brave enough to ask me to dance, I would dance with you. So I danced a lot. I met a lot of people and soon became a regular.

One night Mom and I sat at a table near the entrance when a group of guys came in. Some of them wore leather jackets from the University of Northern Iowa. I could tell they were probably athletes and, from their size, probably football players.

They were happy and having a good time. Most of the guys wore tight Wranglers, Garth Brooks–type country shirts, and cowboy boots. But the one in the middle wore a button-down oxford-cloth shirt, baggy jeans with pleats in the front, and tennis shoes. He parted his hair in the middle and feathered it back on each side. He wasn't as big as the other guys, but he was cute, and he knew it.

Before the guys could even open up their wallets and pay their covers, girls surrounded them. But the cute guy in the middle got most of the attention. There was something about him that made him stand out from the rest. It was as if one of the strobes from the dance floor were aimed right at him, creating a glow. And like bugs on a summer night, every girl in the bar seemed drawn to his light.

The cute guy greeted a few of the girls with hugs and pecks on the cheeks. One of the more aggressive girls grabbed him by the arm and led him to the dance floor. His friends paired up and followed. As he strode past our table, I looked at Mom. "Who is that?"

"I don't know." She surveyed him through narrowed eyes. "But he sure thinks he's all that."

"Well, there are a lot of girls after him."

"I wouldn't call them girls," Mom said. "I'd call them floozies."

When some of the girls from my class showed up, Mom decided to head home. But I kept my eye on the cute one. He was a good dancer, but he didn't take it too seriously. Sometimes to be goofy—and maybe because he liked the attention—he'd show off during line dances by facing his partner rather than standing in the line next to her.

I didn't spend all night staring, though. I spent the night laughing with the girls and dancing with the men who asked.

Over the next few weeks, I noticed that the cute guy and his posse had become regulars on ladies' night. He was still as popular—or more popular—than he'd been when I first saw him. Girls always hung around and asked him to dance. When he sat down, one of the girls would sit in his lap. There was lots of flirting and laughter. But he was also a man's man. Guys came up and slapped him on the back or shook his hand. A few times I thought he glanced my way, but I was busy doing my own thing and didn't spend much time worrying about him.

Besides, by then, I was already dating someone.

I had met Mark at a party, and we hit it off right away. He was shy and more reserved than most of the men I knew in Cedar Falls. He didn't spend nights hanging out at the bar, drinking and dancing. In fact, he wasn't into the bar scene at all.

Mark was originally from Cedar Falls but had moved to Des Moines. The night I met him, he was just in town to visit family for the weekend. We started chatting, and I learned he taught special-needs kids. Before the party was over, we had exchanged phone numbers, and it wasn't long before we were dating regularly. He would come to Cedar Falls to see me, or I'd get Mom and Dad to watch the kids so I could go visit him in Des Moines.

When I started dating again, I had made the decision not to let my dates meet my kids—at least not until I was very sure that we were serious. It was my job to protect them from the ups and downs of my relationships. But after Mark and I had gone out for a few weeks, it only made sense that he meet Zack. Fortunately, Zack took to him immediately. Mark was stable, had a job, and wasn't always looking at other girls—plus he liked my special boy and was good with him.

Mark was exactly the kind of person I needed. Although we went to different kinds of churches, he was strong in his Catholic beliefs and attended mass regularly. It wasn't hard to imagine a future with him.

—————————

Even while dating Mark, I continued to have a good time with Mom and my girlfriends at Wild E. Coyote's. One night late in October, the DJ said, "Grab your partners. We're going to do the barn dance!" An old man asked me to dance, and of course I said yes. I said yes to everybody.

The barn dance was a big circle dance that you started by facing your partner. We moved two steps to the right, two steps to the left, he twirled me away, and I twirled back. Then we bowed, stepped to the side to switch partners, and repeated the steps. Every sixteen counts we switched partners. I started with the old guy, but when the song finished, I ended up with the cute guy—the one I'd seen so many times before.

"Do you want to keep dancing?" he asked.

"I'd love to."

And so we danced. Fast songs, slow songs—it didn't matter. We just kept stepping and stomping, twirling and two-stepping. During a break between songs, he introduced himself. "My name's Kurt. Kurt—" He said his last name, but I didn't catch it because the music had started up.

"I'm Brenda. Brenda Meoni," I said as loudly as I could without yelling. And we started to dance again.

If anyone else wanted to cut in, I didn't see them. I was totally focused on Kurt—so much so that I lost track of time. At one thirty in the morning they announced, "Last call," and at two the dance floor lights flickered, telling us the night was over. People headed toward the door, and we got caught up in the flow. Kurt stayed with me.

I walked to my friend Desia's car because she was giving me a ride home. As we neared her car, I saw her standing next to the driver's door, talking to a guy. She seemed kind of flirty, like she was really into him, but I'd never met him. I assumed they had just met that night and were exchanging phone numbers.

I walked to the passenger side and figured Kurt was about to follow. But before he could say anything, I spoke up. "Listen, I'm divorced with two kids. If you never want to see me again, that's fine."

"Really?"

"Yeah."

He looked surprised. Here's this good-looking college boy who thinks he's going to get my number. Instead he gets my unexpected life story in five words.

He leaned over, gave me a hug and a quick peck on the cheek, and then walked away. *That's the end of that*, I thought. I didn't even know his last name.

Desia grinned as she put the car in reverse, waving to her guy one last time. "That was Doug," she said. "I love him! He's just so cute!"

I half listened as she chattered on about how they'd met that night, what he'd said, what she'd said, and how much she already loved him—even though they'd only just met. But mostly, I was lost in my own thoughts.

I'd just spent the night dancing with the cutest, most popular guy at the bar. And although I should've just enjoyed it and walked away, I couldn't help reliving every moment. But I also realized how stupid it was for me to even think about Kurt-whatever-his-name-was.

I was a divorced woman with two kids. Mark was the kind of guy I needed—good old reliable, stable Mark who taught special-needs children. He was the guy I should be dreaming about. But while I really, really liked Mark and maybe even loved him, he didn't take my breath away like cute Kurt from the bar.

I was wearing my red cowboy boots and a miniskirt. I should have been freezing from the chilly October night, but actually, I felt warm all over. *What am I doing? Why am I even thinking about this?*

Then I told myself it didn't matter. Nothing had happened, and nothing was likely to happen. The next time I saw Kurt at the bar, he probably wouldn't even notice me. I'd done the right thing by telling him about myself.

I let the thoughts go and tried to concentrate on what Desia was saying about her new love.

I hadn't stayed out that late in a long time. When the kids woke early the next morning, expecting to be fed, I was exhausted. I pulled my pink terry-cloth robe over my T-shirt, and I didn't even bother to brush my teeth. I made breakfast for Zack, who was now three and could eat it on his own.

Dad had left for work, and Mom was also gone. She'd probably left a note somewhere, but my eyes hadn't opened wide enough to find it. I started the coffee, got Zack some Cheerios, and started nursing Jesse Jo. Around nine o'clock, just as I finished with Jesse Jo, someone knocked on the sliding glass door.

The vertical blinds were pulled, so I couldn't see who was there. Before checking the door, I glanced at a mirror. My hair was not only messy, but big from all the hairspray I'd put on it last night. I hadn't washed my face, so dark circles from last night's mascara were smudged around my eyes. I pulled my robe closed, which was hard to do while balancing Jesse Jo on my hip. I cinched my belt one more time to make sure the robe stayed closed; then I peeked through the blinds.

"Oh crap!"

It was the cute boy from the bar! Kurt. Kurt something-or-other. But what was he doing here?

He stood on the top step and held a rose. He probably spotted me peeking through the blinds, but if not, he saw what happened next. Zack pushed his walker up to the door and pawed at the blinds to see who was outside. There was no way Kurt didn't see that. I had to open the door.

I slid the door open a foot. "Hey," I said. "What're you doing here?"

"I brought you this." He handed me the rose.

You've got to be kidding me! The whole thing seemed so cheesy. So many thoughts ran through my head, I didn't know what to say.

"I want to meet your kids."

While my brain screamed, *No!* my mouth said, "Come in."

Before I could figure out what to do next, Zack stepped through the doorway and put his pudgy little hand into Kurt's big one. "Come here, Mark," he said.

"Okay," Kurt answered without so much as a glance at me for approval.

"His name's Zack," I called as they walked hand in hand down the hall to Zack's room.

Oh my gosh, oh my gosh, oh my gosh! I just let this guy into my house. Technically, it wasn't even my house; it belonged to my parents. And now my son was calling Kurt "Mark."

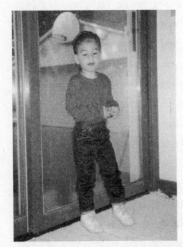

Three-year-old Zack propped against the sliding glass door for a picture before his first day of school

I heard Zack talking as he turned on the radio in his room. Radios fascinated Zack, and he loved to demonstrate them to anyone who showed the least interest. Unfortunately for me, almost every room in the house had a radio. This was going to take a while.

I decided to sit down and wait it out. Jesse Jo needed to be burped, so I held her against my shoulder and started patting her back. Mom's comment from Kurt's first night at the bar echoed in my ears. "He thinks he's all that!" Now he was in her house. *Mom's going to kill me!*

I could hear Zack talking as he took

Kurt from room to room, showing him each radio and alarm clock and how it worked. *And probably still calling him Mark.* I tried to remember what was on my bedroom floor. Probably the bra I'd worn last night. I wasn't always the neatest person. *Great. Just great.*

Jesse Jo let out a good burp. I laid her on a blanket on the floor and gave her some toys to play with. Using a corner of the burp cloth, I tried to wipe the mascara off my face. I tugged the belt on my robe and sat down next to Jesse Jo on the floor. As I shook a rattle in front of her, I realized how awkward I felt just sitting and waiting for Zack's tour to end. But what else could I do?

Kurt was obviously different from the other guys I was used to. He wasn't a marine, for sure. He didn't stand, dress, or speak like a marine. He seemed to totally lack the discipline of a marine. Instead he seemed spontaneous and fun—two things I most definitely was not. I tended toward black-and-white thinking and was usually serious. Kurt, on the other hand, seemed almost childlike.

I was intrigued. Very intrigued.

When Kurt and Zack came back to the living room, I panicked again. *What am I doing?* Kurt and Zack started tickling each other and ended up playfully wrestling on the floor. I raised Jesse Jo up to a sitting position so she could watch. "This is Jesse Jo," I said. Kurt rolled onto his belly and picked up a toy and played with her while Zack climbed on his back.

By now, I was really freaking out.

But Kurt just loved on the kids, playing with them like he'd known them all their lives.

We talked, and he told me he'd gotten my address from Doug. I learned he was twenty-one, four years younger than me. He was a student at UNI and played football. "I'm a quarterback," Kurt said, "but right now I'm just a backup."

I nodded as if I knew what he meant. Despite my years as a cheerleader, I didn't actually know anything about the game; in high school we were just expected to look cute.

When Kurt first started talking, all I could think about was how awful I looked and whether I might be leaking from breastfeeding. But the more he talked, the more I focused on him. *You're cute. You're really cute. And you're a good dancer. But the last thing I need is another cute guy who can dance. I need an ugly guy with a job.*

Kurt asked a question.

"Uh-huh," I murmured, not sure what I'd agreed to.

"Well, I need to get going," he said. I looked at the clock; it was after eleven. He'd been there for more than two hours.

I got up and walked him to the door.

"Will I see you again at Coyote's?"

"Um, yeah. I'll be there on ladies' night."

"Okay, see you then." He opened the sliding door and stepped outside.

I watched him walk down the steps and into the yard, then noticed that my car was the only one in the driveway.

"Hey, where's your car?" It was at least two miles back to campus.

"I don't have one. I walked," he said, grinning. "Bye!"

I saw Kurt during the next ladies' night at Coyote's. He still had his friends, still had his floozies, and still had a girl in his lap. But when he saw me, he left all of them to come over and ask me to dance. There was something about this guy I couldn't refuse. He was exciting, and maybe I needed a little excitement in my life. But best of all, I could tell he liked me. He really thought I was cool, and that made me feel good.

I was pretty sure Mom and Dad wouldn't approve of Kurt. But all we did was hang out at the bar and dance. There was nothing wrong with that.

A few weeks later, I was in Des Moines with Mark. We'd gone out for pizza with a few other couples, friends of Mark. UNI was playing football on one of the televisions, and the guys were more interested in the game than they were in conversation.

"Who's that?" one of the guys asked as a player ran onto the field.

"That's Warner," Mark's best friend said. "Kurt Warner. He's the backup quarterback."

Two years old today, and I look like I already ate the cake!

My daddy's favorite horse, Sport, with me at three years old showing my spunk

One of my favorite places to be, in my mom's arms next to my sister

It's sister's first day of school, and I still got to stay in my PJs and hang with Dad on the farm.

The Carney family in 1970

Me (left) and Kim on the farm

Feeling like the pretty one

We found out very early I had no musical talent, but I could make noise!

Me and my best friend, Flash

A school friend and I riding Flash. Parkersburg, Iowa, 1975

Go! Fight! Win! Cheerleading in the seventh grade

Mom and I taking a moment to talk on the front step. Cedar Falls, Iowa, 1979

Carney family photo, 1981

Chach giving me the dance lessons that would one day help me catch my man

Carney family dressed in plaid, 1981

All-American cheerleader

Good old senior pictures!

The few, the proud . . . A marine!

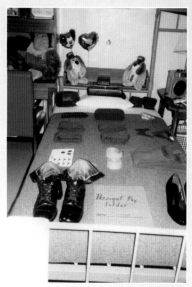

Lance Corporal Brenda Carney ready for inspection!

Back from Okinawa and safe in sister Kim's arms after a year overseas.

Me wearing my dress blues in Mom's kitchen while home on leave

Hanging with the best dad in the world

When I was young, I was Daddy's little girl standing by his truck.

But it wasn't long before I was all grown up and had a truck of my own. Of course, it was just like Dad's.

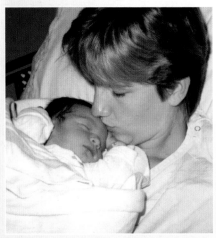

Happy birthday, Zachary Taylor. So in love!

So happy to have Zack home from the hospital, 1989

Zack with his eye patched and using cart for support. Even play was physical therapy for this three-year-old.

Away from his momma for his first Christmas in 1989, Zack was loved on by his grandma and grandpa.

My dad and Zack, such great buddies

Zack on top of the world, mowing the lawn with my dad. I'd say he got the better end of that deal!

Zack feeling for the toothpick at the bottom of the popcorn bowl

Doing it on my own as a single mom

Jesse Jo turns one! I left the party to go break up with my boyfriend so I could start dating a cute, young football player.

GiGi, my favorite resident at the Cedar Falls Lutheran home

Even though I had spent five years being Zack's nurse . . . this is the day it became *official*.

My mom and dad, always hugging and kissing

Jenny Jo and Larry Carney retired after working for more than thirty hard years at John Deere.

Mom and Dad's dream house

After the tornado, only the foundation remained.

At my parents' cabin in Mountain View, Arkansas. This was the last photo I took with my mom.

The sixth-grade photo I found in the convenience store in Mountain View after the tornado

The country girl and the city boy

Two-stepping with my man at Wild E. Coyote's

Kurt and his mom on our wedding day, October 11, 1997

Missing the strong arm of my dad as I walked down the aisle alone

Introducing Mr. and Mrs . . . Meoni (oops, Warner!)

Like father, like son at our wedding

Daddy, can I have this dance? Father-daughter dance at our wedding.

The Warner Four: The early years!

Holding on tight to each other as we get used to the new "normal"

Our first ESPY award show

Look how far we've come! Me and my two best friends growing up (sister Kim and Lynn) sharing a moment at our first Super Bowl.

Momma got a new pair of shoes . . . showing them off as I head into Super Bowl XXXIV

SUPERBOWL XXXIV

A kiss to celebrate the fairy-tale end of the 1999 season

The Warner family "float" at the Super Bowl parade in St. Louis

My infamous hairstyle, and my natural hair color

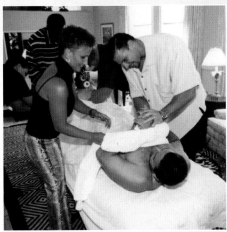

Taping Kurt down for his grand entrance to his thirtieth surprise party

Happy birthday, Jada Jo! (Also in the picture, Uncle Matt, Grandpa Gene, Zack, Kurt, Jesse Jo, Jada Jo, me, Aunt Kimmy, and Kade)

The Warner men: Kurt, Zack, and Kade

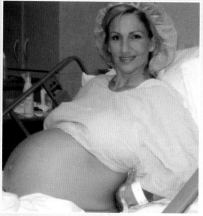

After, with Sienna and Sierra

Before . . .

Sienna and Sierra started out
inseparable; and they still are.
Sometimes I think they are
conjoined twins!

The twins. Arms full of babies, heart full of love.

Sierra and Sienna. Two heads are
better than one.

When you fall asleep in the Warner house, you
never know what will happen!

Me at my boy at sixteen years old

Zack's senior portrait. My baby has come a long way.

The Warner clan flagging a taxi in NYC

Family pic just outside the Central Park Zoo

The day Kurt retired from an amazing career in the NFL

Me and my lover on our romantic vacation in Venice, Italy

The Warner circle of life

It's Kurt! My Kurt! The guy I've been dancing with. The guy who played with my kids.

The guys continued talking about Kurt.

"Is he any good?"

"He's supposed to be," Mark said, "but he's a fourth-year senior and hasn't started yet."

"Where's he from?"

"He went to Regis High School."

"Regis High School?" I said, nearly spitting out my Pepsi. "In Cedar Rapids?"

"Yeah, it's a Catholic high school. You know it?"

"When I was married, I used to live across the street from Regis."

Zack and I used to take walks around the track, and I'd always thought the football players were too noisy. Had Kurt been practicing there when we took those walks?

The conversation continued about stats and football, but I had stopped listening. *What am I doing?* I was in Des Moines, eating pizza with Mark, but the truth was, I wasn't really interested.

I knew Mark had everything going for him. He was a good guy with a good job—he was a special-ed teacher, for goodness' sake!

But he didn't thrill me the way Kurt Warner did.

I thought about the conversations I'd had with God after my divorce. I had promised to put my trust in Jesus and not in any man. God was the one I relied on to provide for my needs. If I ever started dating again, I promised myself that it wouldn't be because I needed a man, but because I wanted a man.

A few weeks later, my family and I celebrated Jesse Jo's first birthday. After I put her to bed, I asked Mom and Dad if they'd watch the kids while I went to Des Moines to see Mark. During the two-hour drive to Des Moines, I analyzed my decision—was I doing the right thing? I knew Mom and Dad wouldn't be happy, but I had to do what I had to do.

I broke up with Mark because I didn't *need* Mark.

And because I *wanted* Kurt.

18

In the Dark

Kurt's popularity at Coyote's and my regular attendance on ladies' night made us something of a couple. When the DJ saw us together, he'd say, "This next one's for Kurt and Brenda," and then he'd play "Fishing in the Dark," by the Nitty Gritty Dirt Band. It became our song. It seemed especially appropriate because I felt like I was a little in the dark about our relationship.

Although we met at the bar and danced a lot, we never went out. In fact, we each continued to hang out with our own friends. Kurt always seemed to have girls hanging on him, and I had continued to date other people.

One guy I dated was fond of wearing a turtleneck with a gold necklace. When Kurt and I danced, he would tease me. "How's 'Necklace'?"

"Necklace is fine," I'd tell him. "How's your harem?"

I had no reason to think we would actually start dating. With all of his girls—and one girl in particular who thought his lap was her reserved seat—it was safer for me not to expect much.

But even knowing all of that, whenever Kurt asked me to dance, I felt like the woman in one of those Calgon commercials—I hoped he would just take me away. There was something so exciting about him. No matter how hard I tried to control my heart, it skipped when he was around.

One night he arrived with a long-haired blonde I'd never seen before. They spent most of the night talking. *Who the heck is she?* I couldn't help but touch my short, dark hair and wonder if she was more his type.

Later that week when we were dancing, I asked him about her.

"Oh, she works at Hy-Vee, a grocery store near campus."

"Is she your girlfriend?" I had to ask, though I wasn't sure if I wanted the answer.

"You don't need to worry about her."

"How serious are you two, because I don't—"

"Don't worry about her," Kurt said. "Just worry about us."

It was my first indication that there was an "us."

I always believed that God had a purpose for Zack's life and that he wouldn't let Zack's injury get in the way of that purpose. But as Zack got older, I realized that my protectiveness might be keeping him from being all that God wanted him to be. I vowed to be intentional about allowing my son to have as many normal experiences as possible.

The first of those had come the previous year, when Zack was two and a half. Neil, Zack, and I had been walking through a department store when Zack heard a bird singing. He knew a bird was out of place indoors, so he let go of his walker and headed toward the sound to investigate. That proved he no longer needed the walker; he was capable of walking on his own. It was a big accomplishment—one that his doctor in Virginia thought would never happen.

Now that Zack was three, he had started taking the bus to a public school that had an early intervention program for kids with special needs. The short bus picked him up every morning in front of the house and returned him in the afternoon. At first I was worried about his being away from me, but he did fine.

My dad also helped Zack extend his boundaries. When Dad mowed the lawn, Zack rode on his shoulders so he could smell the freshly cut grass and explore the yard. And when Zack got a little older, Dad took him along when he went to the lake and stayed in a cabin. He taught Zack to fish, and Zack loved getting his fingers dirty and slimy when baiting the hooks with worms and unhooking the fish they caught. My dad also let him drive a boat, giving Zack verbal cues when his visual ones failed. Through Dad's example, I learned to give my son even more freedom.

Zack's first day of school on the "short" bus. I could just see the top of his head in the first seat.

I had started nursing school full-time in January. I was twenty-five years old and anxious about being back in the classroom. I'd never been much of a student in high school, and though I'd done well in the prerequisite classes, I knew I'd have to work hard to get good grades in nursing school. I also knew that I'd have less time for studying than my classmates who were single and didn't have children.

Each day, Mom got Zack on and off the bus and watched Jesse Jo until I returned. When I got home from school, I took care of the kids until they went to bed, usually around nine. Then I studied.

Whenever I sat down to study, I would start by praying. *God, help me to memorize this fast. Give me a photographic memory.* To my surprise, I found that I really loved what I was learning. I was interested in medicine and the details of the human body. I also found some tricks and mnemonics to help me use my study time wisely.

When I had to remember a long list of symptoms for a disease, for example, I would take the first letter of each symptom and make an acronym. Then when it came time to take the test, I would write down the acronym first and then fill in the letters of the word to complete the symptom. So I would memorize "Fat Unicorns Have Wide Icy Fingers," write down "FUHWIF," then fill in "Frequent urination, Unusual thirst, Hunger, Weight loss, Irritability, and Fatigue."

With that technique and others, I began to get good grades. Everyone thought I was so smart that other students in my class started coming to me for help!

Neil's betrayal had stolen my confidence, but now it was back. Relatives who had worried about me the year before now told me how proud they were of my fresh start. "You're a strong mom, and you're doing great," they'd say, reminding me of how far I had come.

My friends at school knew all about Zack and Jesse Jo. "How do you do it?" they asked. At church, I was the new girl in the singles' group, so they invited me to all of the parties and activities. And of course I was also popular at the bar. For the first time since Zack's accident, I was really happy about my life and feeling good about myself.

On Valentine's Day, I got a card from Kurt. Apparently, in addition to being a football player, he was also a writer, because he'd practically written a book inside the card. "I wanted to give this to you because I think you're beautiful," he wrote. Then he went on about how much fun we had on the dance floor and how he liked hanging out and talking with me at the bar. By the time I finished reading that card, I'd figured out that he wanted to take things to the next level. (He'd also hinted that Hy-Vee girl was gone if I said yes.)

Of course I was interested, but I was still cautious. During the next few weeks, I watched to see if he kept on hanging out with the other girls at the bar. But he didn't. He spent more and more time with me. But he still didn't ask me out on a date.

One night at the bar, while he was telling a story about one of his classmates, it occurred to me that Kurt was just a college student. He probably didn't have money for dates. So I had an idea.

"Would you like to come over on Friday night?" I asked. "We could order pizza and watch a movie with the kids." Although he'd never met Dad, I had introduced him to Mom at the bar, and she had grown to like him. I knew she wouldn't mind. I also knew Mom and Dad went to bed at ten.

"I'd love to," Kurt said.

That's how we started dating. Kurt would come over and spend the evening with the kids and me. After Zack and Jesse Jo went to bed at nine and Mom and Dad turned in at ten, Kurt and I would have long talks. I told him about Zack's injury, Neil's affair, and how vulnerable I felt dating again.

One warm spring night, I walked him to the door, the same sliding glass door where he'd appeared with a rose that first morning after we danced. But instead of leaving as he usually did, he stopped on the first step and turned around. He grabbed my hands and leaned in and kissed me. Then he left.

I slid the door closed, drew the blinds, and made my way back to my bedroom. I was thinking hard. Kurt had obviously made me feel something that Mark had never made me feel, but were tingly feelings enough to base a relationship on? My heart obviously thought so, although it didn't make much sense to my head.

Kurt's second kiss lasted a little longer. On the third one, he grabbed my head and pulled me toward him. Soon we were kissing before he went out the door, and eventually we were making out on the couch before he left. But I was still very cautious—not only to protect my heart, but because I didn't want Mom and Dad to hear us. Their bedroom was just down the hall.

I knew Mom was happy for me. She could see that I had a new zip in my step and a joy I hadn't had in a long time. But I don't think she thought I was serious about Kurt—or that he'd last for long.

I knew Kurt was attracted to me. But I'd have to say his first love affair was with the kids. Zack had taken to him instantly, and although Jesse Jo took a little longer to warm up, it wasn't too long before she was snuggling in his lap.

Best of all, I could see they both had captured Kurt's heart.

And loving my kids, of course, was the quickest route to *my* heart.

The subject of religion often came up in our talks. "Do we have to talk about Jesus again?" Kurt would say when I brought it up. "Can't we just make out?"

But faith was an important issue for me. My relationship with Jesus was central to my beliefs and how I lived my life. Although I wasn't perfect and never pretended to be, it was important to me that the person I dated, the person I could potentially end up marrying, shared my beliefs.

It wasn't that Kurt didn't have faith. He did. Kurt believed in God, and he even occasionally attended the local Catholic church. His faith just wasn't a priority in his life. He didn't pray regularly, read his Bible, or orient his life around Jesus' teachings.

Kurt had heard me talk about Neil's lack of faith and how it had frustrated me, especially when I was the only one praying for Zack's healing. I had felt so alone going to church and praying by myself. I didn't want another relationship where I was the only who believed Jesus made a difference.

Kurt knew how important my faith was, so one Sunday he asked me to go to mass with him. I was open to the experience, but once the service started, I was totally confused. The priest would say something, and Kurt and the rest of the congregation would respond, but I didn't understand how they knew what to say. I looked through the whole bulletin and still couldn't find anything.

"Where's the stuff you're saying?" I asked Kurt.

The priest was heading down the aisle. "Shh. Don't embarrass me," Kurt said.

As the priest got closer, I could see that he was shaking water off some kind of handle. "Wait. He's not going to spray water on me, is he?"

"Stop it!" Kurt whispered. "It's holy water."

"Oh." I thought about that for a second as I watched the priest pass. "Well, what makes it holy?"

"Shh!"

On the way home I continued to have questions. "What do you mean you go to confession to tell the priest your sins? Can't you just tell God?"

Kurt was frustrated, and I had to tell him I wasn't making fun of his religion. I was just trying to understand it. The things he did at his church were very different from the things I did at mine.

The following week, he agreed to come to my church. Unlike a traditional church building with a steeple, our church met in a warehouse-style building. There was a live band, a lot of singing, and some pretty intense preaching. When people started raising their hands as they sang or prayed, I looked at Kurt to see if it scared him. I just knew he was going to run because it was so different from his church.

"Your church was like going to a show," he said afterward.

"What's wrong with that?"

"Nothing, if you want to go to a musical. But if you want to pray, it's a little distracting."

"They were praying," I insisted. It was obvious that we had differences not only in priorities but also in how we expressed our faith. Until we could get those worked out, our relationship would always be limited.

***

In the fall of 1993, Kurt was a fifth-year senior and the starting quarterback for UNI. I attended a few of his games and was happy to be there to support him. Because I supported him, I decided it was okay to ask him to support me with some important things too. And nothing was more important than making sure Zack got the services he needed at school.

At the beginning of each school year, and at least once during the year, I would have to meet with Zack's teachers to discuss his Individualized Education Plan, or IEP. At the meetings, they would review what services they thought he needed and whether they would or would not provide them. In most of those meetings, I had to fight to get Zack the resources he needed—the schools just didn't have enough resources to go around. I hated going to these meetings by myself, so I asked Kurt if he would come with me. To my surprise, he agreed.

Kurt was living in an apartment off campus and still didn't have a car, so I picked him up on my way to the school. When we walked in, I knew there was going to be a small problem. The teacher had set out two of the itty-bitty preschool chairs for us to sit in. While I could make that work, it was going to be difficult for the six-foot-two football player with me.

Kurt didn't let it be a problem. He graciously sat down and pulled the chair as close to the child-size table as he could without bumping his knees.

As the teacher talked about how much Zack had progressed since the previous year, Kurt participated in the conversation, adding his observations and making comments when appropriate. But I had to fight to keep myself focused. I kept tuning out, thinking about how Kurt was exactly the kind of dad I'd always dreamed of for my kids.

I've got to keep this one, I told myself.

Weeks earlier, Kurt and Zack had been playing with a Magna Doodle, a write-and-erase toy that Zack loved to scribble on until the screen was completely black. Kurt had written, "I love my momma" and drawn a little flower as if Zack had written it. Underneath that, he'd added, "I love her too."

"Go give this to Momma," Kurt told Zack, and Zack brought it to me.

I looked at it and smiled at Kurt. But the message scared me. I wasn't sure I was ready for that, for him. So I took the magnetic pen, wrote, "I love my momma too!" and had Zack deliver it back to Kurt. I could tell from the look in Kurt's eyes that it wasn't what he wanted, but I just wasn't ready.

Now, sitting in the tiny preschool chairs and nodding absently as the teacher spoke, I realized I really was in love with Kurt. Although he was only my boyfriend, I had fallen in love with the kind of father he was already being to my children.

And I wasn't the only one who thought Kurt was great. I could tell that Dad really liked him too. That feeling was confirmed on Thanksgiving Day, when he asked Kurt to help carve the turkey. It was as if he had passed the carving knife to the next generation of the family.

But life wasn't all roses and carving knives for Kurt and me. There were people at the bar who didn't like me and didn't think we should be together. My friends overheard his friends encouraging him to date other women. "Why not go out with her?" they said, pointing to a cute blonde. "At least you'd get laid tonight."

"No, thanks," Kurt said. "I've got somebody."

"You're not seriously going to stay with her, are you?" a friend asked. "She's divorced, and she's got two kids."

"You don't know her," Kurt said. "I know what I've got, and I like it."

But Kurt's friends weren't the only ones who weren't happy with me. His mom wasn't exactly a fan either. Early on, Kurt had told me that his parents were divorced. His dad had remarried, but his mom hadn't. Since I didn't know anyone, other than myself, who had been divorced, I was interested in meeting both of them.

My first chance came at a UNI game. Kurt introduced me to his mom, Sue, but she wouldn't speak directly to me or include me in the conversation. She spoke only to Kurt. Kurt's dad, Gene, and his wife, Mimi, were much warmer, but I noticed that Kurt had to keep his parents separate. He would go to one area to talk with his mom and a separate area to talk with his dad and stepmom.

The more time I spent with Kurt's mom, the more I could tell she definitely didn't like me. Right in front of me, she would ask Kurt about his old girlfriend.

"How's Ann doing?"

She loved Ann.

"I haven't really heard," he would say.

Though I'm sure Kurt was embarrassed by his mom's attitude, he didn't let it affect him. But I'd get angry and defensive.

I don't need Kurt, I'd tell myself. And that was true. I was raising two kids on my own. I was in school full-time, and with Mom and Dad's help, paying for it all, with a little bit of child support from Neil. I did not *need* Kurt. But it always came down to the fact that I *wanted* Kurt. I liked what he brought into my life and what he brought into my kids' lives.

19

On My Own

As the months passed and Kurt and I dated each other exclusively, our relationship progressed in every way. Kurt would come over for dinner with the family, and we'd all watch a movie with the kids. Then, after everyone else was in bed, Kurt and I would have our alone time. One night we were on the couch when things got, well, let's just say *passionate*.

"Oh my gosh!" I whispered. "Mom just went by!"

Then the bathroom door slammed shut.

"Oh my gosh, oh my gosh! What do we do?"

"I'm out of here," Kurt said.

"You are not out of here," I said. "We're in this together."

"What do you want me to do?"

"What do you want *me* to do?"

The door to the bathroom opened again, and Mom stomped back down the hall to her bedroom.

Kurt stood up. "I've got to go."

I wanted him to stay, but honestly, what was he going to do? So he left and walked home, or maybe he even ran. I didn't look through the blinds to see. I got myself together and did the walk of shame down to Mom's bedroom. I cracked opened the door and saw that her table lamp was on. She was sitting up in bed. Dad lay next to her, sound asleep.

As quietly as I could, I tiptoed over to her side of the bed. But all I got out was, "Mom—"

"I cannot believe I just caught you doing that," she said.

"I'm twenty-five years old," I protested. "I'm a grown woman. I can have sex if I want to."

"Not in my living room." She took a deep breath. "Brenda, you're a good Christian woman."

I understand now what she was saying, but then I was pretty defensive. I was also afraid of what Mom was going to do. "Are you going to tell Dad?"

"I haven't decided."

I slunk off to bed, not sure what to do or say. I called Kurt. "She's so mad. What are we going to do? What are we going to do?"

"I don't know what *you're* going to do, but I'm not coming back over to that house for a long time!"

Not long after that, Mom suggested I look into getting my own place. And it was a much smarter alternative than the "$&*% or get off the pot" advice she'd given me when Neil and I were living together. Although my funds were tight, I knew she was right. I had been living with my parents too long. We *all* needed a little more privacy.

———

With the help of government-subsidized housing, I would just barely be able to make ends meet. In Cedar Falls, Section 8 housing was located at a busy intersection on Waterloo Road, and when I moved in, the only available apartment was one of the below-ground units. It was dark and dingy. But I didn't care, because it was mine.

The kids shared a bedroom. They each had a toddler bed and a quilt from Mom. I couldn't afford dressers, so I piled their clothes on the floor around the perimeter of the room. They each had a few toys, and I tried to keep those corralled in one corner when they weren't being used.

In my bedroom, I had a mattress and box spring on a metal bed frame, but no headboard. The living-room furniture was mismatched and mostly handed down from relatives, but I still had the mamasan chair I'd bought while stationed in Okinawa. Similar to the round papasan chairs so popular at import stores, this one was oval and slightly bigger. I had moved it with me everywhere I went.

Money was tight, especially with both kids still in diapers. Food stamps helped me make ends meet, especially at the end of the month. Although I appreciated the government assistance, it still wasn't easy to take. Every time I used food stamps at the grocery store, I felt like people were staring at me and making negative judgments about me as a person and as a single mom. I was still rebuilding my identity after my divorce, so to feel scrutinized and judged was humbling. But I held my head up and kept my shoulders back because I was strong enough to endure the embarrassment so my kids could eat.

I just wished it didn't have to be so hard. Many times I would pray, "God, please just have somebody give me a hundred dollars to help me make it to the end of the month. Holy Spirit, please tap a Christian on the shoulder and show them I need help." But it never happened. Today, when I work through our foundation to help furnish a home for a single mother, I wonder if that young mom is looking at me and thinking, *She has no idea what I'm going through. She's got everything.* But those days of being a single mother remain fresh in my mind. It's one of the reasons it's such a blessing for me to give now, because I know what an extraordinary blessing it would have been to receive then.

———

It was spring, and Kurt's graduation was coming up soon. One day while I was washing dishes, he came into the kitchen and asked me, "Are you going to follow me someday if I make it?"

"Follow you where?"

"To the NFL."

I knew that had something to do with football, but I really had no idea what it was. Rather than agree to something I wasn't sure of, I turned to him and said, "Oh, yeah, and I want to be a model. Are you going to follow me?"

"I'm being serious."

Kurt always said he wanted to play football professionally; he'd never used the word *NFL*, and we'd never really talked about what professional football would look like. I just knew it meant he would get a paycheck for playing. And as long as he got a paycheck, I was fine with that. We would do whatever we had to and make it work somehow. "If we're meant to be," I told him, "then yeah, I'll follow you."

In my mind, though, there was still something big in the way of our being together. Kurt didn't swear, lie, or steal. He treated everyone around him with respect and kindness, and if you were in need, he would give you the jersey off his back. But he had never prayed a prayer making Jesus the Lord of his life.

When I encouraged him to pray that prayer, he just brushed me off.

"What for? God has always been a part of my life."

At the time, I really didn't think about there being a conflict between my belief in living as the Bible taught and the fact that I was sleeping with Kurt (although that would change later). I just figured sex was something everyone else was doing, so what was the harm in my doing it too?

But that didn't mean I'd given up on my faith or that we stopped arguing about it. Jesus hadn't become any less important to me, just as Jesus hadn't become any more important to Kurt.

One day, I noticed little blisters erupting in patches all over Zack and Jesse Jo. Although I was still in school and not a registered nurse, I made my first diagnosis—chicken pox. More spots broke out on both of them during the next few days, but Jesse Jo's were so severe that they even erupted between her legs. I took off her diaper, then Zack's diaper, and let them run around the apartment naked. Why not? We weren't leaving, and no one was coming over.

I worried about what they'd do when they had to *go*, but I shouldn't have. Neither one of them wanted to just stand there and pee, so they would race to the toilet and do their business there. We had a few close calls. But by the end of the weekend, the chicken-pox lesions had scabbed over and they were both completely potty-trained. How cool was that? I felt like mother of the year.

But that was the high point of our apartment living. After several months, my money ran out. I just couldn't swing living on my own. I had to move back in with Mom and Dad, but this time they moved my bedroom to their basement. The floors were cement, there were cobwebs on the ceiling, and it was always cold, but at least the basement offered a little more privacy.

Soon, I would need all the privacy I could get.

After graduation, the Green Bay Packers invited Kurt to their training camp. He was thrilled. He longed to play in the NFL, and this was his big chance. He packed his things, moved them back to his mother's home in Cedar Rapids, and headed to Wisconsin. He was gone for five weeks, but he ultimately didn't make the cut.

Since Kurt had given up his apartment in Cedar Falls, he didn't have a place to live when he got back. Mom was scheduled to have surgery on her foot, which meant she wouldn't be able to watch the kids while I was in school. So the best idea seemed to be for Kurt to move into the basement with me and take care of the kids while I was in class. Normally, Mom wouldn't have supported such an idea, but there didn't seem to be a lot of alternatives.

All that fall, Kurt watched the kids during the day while I was in school. When I got home, I took over so he could head off to football practice at the university. He continued to work out with the team so he could stay in shape and be available in case scouts came through.

We didn't get to see a lot of each other during that time, but I did get to observe Kurt's character, and I liked what I saw. To help out with expenses, Kurt took a night job stocking shelves at the grocery store for minimum wage—$5.50 an hour. It touched me that he would humble himself to take a low-paying job to help support my kids and me—and he was just my boyfriend. It wasn't what I was used to.

After meeting Kurt's mother, Sue, at that UNI football game, I had told Kurt that she didn't like me.

"She likes you," Kurt said.

"No, she doesn't. I can tell."

"She likes you. She just doesn't know you. You need to spend more time together."

169

That reminded me of so many similar talks I'd had with Neil, trying to convince him that my mom really did like him when it was obvious she didn't. I knew what it felt like to be caught between two people whom you loved but who didn't love each other. I wondered if Kurt was telling his mom how much I liked her and if she wasn't buying it either.

One Saturday Kurt and I took the kids to Cedar Rapids to meet Sue. She lived alone, and as soon as we walked inside, I knew her house wasn't a great place to bring little kids, especially one who was blind. Her house was cluttered with little knickknacks that covered every surface, including lots of pictures of Kurt. Sue and Kurt were very close, and his moving in with my parents and me had to be hard for her. I thought she must be a very lonely woman, and I hoped our visit would bond the two of us somehow.

But as with every other time I'd been with her, she barely spoke to me. If I started a conversation, or if one of the kids said something, she'd interrupt. "Kurt, do you remember when . . . ?" Even during the meal, her conversation was directed solely at Kurt. She had always been cold to me, but now she was acting the same way toward the kids, and I could feel my anger growing. It was a completely different experience at Kurt's dad's house. Gene and Mimi were always warm and loving toward the kids and me, which made me want to spend more time with them. Of course, that only upset Sue.

Sue and Gene were the first divorced people I had observed up close. After seeing their behavior, I changed mine. I vowed never to speak negatively about Neil and to make sure Neil and I always communicated to each other, not through the kids.

Although Kurt and I were dating seriously, we weren't yet serious about our future together. Kurt still had hopes of playing professional ball, and I was just trying to get through nursing school. We talked about spending the rest of our lives together, but money was tight for both of us, and neither of us was in a position to make that happen. Besides, I'd learned my lesson with Neil. No matter how much I liked a guy—and at this point I loved Kurt—I wasn't jumping into another marriage until I was absolutely sure about *everything*.

Ever since my divorce it had been hard for me to trust, and I got jealous easily. When something set off an alarm bell in our relationship, it was like the drills we used to have in Okinawa. I guarded my perimeter, focused on the threat, and shredded every bit of evidence that there was once a good relationship. It wasn't a healthy way to handle trust issues. But at the time, it was the only way I knew to protect my kids, and just as important, my heart.

20

The Bachelor Party

I had known my friend Desia since we were both ten years old. She was the one who'd driven me home from Wild E. Coyote's the night Kurt and I first danced together. She'd met Doug that night, too, and all the way home she'd talked about how cute he was and how she was going to marry him.

That conversation turned out to be more than just idle chatter. Desia and Doug's relationship grew, and a little over a year later, they got engaged.

Desia asked me to be one of her bridesmaids, and she wanted Zack and Jesse Jo to be the ring bearer and the flower girl. My parents were invited because they'd known Desia as long as I had, and Kurt was invited because he was Doug's friend. The four of us hung out at Coyote's, so Kurt and I heard all the wedding details long before it actually happened.

Several weeks before the wedding, Kurt told me that some of the guys were going to throw Doug a party. "It's going to be at Mike's house, and we're just gonna hang out and drink and stuff."

"Do you mean a bachelor party?"

"More like a guys' night out."

"What are you guys going to do?" Mike lived on a large farm in central Iowa, so I wondered what "guys' night out" would mean if there wasn't a movie theater or other entertainment available.

"I don't know. We'll probably have dinner, and if it's warm enough, we might throw the football around. If not, I guess we'll play poker and smoke some cigars. There'll probably be some drinking. I hear Mike is ordering a couple of kegs."

I didn't feel right about what I heard, but what could I do? I couldn't tell Kurt not to go. He and Doug had been friends for a long time.

On the afternoon of the party, Kurt decided he would stay at his mom's house that night. It would probably be a late night, and his mom lived closer to Grinnell, where the party was being held. I thought that was a good idea.

I was asleep in the basement when the phone rang. It was shortly after midnight, and I was expecting a call from Kurt. He was supposed to call me as soon as he got to his mom's house so I'd know he'd made it safely. I grabbed the receiver quickly so Mom and Dad wouldn't hear the ringing upstairs. But it wasn't the call I was expecting.

"Brenda?" It was Desia, and she was crying. "They had a bachelor party, and there were strippers!"

"What?" I sat up in bed, now fully awake. "What are you saying?"

"There were naked women at the party. Strippers. I'm breaking up with Doug, and I'm calling off the wedding!"

"Wait a minute. How do you know there were strippers?"

"Doug called me. He said he didn't do anything with them, but I don't care. They were there!"

It wasn't very sensitive of me, but I asked the first thing that came to my mind. "What about Kurt? Did he do anything?"

"I don't know," she said. "Doug's still at Mike's house. I've got his number if you want to call him."

We talked for a few more minutes, and then I told her I was going to call Kurt. "I'll call you back if I learn anything else."

Mike's phone rang for a long time before someone answered. "Can I talk to Kurt?" I asked.

"I don't think he's here," the person said, slurring his words. "I haven't seen him in a while."

I tried Kurt's mom's house. "Hey, Sue, I am sorry to wake you. Has Kurt gotten there yet?"

"No, he's not here."

"Could you just leave him a message to call me as soon as he gets in? It's kind of important."

"I'm in bed, but if I hear him come in, I'll have him call."

I pulled the phone into the basement bathroom so Mom and Dad wouldn't hear me and then called Desia to tell her I didn't know anything more. Then I waited for Kurt to call. I leaned against the door and tried to figure out what to do next. Eventually one of the guys called to let me know Kurt had passed out on the gravel drive in front of Mike's house. He was sleeping it off. He would have Kurt call me in the morning.

I crawled back to bed, angry and hurt, but also praying that Kurt hadn't done anything stupid. During the few hours of darkness that remained, I didn't sleep much. I lay awake, thinking about what it had felt like when Neil cheated on me.

If Kurt has done the same thing, there's no second chance. I am done with him too.

———————

Kurt called me the next morning from his mom's house, and again I carried the phone into the bathroom so I could close the door.

"What happened?" I asked.

"Oh, it was a crazy party," Kurt said. "We all got drunk."

"Desia said there were strippers."

"Well, yeah, there were."

My fingers gripped the phone tighter, and my heart raced. "What did you do?"

"I didn't do anything."

"You did nothing?"

"No, I didn't do anything."

Obviously, I was getting nowhere with that line of questioning, so I tried another one. "Well then, what did the strippers do?"

"They danced and stuff."

"Were you there when they were there?"

"Yes."

"Were you in the same room with them?"

"We were all in the same room."

"Were you near them?"

"Well, I, uh . . . I danced with one of them."

"You danced with a stripper?"

"Yeah. You know; we were drunk, and we just danced."

I couldn't believe it. My questions came faster. "What was she wearing?" I had to know all of the details.

"Well, uh . . . she wasn't wearing anything."

"She was *naked?* You danced with a *naked* woman?"

"I'm so sorry. I'll never do it again. I was too drunk to know what I was doing."

"I can't believe you! You danced with a naked woman, and now you're telling me you did it because you were drunk? Like that matters! If you committed a crime, you would go to jail whether you were drunk or not!"

"I'm sorry. I am so, so, sorry."

I heard the remorse in his voice, but I didn't care. I didn't have to think about what to do next. No explanation or second chances could change what he'd done. "You touched another woman's naked body. I am done. Done. Done. Done!" I hung up the phone before he could say another word.

I didn't tell my parents right away that I'd broken up with Kurt, but Mom figured it out the next time he called.

"It's for you. It's Kurt." She set the phone on the kitchen counter.

"I don't want to talk to him," I said.

She picked the phone back up. "She doesn't want to talk to you. Sorry."

The same situation was repeated several times that day. Eventually she no longer had to ask me. She just told Kurt, "Nope. She doesn't want to talk to you."

Desia and Doug patched things up and continued with their wedding plans. But my feelings stayed the same. Kurt and I were done.

Apparently word got out at Coyote's that Kurt and I were no longer together. More guys came and asked me to dance. I also learned that my cousin John's friend Shane had always been interested in me. When Shane heard that Kurt and I had broken up, Shane called and asked me out to dinner. I agreed.

Shane was my age, and he owned a farm. He was a great conversationalist, and we had fun at dinner. At the end of the night, he asked if he could see me again.

"I've got a lot going on the next two weeks," I told him. "My friend's getting married, and I'm her maid of honor. But how'd you like to be my date at her wedding?"

"That would be great."

I wrote down all of the information and gave it to him. "I'll already be there to help Desia, so I'll just meet up with you at the church."

Early on the day of Desia's wedding, Dad dropped me off at her hotel so I could help her get ready. Then Dad returned home to help Mom get Zack and Jesse Jo ready. They would bring them to the church, and I would meet them there.

After Desia and I got ready in the hotel, we left for the church. I was a little nervous. I knew Kurt would be there, and it would be the first time I'd seen him or talked to him since the bachelor party. I wondered how he would react when he saw me with Shane.

As I stood in the back of the church and waited for the music to start, I bent down and reminded Jesse Jo and Zack one last time what they were supposed to do. "Walk all the way down to the end of the white carpet, and then you can go sit with Grandma."

The music started, and my babies walked down the aisle. I couldn't help but be proud of them. They looked so adorable all dressed up in their wedding clothes, and they were smiling and enjoying the spotlight. I thought back to Kim's wedding, when Zack had worn that little tux. Back then, we hadn't been sure he would ever sit up. Now he was walking down the aisle with his little sister.

As soon as Zack reached the front of the church, he headed straight for the piano and, before anyone could stop him, he'd plunked out three notes. Mom tried to pull him away, but he didn't like that. "I gotta play!" he yelled. The whole church laughed; it was so cute. Mom led him to her pew and got him and Jesse Jo settled just as the processional started.

I walked slowly down the aisle, trying not to trip in my heels. The church was packed with people, but of course, the first person I noticed was Kurt. I scanned the pews, looking for Shane. Where was he?

Throughout the ceremony I plastered a smile on my face to hide my concern while I continuously scanned the congregation. I didn't see Shane anywhere. Afterward I stood next to Desia in the receiving line and shook hands with all her friends and relatives. "She *is* a beautiful bride," I must have said a hundred times.

Still no Shane.

When Kurt walked through, I could see lines in his face I'd never noticed before. There was a deep sadness in his eyes. He obviously wanted to say something to me, but I quickly reached for the next person's hand, forcing Kurt to keep moving. I continued looking for Shane, but out of the corner of my eye, I saw Kurt go straight to Zack and Jesse Jo. They both ran up to him and jumped into his arms. *Crap!*

"Brenda, c'mon. We need to go," Desia said. "The limo's here."

I got into the limousine with Doug and Desia and other members of the wedding party. It was a twenty-minute drive to Waterloo for the reception. The conversation in the car was all about the wedding, but all I could think about was the reception. *Come on, Shane. You'd better be there!*

We arrived at the hall and made our way to the head table. I took my seat next to Desia and looked around the room. Zack and Jesse Jo were sitting at a table with my parents—and with Kurt! Why was he sitting there?

He'd brought Zack a radio in the shape of a Dallas Cowboys helmet. It was the one from Kurt's room; he'd listened to it growing up. Now Zack was busy fiddling with the dials. Jesse Jo had a new coloring book and crayons. *Great, he's bribing the kids!*

Doug and Desia took to the floor for their first dance as husband and wife. I continued to search the hall for any sign of Shane. I knew I only had about three minutes to find him. The next dance was supposed to start with the wedding party dancing together, and then halfway through the song, our dates were supposed to cut in.

The song started while I was still scanning the room for Shane. No sign of him. I took the floor with the best man, and then a couple of minutes into the song, I saw Kurt striding across the dance floor.

"Can I have this dance?" he asked.

I didn't say a word, but the best man stepped away. *Everybody's watching. Everybody knows all about this drama. Don't make a scene.* I took his hand.

"It's so good to see you," he said.

I didn't say anything.

"I need to talk to you. We need to talk. I love you, Brenda, and I miss you."

He kept on talking, throwing it all out there, doing everything he could to get me to say something, but I refused. The dance ended, and I returned to the head table without talking to him. With his head down, Kurt slowly walked back to the table with my parents and kids.

Shortly afterward, I spotted Shane sitting at the bar and talking to Tina, a girlfriend of mine. How long had he been there? I walked over to talk to them, but I could immediately tell they were both drunk.

"What are you doing?" I asked Shane.

"Well, I was embarrassed to go to the wedding by myself, and so was she," Shane said. "So we skipped out and went to a bar for a few drinks first."

"Get out of here!"

"What?"

"Go!" I said, trying not to raise my voice.

"What are you talking about?"

"You're no longer invited. I invited you, and now I am uninviting you. Just go!"

"What? You're crazy!"

"Go!"

"Fine!" He stood up, got his balance, and stomped out of the room.

The night had not turned out like I planned. I was alone, and my kids were loving on Kurt.

Around ten o'clock, Mom came over to tell me that she and Dad were leaving. "I'm taking Jesse Jo and Zack back home so they can get to bed."

When I looked at her, I knew she could see the pain in my eyes. "Mom, what am I going to do?"

She looked me right in the eye and said something that surprised me. "We never gave you a chance to forgive Neil. This time I think you need to consider forgiveness." Then she left.

I was stunned. "This isn't how we do it!" I wanted to say. "We're fighters! We wait for the guy who deserves us."

I got a drink from the bar. Then I got another one.

I started dancing with some of the guys at the wedding, and with the drinks and dancing, I actually had a good time. The reception ended and I was gathering my stuff when I suddenly realized I didn't have a car. Dad had dropped me off at the hotel hours earlier. Now he and Mom had left me without a ride.

I was trying to figure out my options when Kurt approached me. "Please let me take you home."

I glared at him. But then I handed him my stuff, took off my high heels, and followed him to his car.

All the way back to my house, Kurt pleaded his case. He told me how sorry he was, how much he missed and loved me. When we finally parked in my driveway, I had a few things to say.

"No man who deserves me would touch another naked woman. Period."

"I know. You're right."

"A man who loves me won't even *want* to be near another naked woman."

"I'll never do it again. I promise."

"I've been cheated on once, and I will not let it happen again. You have no idea what it feels like to be nearly eight months pregnant and have a man cheat on you with another woman."

"You're right. I don't."

"I don't deserve this."

"No, you don't, and I am so sorry." By now he was crying. "Please just give me another chance. I miss you. I miss the kids. I need them in my life. I love them, and they miss me. I promise I'll never let it happen again if you will just give me another chance."

"What happens the next time you go out and have too much to drink?"

"I've never gotten that drunk before and I promise I'll never do it again."

I could tell Kurt was sincere in both his apology and his promises. I was touched by how sweet he was being, especially in his love for the kids. He had obviously thought the situation through and seemed willing to do whatever it took to get me back.

"If we were ever to get back together—and I say *if*—there would have to be some rules."

"I'm okay with that. I love you, and I'll do anything."

"The first rule is that you don't dance with naked women. You don't even stay in the same room with them. I don't care if you're drunk. I don't care if it's a bachelor party. If there are naked women, either they leave or you leave."

"That's not a problem."

"I don't know what all the other rules are yet, but the man who deserves me will act like he deserves me and not be hanging out with other women."

"I understand."

"I know you didn't do the same things the other guys did, but to me that's not even the point. A guy who deserves me wouldn't even go there because he wouldn't want to take a chance on hurting me. If you're going to be with me, you need to know even *being* in a place like that is hurtful to me because of what happened with Neil. And I'm not going to date a guy who doesn't care if he hurts me."

"I am so sorry, Brenda. I never meant to hurt you. I just never looked at it like that. I love you, and in the future I'll be more careful so I never hurt you again."

Kurt's willingness to do whatever it took softened me a bit. "I admit that I'm more jealous than other women you could date, and that's going to make it harder on you. You'll have to pay the price for the actions of my first husband. My standards are just going to be higher than other women's standards."

"That's okay. I'll live up to them. I promise." Tears were still sliding down his cheeks. "I don't ever want to hurt you again. Please, Brenda, just give me another chance. I'll earn your trust; I promise."

I hugged him and told him I'd think about it, and I told him he needed to think about it too. I knew I was asking a lot, but if we were going to get back together, he needed to be willing to live by my rules.

We'd been in the car for hours, and it was really late when I walked into the house. Mom was waiting for me. "How's my baby girl?"

"He says that I can trust him, but I don't know."

Instead of offering advice, she simply said, "It's a decision you're going to have to make."

I lay awake for a long time that night, going over everything we'd talked about. I thought about the good times Kurt and I had had, and I thought about the bachelor party. In the end, I thought about him at the wedding and the reception, hanging out with Jesse Jo and Zack, and I knew I wanted him in my life.

But could I trust him?

I prayed about that for a while, laying out my dilemma before God. And somewhere deep inside, I felt I heard an answer: *Trust me, not man.*

I realized that even if the guy I was dating or was married to was perfect, in the back of my mind there would always be a seed of distrust. That was the unwanted gift that Neil had given me. But God was showing me that I didn't have to have a perfect man or even to trust him completely. Instead I could put my trust in my heavenly Father.

I fell asleep that night knowing I would call Kurt in the morning. Somehow we would find a way to work all this out.

Because Kurt Warner was still the man I wanted.

21

Long Distance

On a Friday night, Kurt and I drove to Des Moines and checked into the Ramada Inn. It was the nicest hotel we'd ever stayed in. Better yet, we weren't paying for the room. The owners of the Iowa Barnstormers, a new Arena Football League team, wanted to meet Kurt, so they were paying the bill. The next morning I went to take my nursing boards, and Kurt went to meet with the Barnstormers.

I passed my test and got my nursing license, and Kurt signed a contract to play arena football with the Barnstormers. We were both excited about following our new callings in life. The bad news was that I already had a nursing job in Cedar Falls, and Kurt would be moving two hours away to Des Moines to play football. Our relationship would now be a long-distance one.

———

I moved out of the basement about the same time Kurt left for Des Moines. With my new job at a nursing home, I could afford to move the kids into our own apartment.

Although Kurt and I would be separated physically, we did have a plan to be together. Kurt would come back to Cedar Falls on his off days, and the kids and I would visit him in Des Moines when he had home games. It actually worked out pretty well. We probably saw more of each other than we had while living together and working opposite shifts.

My new job was at the Cedar Falls Lutheran Home. It was affiliated with the nursing school, and I had done some of my clinical work there, so I was familiar with the place and knew some of the employees. The home had three wings. I was put in charge of Wing C and was responsible for the sixty-two patients who lived there and for supervising the nurses' aides who worked with me.

I welcomed the challenge and enjoyed the work. But most of all, I loved the patients, who taught me some important life lessons.

Gigi was ninety-two and one of the oldest patients in the home. She was four foot nine when she stretched. Arthritis had deformed her fingers, wrists, and elbows, but she didn't let that stop her gnarled hands from pinning up her beautiful white-gray hair into an updo every morning. She was legally blind and wore thick glasses. And instead of keeping flowers in her room, as the other old ladies did, she hung up sports posters.

Gigi's room was by the nurses' station. Sometimes she used a little walker to take itty-bitty steps on the rare occasions that she ventured to walk from her room, but mostly she used her electric wheelchair. During my breaks, I would sit and talk with her. I didn't share her passion for sports, but I loved everything else about her. I especially enjoyed hearing stories about her life.

Gigi had gone to college and then worked as an administrator for another college at a time when most women stayed home and had babies. She had never married and instead had focused on her career. I had become a mother at such a young age; I couldn't imagine being the kind of career woman she once had been.

I asked her once if she'd ever regretted not getting married. The strength of her answer inspired me. "I fell in love once," she said, "and he asked me to marry him. But he didn't want me to work, and I wanted to work, so I told him no."

Gigi loved to hear stories about Zack and Jesse Jo, especially Zack. I would bring the kids up for a visit each week, and they would spend time with her. Jesse Jo would sit in Gigi's chair and sing. Zack played with her talking clock and tried to mimic the robotic voice.

A die-hard football fan, Gigi had spent years listening to UNI games on the radio, so she knew about Kurt. She also followed the Barnstormers.

On game days, I would stop in her room and listen, or she would give me her radio to put on the med cart so I could listen while I worked. I counted on her to keep me updated on the score and how Kurt had done.

Gigi inspired me with her sharp mind and her zest for life. But another woman, Mary, touched my life in a different way. Mary was so fragile that she barely spoke. She didn't have enough strength to move her own limbs. My team and I were responsible for moving her skeletal body so she wouldn't get bedsores. I combed her hair every day, and if I had time, I would braid it, thinking that might make her feel spunkier.

But frail as Mary was, her gentle spirit was a gift. She was always at peace, and just going into her room made me calmer. Whenever Mary saw that I was in the room, she would reach out to touch me with her bony fingers. She never complained, and she always made me feel special.

In all the time that I worked with Mary, she never had a visit from family. I wondered how that could possibly happen. And more than once I found myself thinking, *Her family is missing out.*

Not every resident was nice, of course. One old woman, a former school-teacher, had a mean streak a mile wide. No matter what I or the other nurses did, we could never do anything right for her, and she yelled at us often.

I pitied the poor students that woman had taught in her classes. But I have to say she was an exception. Overall, I loved the people I served at the nursing home. It was a joy to be able to make a living doing work I thought was important, work I could do well.

When Dad retired from John Deere in the spring of 1995, he and Mom announced that they wanted to move to Mountain View, Arkansas. I wasn't surprised. They had visited Arkansas many times when my grandparents lived there, and Mom still had family living in Mountain View, including some cousins and her mother, Chach, who had moved back to Arkansas after Grandpa died.

Mom and Dad planned to build a tiny, two-bedroom cabin by the Spring River, where Dad could fish. It would be the perfect spot for them to enjoy the rest of their lives.

I was sad to see them go, of course, but now that I was working and able to pay rent on my own, it was time for me to stand on my own. Being a single mother still challenged me financially, especially since now I would have child-care expenses, but I think my parents looked on their move as a weaning process. They would still be there for me if I needed them, of course. Arkansas was just a ten-hour car ride away, and we'd been making that drive my whole life.

At first after they moved, I called a lot for help.

"I've never done this. Can you talk me through it?"

"How do I handle this?"

"Can you send me some money?"

Although we were separated by distance, knowing Mom was only a phone call away helped a lot. Mom's approval was still important to me, especially now that I was doing everything by myself.

———

Kurt and I continued dating despite the physical distance between us. The kids and I would go hang out with him in Des Moines, and Kurt would come stay with us in Cedar Falls. We'd still go dancing at Coyote's, and of course, he was as popular as ever.

I'd known I was in love with Kurt ever since that first IEP meeting he attended with me, but I'd needed time to know what kind of a husband he would be. Ever since the bachelor party episode, Kurt had been as close to perfect as a boyfriend could be. He really had lived up to the promises he'd made in the car after Desia's wedding. He was loving, attentive, and faithful.

Around this time, I started to believe that God was calling us to get married and spend the rest of our lives together. Kurt and I even talked about it. But Kurt wasn't hearing the same call. Not yet.

"I just want to be sure," he said.

"What will it take to make you sure?"

"I don't know."

"Well, then how will you ever know?"

"I don't know."

"Well, what do you need? Do you need God to smack you on the side of the head with a two-by-four?"

"I hope he does! At least then I would know." He seemed genuinely confused.

But I couldn't understand how he didn't know by now. We'd been dating for three and a half years. That had been long enough for me. What else was there for him to know?

I did get it that he was preoccupied with his new job. He'd always wanted to play professional football, and although the Arena Football League wasn't quite what he had dreamed of, he was happy to be on the field again. He was working hard and making more money than he ever had. He was also enjoying a bit of the popularity and fame—if you could call it that—that went along with being a Barnstormer.

But that fall I noticed some subtle changes in Kurt that concerned me. He seemed distracted and a little more full of himself than usual. I wondered briefly if success could be going to his head, but then I dismissed the thought. Surely it was natural for him to go through an adjustment period. Whatever it was, we would work it out.

One evening, Kurt showed up unexpectedly in Cedar Falls and said words that no one in a relationship wants to hear: "We need to talk."

His face looked tense, and he was nervous as he came in. I sat in the mamasan chair while he paced. "I just feel like this relationship is going too fast and you're pressuring me to go to the next level. I don't know what I want, and I don't know if I'm ready. So I just want to take a break."

I didn't have to say anything. I knew the look of shock on my face told him how unexpected this was.

He crossed the room to where I was sitting. "Here." He handed me a piece of paper. A cashier's check for fifteen hundred dollars.

A check? It was more money than I'd ever seen. But still—a check?

"You're paying me to break up with you?"

"No, I just want to help out."

"You're handing me a check, and you think that's going to make everything okay?"

"Just put it in an account for the kids and use it as you need it. I just need a break," he said as he grabbed his coat and left.

I sat there stunned. I wasn't sure what was worse—that we had broken up, or that he had paid me off to do it. But I was in a different place than I had been in the past. I didn't panic or make any rash decisions. I was confident that Kurt just needed a temporary breather from our relationship and that once he looked around and realized what we had, he would return.

I promised myself that I would give him whatever time he needed without pressuring him. But that didn't make his being gone any easier. I missed him like crazy. So did the kids. I was still really into country music, and it seemed that every song I listened to over the next few days related to my poor broken heart.

I thought about Kurt all the time, but I also remained true to my promise not to call him or pressure him. During those lonely days, there were times I considered just giving up on him. But then I would think, *I love that man. Doggone it, I am not walking away. I am not!*

Kurt called a couple of days later. "How are Jesse Jo and Zack doing?" he asked.

"They're fine," I said. I knew the question was just his excuse to call, so I took the opportunity to find out more about where his head was. "So tell me: what's the real reason you broke up with me? Is there somebody else?"

"No, there's nobody. I just wanted to take a break."

"You just think the grass is greener without me, don't you?"

"No, I don't."

But whether he knew it or not, I knew that was part of it. He was in a new city, had a brand-new career, and wanted to see what else was out there.

For the next two weeks, we had a few more conversations about our breakup, but we didn't see each other. He didn't come to Coyote's, although I continued to go on my own. Finally he again showed up unexpectedly at my door and began to plead his case.

"I love you and I miss you," he told me. "I miss the kids. I want you back."

I asked him a lot of hard questions, and his answers confirmed that he was ready to be in this relationship for the long haul. I forgave him, and we got back together.

Although Kurt had come to terms with his feelings for me, there were still some things we needed to resolve before we could ever get married.

The break reminded me that Kurt and I looked at the world differently and that if we married, we needed to be on the same page for the kids' sake. I wanted faith to be just as important to my kids as it was for me. If Kurt and I got married and we couldn't agree on the role of Jesus in our lives, then how could we agree on what to teach our kids? How do you make decisions as a couple about what is best for a child's future if you don't share the same values?

We continued to have discussions about faith, and when Kurt offered an opinion on religion, I would ask him, "Why do you think that?"

He hated that question because often he had no grounds for what he thought.

"Well, why do you believe the things you believe?" he asked me once.

"I believe them because the Bible says they're true."

He gave me a funny look, as if he'd never thought about the Bible being a source for answers about his faith.

In another conversation he got really animated. For instance, he said, "God helps those who help themselves."

"Where does it say that in the Bible?" I asked.

Again, that funny look. He had no idea.

"Well, you need to find out why you believe that or find out what the Bible says about it."

Kurt didn't like being challenged like that because it forced him to wrestle with his own thoughts and ideas. He would have ignored the whole subject, but I wouldn't let him.

After a particularly difficult conversation when Kurt couldn't really defend his beliefs, he came up with this snappy retort: "Who cares about all that? It's not important. We can each have our own thoughts and views, and we can still get along and be together."

That was our problem right there. To him, faith wasn't important. To me it was eternally important.

But Kurt could see how passionate I was when we talked about faith. It took some time, but ultimately, I think my passion sent him searching for his own answers. He realized I had something he didn't—a relationship with Jesus. And although he would have preferred for me to just shut up and make out with him, he also wanted what I had.

Either that, or he wanted to prove me wrong.

———————

At work, Mary wasn't doing well. She was slipping away quickly and didn't have long to live. During the previous week, she had weakened considerably and slowly curled into a fetal position. She wouldn't eat, and each breath sounded like her last. Her eyes remained closed, and when I came into her room, she didn't reach out to touch me anymore.

I knew she was going to die, and she was going to die alone. My only hope was that perhaps angels would show up at her bedside when it happened.

After my shift ended, I went in and sat with her. I talked to her and held her hand. While I was praying for her, I heard her take one last gasp of air, and then she stopped breathing. It was the first time I had ever watched a death while it happened. It was beautiful and peaceful.

No angels appeared. But that night, one left.

22

The Worst Call

Of all the places I have lived, the house with the crooked floors was the most memorable. The hundred-year-old house sat directly across the street from the nursing home, and the nursing-home owners rented it to me for three hundred dollars a month.

If you looked at that house from the outside, you could tell it was physically crooked, as if the foundation was sinking. The living room and kitchen rose away from the front door, so you actually had to walk uphill from the front of the house to the back. The kids kept their toys in the living room, but since the floors weren't level, the balls and the toys with wheels, like Jesse Jo's little shopping cart, would always roll to the same corner of the room, by the door.

There were two bedrooms—neither of them had closets—and one small bathroom. The carpet was thin, and the appliances were dated but functional. A washer and dryer sat on the cracked concrete floor of the unfinished basement. The place smelled of mildew and rotting wood.

We didn't have much in the way of furniture. I still had the mamasan chair and a hand-me-down sofa that smelled like my parents' dog. The TV sat on a cardboard box I had covered with a piece of fabric. If the TV stayed on it too long, the weight of the set plus the moisture in the air would cause the box to sag, and I'd have to replace it. In my bedroom, I still had the mattress and metal frame, but I had added a plastic, zippered wardrobe from Walmart to hang my clothes in.

I also bought the kids a hamster. We used a couple of cinder blocks from the basement to make a table for the hamster's cage. As far as the kids were concerned, home was where their hamster was.

The kids and I visited Kurt most weekends. Although we saw each other as often as we could, we still weren't spending as much time together as we would have liked. Even during the off-season, Kurt worked at the YMCA in Des Moines. So when the kids' spring break fell the week before Kurt was supposed to start his second season with the Barnstormers, we decided to both take a week off of work and take a trip together—something we hadn't done since the weekend I took my nursing boards.

We booked a discounted flight to Las Vegas and found a cheap hotel. Although my parents had moved to Arkansas, they were always willing to babysit the kids. At that time, Zack was seven and Jesse Jo was four, and they loved going to Grandma's, where they would get to stay up late to watch TV, drink sodas, and eat popcorn with Papa. Though Mom and Dad had been in Arkansas for a year, they had just moved into the home they'd built near the river. It was very small, but Mom loved decorating it with her country accessories. She had spoons hanging on the wall and pink and mauve country trinkets in every room.

It felt like home to me. For the kids, it was like a vacation resort.

Kurt and I drove Zack and Jesse Jo down and dropped them off at my folks', then we drove back to Des Moines, where we caught our flight to Las Vegas. We had a good time being away together before flying back to Des Moines. Then, we made the trip back to Arkansas to pick up the kids.

When we left, I looked in my rearview mirror and watched Mom as she stood on the porch, waving good-bye. She was crying.

Then I heard crying from the backseat too. Jesse Jo was bawling.

"What's wrong, Jesse Jo?"

Through her sobs and sniffles, she choked out, "I feel like I'm never going to see her again."

"It's okay, sweetheart, we'll see them in a few weeks at Aunt Kimmy's house." A few tears ran down my cheeks too. I was glad Jesse Jo loved and missed my mom as much as I did.

The Saturday after Easter, Kurt had an exhibition game in the Quad Cities. The kids and I met Kurt at Kim and John's house in nearby Eldridge, Iowa, and we all went out to eat together. Then Kurt caught up with the team while the rest of us went back to Kim's house until the game started. This particular Saturday was also Dad's birthday. Mom and Dad had planned to join us at Kim's for a celebration, just as I had told Jesse Jo when we left their house a few weeks earlier. But at the last minute, they'd had to cancel.

We were hanging out in Kim's kitchen, getting ready to call Dad and wish him happy birthday, when Zack knocked a plant off the table and the pot broke. "Be careful, Zack!" Kim said harshly.

"You don't have to be so mean," I said.

"I wasn't mean. He should be more careful."

We started to bicker like we did when we were in high school and I'd hidden her favorite sweater. I didn't like it when she corrected my kids, and she didn't think I corrected them enough. Looking back, it doesn't seem that important, but at the time it was a big deal.

Kim called Dad. "We bought you that electric drill you wanted. I'll get it in the mail this week."

Great, I thought. *We don't have money to buy him anything, and there she goes, showing me up again.* She had a way of making me feel inferior, and it made me mad.

I spoke with Dad next and wished him a happy birthday. I told him I would get him a tool he wanted and bring it the next time we came to Arkansas. When we were done talking, I asked to speak with Mom.

While she was coming to the phone, I stretched Kim's phone cord into the other room so I could have privacy. As soon as Mom said hello, I let her know what was going on. "Kim's driving me crazy!"

"What happened?"

I told her about Kim's attitude that day and how I thought Kim was too harsh with Zack.

"You know that your sister loves your kids. You guys need to figure out how to get along. You might only have each other someday."

Obviously Mom wasn't going to take my side.

After the game, Kurt went back to Des Moines with the team, and I drove back to Cedar Falls with the kids. We spoke on the phone later that night, and I told Kurt what Mom had said.

"She's right. You two need to get along."

Nobody was taking my side.

———————

I wasn't sure if they hadn't gotten enough sleep or if they'd drunk too much soda the day before, but the next day the kids were driving me nuts. With summer approaching, I knew I was going to need a break.

When I got home from church, I called my parents. Dad answered.

"Could you and Mom take the kids for a week when they get out of school in May?" I asked.

"Honey, we'll take the kids anytime and for as long as you want us to," he said. "But can your mom call you back? She's lying down right now. She's got a headache; you know how she gets those headaches."

I did know. Mom was still a bit of a hypochondriac. If she was lying down, it probably meant she'd watched a medical show the night before. "Just have her call me when she gets up."

"We're getting baptized tonight," Dad said.

"Are they making you do that *again*?"

"If we want to be members at the church, we have to be baptized there."

That made sense; it was typical of small Southern churches to do that. "Then just have Mom call me tonight after the movie." Mom and I always watched the *ABC Sunday Night Movie* and then called each other to discuss it afterward.

"I'll have Mom call you. Kiss those kids for me."

"Will do. I love you."

"I love you, too, sweetheart."

If I had known it was the last time I would ever speak to him, I never would have ended the call.

———————

I put Zack and Jesse Jo to bed; then I sat in my mamasan chair with an RC Cola to watch the *Sunday Night Movie* and wait for Mom to call. Shortly after ten, the phone rang. I got up out of the chair and walked toward the kitchen. The phone sat on a half wall that separated the living room from the dining room. I set down my soda and picked up the receiver.

"Sweetheart?"

It was Kim. We hadn't talked since I left her house the day before, and I wasn't sure I was ready to talk to her now. "Kim, Mom's going to be calling," I said. "The movie's over, and I'm waiting for her to call. I need to go." I couldn't help but gloat a bit by letting her know that Mom was calling *me*.

"Sweetheart," she said, speaking slowly, "Mom and Dad were killed in a tornado."

"What?"

"Mom and Dad were killed two hours ago."

"No!" I screamed. "No, no, no!" I started sobbing. All week long I'd seen the advertisements for a new movie called *Twister*. The trailers showed images of tornadoes swirling with debris, and a cow flying through the air. I knew it was just a movie, that the images weren't real. But Kim's words didn't seem real either.

"At seven thirty a tornado hit Mountain View. It killed both of them. Chach called me. She's okay, but Mom and Dad are both gone."

I shook uncontrollably, and I squeezed my eyes shut, trying to keep from losing it completely. I couldn't stop thinking about my earlier conversation with Dad, when he'd said they were under a tornado warning.

"Momma, what are you crying about?" Jesse Jo walked in, rubbing her eyes. My crying had woken her up.

I grabbed her and held her tightly against me as I continued to shake. I could hear her crying, too, although she had no idea why she was doing it.

Kim was still talking. ". . . we'll figure out plans and—"

I saw people walk up to my door. "Kim, there are people here. It's Aunt Loie, Uncle Francis, and Lance. I've got to go."

"I'll call you back. I love you."

"I love you too."

I hung up with Kim and immediately called Kurt. "Get here! Get here as fast as you can! Mom and Dad were killed in a tornado!" Then I hung up the phone.

The front door was open, and the screen door was closed but not locked.

My aunt had seen me on the phone, so they let themselves in. Immediately I felt self-conscious. All I was wearing was a big T-shirt and panties.

My aunt hugged me, and I tried to tell her what had just happened to my parents, but I couldn't stop sobbing. I knew I wasn't making much sense. Later, I realized they already knew. Kim must have called them and asked them to come over, then stayed on the phone with me until they arrived.

I sat down in the mamasan chair and pulled the T-shirt down over my knees. Someone handed me tissue, and I cried and cried. More people came—relatives, my friend Stacy.

Jesse Jo would twirl and dance in her nightgown, showing off her new Walmart nightie to the latest visitor. But then her questions would start again. "Momma, why are you crying? Why is everybody here?" She sensed something terrible had happened, and she was scared. I needed to tell her something. So the next time she asked me what was going on, I pulled her onto my lap. I looked at her sweet little face, the dimples on her cheeks, and her inquiring dark eyes. Dark ringlets, messy from sleep, framed her face. I tried to stop crying, but the best I could do was slow it down enough to get the words out. "Grandma and Papa died. They went to heaven, and we're going to miss them."

Jesse Jo burst into tears and cried as I'd never seen her cry before. She buried her head in my chest and screamed, and I hugged her. *Oh, please don't wake your brother!* Although I could tell my four-year-old daughter what happened, I didn't want to tell Zack. I was always protecting that child.

I looked up and saw Kurt coming in the door. I jumped up and ran into his arms, and he just held me as I cried on his shoulder.

Friends and family tried to comfort Jesse Jo, and eventually she fell asleep again. Someone put her to bed. Then, one by one, everybody left except Kurt.

I don't think I slept that night. At least I don't remember sleeping. I just remember holding Kurt and both of us crying.

23

The Damage

Sometime during the night, a plan was made. Kurt would drive the kids and me to Kim's house, and then we'd drive to Arkansas together while Kurt returned to Des Moines. He would then fly to Arkansas to be there for the funeral.

The next morning, I packed our bags, and Kurt helped me load them in the car.

On the way to Kim's house, I told Zack that something had happened to Grandma and Grandpa and that they were now in heaven. I wasn't sure how much of it he understood, but I told him over and over again how much they had loved him.

Jesse Jo had obviously overheard conversations from the night before, so on the ride to Aunt Kimmy's, she asked a few more questions. "Why did the tornado hit Grandma and Papa's house?" I tried to answer in ways she could understand. But the truth was, I had the same questions, and there just weren't any easy answers.

After we got to Kim's house in Eldridge, we loaded up her minivan. Then we all squeezed in—Kim and John; their two girls, Alexandria and Victoria; my kids and me. There was so much luggage, we had to scoot the back bench seat up as close to the middle seat as possible. Ali and Tor sat in their car seats in the middle, and I sat in the back with Zack and Jesse Jo on either side of me. We were so cramped, my knees touched the seat in front of me and the kids kept kicking it. But I hardly noticed. I was too numb.

Even from the back of the van, I could tell when Kim started to cry. Her head would drop and her shoulders would shake. She'd turn around to look at me and her girls would see her crying, then they'd start crying and I would too. Jesse Jo kept looking at me as if to ask, "Are you okay?" I didn't know how to answer her.

All Zack wanted to do was listen to the radio. But driving ten hours south meant that we kept driving out of signal range. Because of the static, I kept asking John to change the station. He probably didn't even want the radio on, and all the station changing probably drove him crazy, especially when Kim kept turning down the volume. Each time she would do that, I would think, *Just let Zack have the radio. It's the only thing he's got.*

Whether it was from shock, grief, or lack of sleep, my thoughts during those ten hours were jumbled and didn't make much sense. One minute I'd be wishing I could have held Mom and Dad as they died or said, "I love you" one last time. A few minutes later I would think, *Maybe someone made a mistake identifying the bodies. Maybe they didn't really die.* Or, *Maybe one of them is still alive, but since they found a couple, they just assumed it was the two of them.*

Of course I didn't really believe any of that. Chach had told Kim that Mom and Dad had died instantly. But regardless of what I knew to be true, my brain wasn't working right, and hopeful thoughts like those would pass through my mind. It just didn't seem possible to believe that *both* my parents were dead. I wasn't sure I even knew what death was. I knew my grandpa had died, and I had held Mary's hand when she died, but what did it really mean anyway?

As we got closer to Mountain View, I saw the damage. We'd been there just a few weeks earlier, so I recognized what should have been there and what was no longer there. I felt as if I was seeing everything in slow motion.

Kim and John hadn't been to the new house yet, so I needed to give them directions. "When we get to the bottom of this hill, there'll be an RV park, and after that, take a left and then—"

The RV park came into view. "This is bad. Oh, this is so bad." The RV park looked like someone had kicked over a pile of Lincoln Logs. Motor homes were strewn across the field at odd angles. One was upside down and was smashed to half its height.

"Look at that!" John said.

"Oh my! Look at that!" Kim said.

We kept thinking we had seen the worst, but then we'd spot something even more devastating. I tried to stay composed so I could continue to give John directions.

"Continue across the bridge," I told John. "Mom and Dad's street is just on the other side of the bridge. You'll need to take a right."

As we crossed the bridge, I saw that the houses by the river were now piles of rubble. "Those were homes! Those were homes!" I said, pointing at the debris. I felt like some kind of sick tour guide, pointing out all the things that used to be.

We turned onto Mom and Dad's street. There was a house, then another house, and they both looked just fine. Farther down the street, there were more undamaged houses. *But Mom and Dad's house should be here somewhere! Where is it? Oh my—*

I started pulling on the door to get out of the van, but it wouldn't open. Frantic, I pulled harder and harder. "Brenda, stop," John said. "We're still moving. The child locks are on." He pulled the van over to the side of the road and ran around the van to let me out.

"This was their house!" I screamed. "This was their house!" John opened the door, and I ran into the street, leaving Zack and Jesse Jo behind, not thinking of anyone else. "This was their house!"

Everything was gone. Just . . . gone.

To say the house had collapsed would imply that parts of it were still there, but they weren't. All that remained was the foundation of their house. Even the foundation of the garage had disappeared.

I stared at the scene for the longest time. It was surreal. The day was beautiful. The sun was shining, and people walked around holding on to each other for strength and comfort. Occasionally someone stooped down to pick something up. They were quiet and respectful, almost ghostlike, as they drifted from one debris field to another. The smell of wisteria and fresh pine from the newly snapped trees filled the air. Although there were media trucks and emergency vehicles, the only loud sound was the *thwump, thwump,* of the news helicopters overhead. Occasionally we'd hear a burst of crying when one of the searchers found a particularly meaningful object.

I spotted a small pile of what looked like junk on the corner of the foundation. I walked over to look at it. Someone had apparently put it there for us to find. In the pile, I found the roof from one of the birdhouses Dad had made. And one red shoe—Mom's.

Dad's hands touched this roof, I thought. *Mom's foot wore this shoe.* But there was nothing in the pile larger than the shoe.

I looked up the hill. As far as my eye could see, there was only damage. Siding stuck in trees. Fragments of furniture. Twisted metal.

A line of cabins had once run along the top of the hill. My cousins owned them. Five of them were now rubble, but one was left standing as if nothing had happened. Mom and Dad had stayed in one of those cabins while building this house. We had even stayed there once when we came to visit.

I followed the path of destruction back down the hill. Big, strong, beautiful trees that had been budding new leaves a few weeks ago were now splinters. It looked like a bomb had gone off.

I picked up Mom's red shoe and turned it over in my hands. I still refused to believe she was gone. Missing, yes. But gone? I thought about the *Twister* trailer and the stupid cow flying through the air. *Did the tornado pick up Mom and Dad? Did they fly through the air too?*

I still didn't know where Mom and Dad were, and part of me still hoped we'd find them alive. It was as if I couldn't comprehend the damage in front of me. So I kept searching the street and the horizon, thinking Mom and Dad might see us and come over.

I started talking to God. *I know you're big enough to stop a tornado. And I know that even if a tornado hit a house, you could still save the people inside. I even trust that if the tornado hit the house and people went flying, you could help them to survive. You could help them be alive somehow, somewhere.*

By now, Kim and John were standing on the foundation with me, all of us staring at the unbelievable destruction. A man walked up to us. "Are you Larry and Jenny Jo Carney's girls?" We told them we were. He told us how sorry he was that the tornado had hit their house. He said he'd been looking for their belongings and that if he found anything, he'd make sure we got it back.

"Did they tell you where your parents are?" he asked.

"No," Kim said.

"They're at the morgue downtown. It's the house with white siding on Main Street," he said. "At least they didn't suffer. I heard they died instantly." He patted my shoulder, then lowered his head and left.

I could barely breathe, and I couldn't stop shaking. I sat down on the concrete steps that led up to the foundation. That's when I saw their initials: "L&J Carney 1995." Mom and Dad had scrawled those letters in the wet cement to signify their love and the happiness of a new house. Now the same letters read like a memorial to their death.

The only thing left of Mom and Dad's dream house—the step with their initials. Later we cut it out and made it into a bench that sits in our front yard.

It was late by the time we got to the Motel 6 where we had reservations. Kim and I kept busy, feeding and bathing the kids. I must have slept that night, but when I woke up the next morning, I didn't feel like I had. My eyes burned, and I moved slowly.

We went over to Chach's house and talked with our relatives. Someone offered to watch the kids while John drove Kim and me to the morgue. Mountain View is a sleepy little town with one blinking stoplight, so the place wasn't hard to find. The man was right; it had once been a house. But now it was a combination funeral home and morgue.

When we walked in, the front rooms were quiet and dark. My uncle and two cousins were there. An old man dressed in a dark suit met us, expressed condolences, then motioned for us to follow him.

We entered a brightly lit, white-tiled hallway. The man led us down this long hallway toward an addition that had been built onto the backside of the house. Near the end of the hall, I saw two gurneys pushed against the left side of the wall. I could see feet sticking out from underneath a sheet on the first one. Dad's feet. I looked at the second gurney and I realized that must be Mom.

"Darlin', I am sorry your parents are here in the hallway," the old man said in his slow Arkansas drawl. "There was no more room for 'em in the morgue."

As I approached Dad, I saw that the sheet covered him from his ankles to his chin. I could see his head at the top. It was huge. My nurse's training kicked in and set off all kinds of alarms. Dad hadn't died immediately! He must have suffered for at least a while, because a body doesn't swell unless it is alive. *Did anybody realize he was alive? How long was he alive?*

I wanted to tell someone. I wanted to ask questions. But Kim was right next to me, and I didn't want to upset her. My mind raced with possibilities as I looked at his swollen head, so I forced myself to look at his large, muscular feet. Thirty years of hard work had made them strong.

Kim stepped forward to see Dad, so I stepped back and moved toward Mom's gurney, toward her face. It was completely flattened. She had obviously been hit in the face. Her nose, the nose she used to hate, the nose that looked just like mine does now, had been smashed in. She'd had her yellowed teeth fixed several years before. Now her beautiful white teeth were all pushed in. Her flattened face barely resembled itself.

She would not want anyone to see her looking like this. I knew that family would want to come in and say their good-byes, but in that moment I made a decision. *Nobody else is going to be allowed in here to see my mom, because she wouldn't want this.*

I stepped back so Kim could see Mom. I never moved the sheet on either Dad or Mom to take a look underneath it.

I wish I had. Or at least I think that now. But perhaps it's best that I didn't.

The old man took us into an office and asked us about our plans. Kim and I agreed that no one should be allowed to see Mom and Dad and that they should be cremated. He seemed to have anticipated our request and had the papers all filled out, ready for us to sign. One of the family members had probably already told him about Mom's desire to be cremated.

The memorial service would be held the next day at the same church where Mom and Dad were supposed to have been baptized. Had they gone to the church as originally planned, they would have both survived the tornado.

24

Final Arrangements

Back at Chach's, the Woodyard family coped the best we could. There were lots of tears, some laughter, lots and lots of food. Chach lived in an apartment in a retirement community, so her place was rather small. Once we arrived and when other relatives started showing up, the place got really crowded, really quick. There was nowhere to sit and not much to do other than play with the kids. People I didn't know kept dropping off casseroles as a gesture of comfort, but no one wanted to eat a bite.

Later in the day, Kim and I went to the bank to close Mom and Dad's accounts and to the State Farm office to fill out paperwork. When we got back to Chach's, I went into my grandmother's bedroom and made calls to cancel credit cards and other accounts. Someone had found Mom's wallet in the debris, so I pulled out every card and called the number on the back.

"She was killed in a tornado Sunday. What do I need to do to close this account and tie everything up?" I must have asked that question a dozen times. I also called my pastor in Cedar Falls and started making arrangements to have a memorial service at my church on Saturday. I was in a daze, doing what I had to do without really thinking about what I was saying. I was trying to hold it together, and as long as I had something to do, I thought I could make it through.

While looking for the next phone number to call, I heard Chach's front door close as someone else came in. Then I heard someone say, "Hey."

"Hey," came several replies.

I knew it had to be Kurt. One of my cousins was supposed to pick him up from the Little Rock airport and bring him to Chach's. I stepped into the hall and motioned him into the bedroom. As soon as he entered the room, I shut the door and ran into his arms.

"Dad was alive," I said. I could finally say it, and when I did, I started crying uncontrollably.

"What? What are you talking about?" Kurt held me tightly. "Breathe, Brenda. Just breathe and tell me what happened."

"Dad was alive! They're all saying he died instantly, but he was alive! He was alive!" Kurt must have thought I was crazy, so I explained what I knew from our trip to the morgue.

"Did anybody know that?"

"Nobody said a thing. They just keep telling us that he died instantly, but he didn't!"

I couldn't stand the idea of Dad's dying slowly. I guess I thought that perhaps if someone had found him alive, maybe they could have saved him. It bothered me to think that he had suffered.

There were so many questions I couldn't answer. Kurt couldn't answer them either. He just held me tight and let me cry.

The next day, before the memorial service, I told Kim that I wanted to take Kurt to see where our parents' house had been. He'd been there with me just weeks before, and I wanted him to see the devastation. The rest of the family was loading up food and flowers to take to the church, so we had a few minutes.

Kurt and I and the kids got into the minivan with Kim and her family. On the way we stopped at a flower shop, picked up an arrangement, and put it in the back of the van. When we turned onto their street, I started doing the tour-guide thing again. "Look at this, Kurt. Just look at this. Do you remember what was here a few weeks ago? It's gone!"

When we got to Mom and Dad's land, Kurt walked off into the distance to get a better look. I sat on the stairs and studied the letters Mom and Dad's fingers had traced: "L&J Carney 1995." Once again, the scene around me seemed peaceful. All of our talk was about the violent storm, but it was another beautiful spring day.

Around us, people continued to sift through the debris, trying to recover whatever shards of their life were left. Occasionally, a complete stranger would come over with an object. "Is this your mom and dad's?" they'd ask. Or, "I found this. Do you recognize it?"

Some of my cousins were there also, looking through the rubble before heading off to the funeral. One of my cousins tried to put a smile on my face when he brought over another of Mom's shoes. "Look what I found!" he said. I nodded and thanked him, but all I could think was, *Yep. It's one shoe. But where's her foot?*

"We need to go," Kim said.

I stood up and looked for Kurt. I couldn't see him anywhere. "Kurt!" I yelled, looking toward the hill. *C'mon! We gotta go, dude. Where are you?*

"Kurt! Kurt, it's time to go!" I yelled again.

Minutes passed, and he still didn't answer my calls. Now I was getting mad. *I'm going to be late to my own parents' funeral.*

I called again, "Kurt! Where are you?"

A wooded area with a creek ran between Mom and Dad's house and the hill where my cousin's cabins had stood. Suddenly, I heard the sound of branches breaking. Through the branches, I made out Kurt coming toward us. As he got closer, I saw he had mud on his good pants.

"Where have you been?" I asked angrily.

"I found this." He opened his hand. A crumpled piece of torn paper lay in his palm. Through tears, he said, "I think it's from your mom and dad's Bible. We need to keep it."

I didn't bother to read the Bible passage. I just turned to head toward the car.

"And I found this," he said. I turned back, and he held out some other papers. "It's your parents' will."

I was still worried about getting to the memorial service on time, but inside I thought, *Wow! You found the will!* I remembered all those ghostlike people slowly sorting through things. None of them had found the will. But Kurt had.

"I was just taking a walk," Kurt said, "and something told me to jump the creek. So I did, and on the other side there were all these pieces of white paper everywhere. But something told me to pick up this one, and I couldn't believe I'd found it!"

I looked at the tears running down his face, and my anger disappeared. I wasn't the only one suffering here. Kurt had also lost people he loved, and he needed time to absorb it all. But it was sweet to see that he had a look of awe on his face, as if the experience of finding the will had been a spiritual event.

I slipped my hand into his, and we walked back to the van together.

At the church, Kurt tried to wash the mud off his pants the best he could while Kim and John made sure everything was ready for the service. Kurt and I finally entered the sanctuary and sat on the front row. Our flower arrangement had been placed in the middle of the altar, and Mom and Dad's picture was tucked in among the blooms. It was the one they'd had taken the year before when Dad retired.

I spent most of the service trying to keep my kids quiet, so I didn't hear a word the preacher said. I heard a lot of crying, but I didn't cry much. The whole funeral just felt . . . useless. We were all just sitting there, not doing anything. I couldn't wait for it to be over.

Afterward, everyone was invited downstairs to the fellowship hall. I didn't want to go, but I knew I had to. "Thank you for coming," I said over and over. What I really wanted to say was, "How do I get out of here?"

My escape came soon enough. Kim had arranged for somebody to watch our kids so we could take Mom and Dad's ashes to the river. I made my way to the parking lot with Kim, John, and Kurt. Kim was carrying the two small, black boxes.

"Are you ready to go do this?" she asked.

I nodded. "Yes."

Kim and John got in the car. I lingered outside for a minute longer, staring at the cars lined up in the gravel parking lot. Kurt reached to open the door, but I stopped him.

"What's up?"

"Listen, if you're not going to marry me, then it's really stupid for you to be here right now. This will be a memory I will always have, and if you're not going to be a part of the rest of my life, then I don't want you as a part of this memory. So if you're not going to marry me, then you shouldn't come along."

"It's okay, Brenda."

"I'm serious," I said.

I am sure he thought I was crazy. He probably wanted to say, "Look, your parents just got killed, and we're going to scatter their ashes. This isn't the time to talk about marriage."

But what he said was, "I love you. Let's get this done." He opened the door and climbed into the middle seat behind Kim.

I climbed in after him.

―――――

We crossed the same bridge toward Mom and Dad's place, but instead of turning right, we turned left and headed for the boat ramp. As we drove, Kim said something funny. I don't remember what it was, but I do remember that I snickered. Whatever it was got funnier, and we both started giggling. Kurt and John sat stoically, not saying a word.

"Which one do you want?" Kim said, turning around and holding out the boxes.

"Who's who?" I said before I even realized how dumb that sounded. We laughed again, harder this time.

"That's not funny," John said, but we couldn't stop laughing.

"Who's who?" Kim howled, a little hysterically. "That's funny! Who says that?"

By the time we pulled onto the boat ramp and parked, Kim and I were laughing so hard we were crying. Kim handed me whomever, and she took who was left, and the two of us walked down the long concrete ramp to the river. As we got close, a fishing boat crossed in front of us, and water lapped up around the banks.

This is just a normal day for those fishermen, I thought. It wasn't until later that I realized they weren't fishing. They were looking for debris from the tornado.

Kurt and John hung back a bit. I think they were scared we were going to totally flip out. But by the time we reached the water, we'd both calmed down.

I went first. I knelt down on the concrete and shook the box gently to release the ashes into the water. Neither of us said anything, but we were both crying. We watched as the ashes floated down the river. As I stood up, John put his arm around Kim to comfort her. Then I stepped back so she could have her turn.

Kim got her box and knelt down, but instead of shaking it gently, she opened it and shook it hard. A puff of ashes came out, and much of it landed on her face, as well as on her shirt and her camera. We started to giggle again, but then Kim started gagging because some of the ash was now in her mouth. She freaked out, jumping around and trying to brush the ashes off.

"Oh my gosh," she kept saying. "It's in my nose! It's in my nose!" And that made both of us laugh harder than ever.

I looked at Kurt and John, their eyes wide in horror, and I could tell they thought we'd crossed the line.

"That's not funny!" Kurt said.

Their anger only made it worse. Kim and I burst out into belly laughs.

"Really?" I said to Kim. "You couldn't just let the ashes go? You had to mess it up?"

The guys were so mad, they couldn't take it any longer. "You're going to hell," John said, "and we're not going to be a part of this." Of course that brought on a fresh wave of laughter. By then, I was laughing so hard I had to cross my legs so I didn't wet my pants.

John and Kurt stomped off to the van. Kim and I slowly got a grip; then we walked back up the ramp together. The guys were both in the car when we returned. We were still laughing and making jokes. Kim got a Kleenex and tried to wipe the ashy dust off her camera, and we joked about how the pictures would turn out.

The guys just stayed mad. We honestly tried to stop laughing, but their anger just kept it fueled. We would quiet down, but then one of us would say something, and then it'd start all over again.

Some people would think our laughter was very disrespectful. Maybe it was. But for Kim and me, it released a lot of pent-up stress. It was also a real bonding moment for us.

But not for the guys. It took them a long time to get over it.

My cousin drove Kurt back to Little Rock that night so he could fly home and catch up with his team. The kids and I hung out at Chach's, and I tried to eat, but I still couldn't manage it. We stayed one more night at the Motel 6 and then made the long drive back to Iowa on Thursday.

When we got back to Cedar Falls, Kim and I met with the pastor to plan the memorial service. Kim remembered that Mom loved "The Old Rugged Cross" and asked if that could be sung. Since he didn't know my parents well, the pastor wanted to have a time when people could get up and share memories of Mom and Dad. He asked if Kim or I wanted to speak. We looked at each other for a minute and then shook our heads and said no. That would have been too much.

At the service, I sat once more on the front row next to Kurt and the kids. Just as in Mountain View, I spent most of the service worried about Jesse Jo and Zack. I wanted them both to be good and sit still, but I also wanted to make sure Jesse Jo didn't cry too much. As usual, Zack had a Rubik's cube and a radio to play with. We always had to make sure we'd taken the batteries out of the radio before we went somewhere quiet.

The last time the kids had been in this church with me was at Desia's wedding. Mom and Dad had been there that day, fussing over Zack and Jesse Jo. Looking down the pew at Kim and John and their girls, I was unprepared for how the same space could have such a different feeling. Desia's wedding was bright and happy, despite my issues with Kurt. Now the church felt cold and gray, and Mom's favorite hymn playing on the organ seemed so heavy. Even the music felt like death.

While the pastor spoke, I heard sniffling and crying from behind me. Kurt put his arm around me, and I was comforted by his strength. But though I knew he loved me, I also knew he couldn't fully understand what I was going through. Only one other person could do that—Kim. I looked at her sitting with Ali and Tor and knew that she was hurting as much as I was.

Less than a week ago, on the phone, Mom had said that Kim and I needed to get along. She'd said that one day we might be all we had. But neither of us had thought that day would come so soon.

After the service Kim hugged me and we both cried. I wanted her to hold me and make it all feel better, but even through her embrace I could feel her brokenness. Her grief only made me sadder. Everyone else at the service had lost a brother, sister, or friend. Kim and I had lost both of our parents and more. We also had to each watch our sister face heartbreaking grief and be unable to console her.

We did the fellowship hall thing again, but this time the atmosphere was a little lighter because we knew more people. At the memorial in Arkansas, there were many people from Mom and Dad's church whom we had never met. But in Cedar Falls we were together with Dad's mother, his nine brothers and two sisters and their families, the Iowa Woodyards from my mom's extended family, and friends we had known all our lives. One of dad's friends told stories about how Dad hated to be goosed and how he'd scream no matter where he was. So they would wait for the right situation and then goose Dad so he would scream in public and embarrass himself.

It felt good to have more laughter—especially since I couldn't seem to cry anymore. Apparently I had already cried out every tear. For the first time I could remember, I actually wanted to cry and couldn't.

After the memorial service, Kurt had to go back to Des Moines. That night after I got home and got the kids tucked in bed, I thought about how good he had been to me all week. I had experienced an extremely traumatic situation, and he had stood by me the entire time.

He'd been incredible—talking to the kids when I couldn't and letting them know I was sad but I still loved them, putting up with Kim and me losing it on the boat ramp. And, of course, choosing to come with me to do the ashes after I'd given him that unexpected ultimatum.

I knew in that moment that Kurt was going to be mine. And I also knew I would take him just as he was, without insisting he act just the way I wanted or believe exactly as I believed or conform to all my rules. Kurt Warner was everything I wanted for my kids.

And for me.

25

Questions Remain

If the devil was trying to destroy me, if he wanted to take me out, taking my parents from me was the way to do it.

What had happened to Zack was horrible. So was all the stuff I had to endure after that. But at least Zack and I were still alive. Mom and Dad were dead.

I had moved back in with Mom and Dad so many times because I couldn't afford to live on my own. Whenever I screwed up, they had always been there to catch me. They were my biggest cheerleaders and had always provided me a safe place to fall. But now that had all blown away. If I couldn't pay my bills, if Kurt dumped me, if I needed a place to regroup, I had no one to turn to, nowhere to go.

Most of all, Mom and Dad were the people who had always loved me unconditionally. Now that they were gone, who would love me that way?

It turned out that I wasn't out of tears after all. In fact, some days I cried so much that I'd think each breath was going to be my last. I was never suicidal, but there were times I just wanted to get away from the pain.

But of course, I still had Zack and Jesse Jo. Their presence brought me so much comfort, and they also provided distractions to keep me moving. There were lunches to make. Laundry to do. Baths and bedtime stories. So whenever I thought I just wanted God to take me away, he'd remind me that it was time to pick up one of the kids or make dinner, and the grief would pass for a while.

Life moved forward, as it always does. With the arena season in full swing, Kurt traveled more. The nursing home let me have a few more weeks off work. Zack went back to school, and family members would take Jesse Jo for an occasional afternoon so I could get things done at home. There was still so much insurance paperwork to handle, as well as final bills to pay and other estate issues.

About halfway through the process, I opened a notice from the morgue but was confused by the zero balance. So I called them. "I'm trying to get everything worked out. What do I owe you for the cremation?"

The woman said in her southern Arkansas drawl, "Oh, darlin', you don't owe us a thing. The Red Cross took care of that."

I hung up the phone and stared at the open checkbook, the pile of paid bills, and the bigger pile of unpaid bills. And I burst into tears. It was such a blessing that somebody cared. Not having to write a check for my parents' cremation was a big deal to me.

Grief sneaks up on you when you least expect it.

For months, I'd be driving in Cedar Falls and catch a glimpse of someone driving a truck like my dad's with a driver who looked familiar. I'd think, *That's Dad!* Then the driver would turn, and I could see he didn't look anything like my dad. And I'd have to pull over because suddenly I couldn't see to drive.

I would open a can of soup for the kids and remember Mom making the same soup for me. Then there would be tears on the counter before I could get the soup into the pan.

Suddenly, little things had big meaning. I would find papers my mom had signed with that distinctive letter *y*, and a rush of memories would come flooding back.

When Mountain View residents picked up stray objects that might belong to victims of the tornado, they took them to the fire station. Chach and my cousins who lived there would go to the station periodically and identify anything that had belonged to Mom and Dad. Over time, they identified a total of ten quilts that Mom had made. They were found over a ten-mile radius from the house—some torn, others in perfect condition. We also got a box of photos back. Other items seemed random—like that red shoe—but they were significant because Mom or Dad had once touched them.

Kurt carried the torn Bible passage with him for a long time. It was something from Isaiah, but when we read it in context, it didn't seem to have any deep spiritual meaning for either of us. Eventually, after his grief settled down a bit, he put it away.

Grief would cause me to act in unpleasant ways. Sometimes the pain made me lash out at those who were closest to me. One day I yelled at Kurt, "It's so unfair that you have three parents and I don't have any."

I knew that was a horrible thing to say, and of course I didn't wish that his parents were dead, but I just felt so alone. I didn't know anyone other than my sister who had lost both parents. I didn't know what grief was supposed to look or feel like. People had expectations about what grieving should look like and how long it should last, but I didn't share their expectations. Just as I didn't have a role model for what being divorced looked like, I didn't have a role model for how to handle my sorrow.

As the weeks went on, I sensed that people thought I should be getting over my grief. They wouldn't say anything, but they would give me a look that said it all. *It's been six weeks. When are you going to stop this?* they seemed to think. *You're still crying?* Or they would tell me about someone they had lost, including details about how the person had died. I thought that was weird. I knew they were just trying to connect with me, but I didn't need to connect with more loss. I needed comfort for my *own* loss.

I also know people thought they were being kind when they quoted Bible verses and religious platitudes to me. But it wasn't my faith that needed healing. It was my heart. Well-meaning friends and family would say things like, "God just needed two more angels in heaven," and I'd think, *I need them here!*

Although I knew Kim would understand, I hesitated to pour out my sorrows on her, and she seemed to hesitate with me as well. We both knew good days were rare during those early weeks, and we didn't want to risk calling and bringing the other sister down.

Surprisingly, the person who helped me the most wasn't someone who shared my faith. It was Kurt. He would sit for hours and hold my hand and listen to me talk, or he would hold me while I didn't say anything at all. He didn't quote Scripture—he didn't know any—but I think he also sensed that wasn't what I needed. He didn't tell me that I shouldn't be angry with God. He just agreed about how horrible it all was.

Best of all, he'd step up and take care of my kids when I just couldn't do it. He'd tell Zack and Jesse Jo the things I wanted them to hear but couldn't find words to say: "Your momma is crying because she misses Grandma and Papa" and "Your grandma and papa loved you so much."

He was the one to help them through the grieving process when I could barely help myself. How do you help a child grieve when you're a grieving child?

He never judged me.

He never told me how to handle my grief.

He just stood next to me and held me when I couldn't stand on my own.

Holidays and birthdays during the first year after Mom and Dad's death were the hardest. As time went on, memories started to fade, and I didn't want that to happen, so I worked hard to remember what Mom looked like, the smell of her White Diamonds perfume, the feel of her favorite sweater. I tried to remember how the smoke curled from Dad's Pall Mall cigarettes and what it felt like when, as a child, I blow-dried his hair into an Elvis do.

Less than a month after their death, Kurt and I visited his mom's house for Mother's Day. It was obviously a bad day for me because everything reminded me of Mom. We went out to eat, and during dinner I tried to remember things about my mom. Innocently I asked Kurt, "What did we do last year for Mother's Day?"

"I remember exactly what you did," Sue said curtly, almost accusingly. "You went to *your* mother's house for Mother's Day."

I sat there for a moment, stunned, trying to take in what she had said and how she had meant it. I could feel tears forming in my eyes, and I didn't want her to see me cry. I put down my fork, took the napkin off my lap, stood up, and walked out.

Kurt followed after me. "I am so sorry she said that! I'm sure she didn't mean it the way it sounded."

"That's it!" I said. "I'm out of here." Her words had been like sandpaper on already-raw wounds. I went outside and waited in the car for everyone to finish. It didn't take long.

That night, I was sorting through some of Mom's things when I spotted a letter in her handwriting. I picked it up and read it. It was a letter she'd written to me shortly after she'd moved to Arkansas. She talked about how beautiful it was around her new home, and how many friends they had made. Apparently I had complained about Sue in a previous letter to her because her response to me in this letter was, "I know this is difficult, but surround yourself with people that bring good into your life."

To me, this was a message from the grave. I told Kurt that night, "Your mom isn't bringing good into my life, so I need to separate myself from her."

"You can't do that," Kurt said. "She's my mother."

"I'm sorry to have to put you in this position, but I will not have her in my life. You need to decide what that looks like for you."

He tried to argue with me, but I wouldn't budge.

———

About a month after Mom and Dad's deaths, Kurt said, "Why don't you just move down to Des Moines so we can be together?"

I had returned to work a few days earlier, but my heart hadn't been in it. I wasn't ready. So I'd gone in the next day and asked my boss for more time. "I can't do this right now."

"Take all the time you need," my boss, Melissa, had said. "Your job is here when you want it." She was a good friend, and she understood what I was going through.

The kids and I packed up our mismatched furniture and that mamasan chair and moved to Des Moines, where we put it all into storage. Then we settled in with Kurt and his roommate.

———

Years later, after Kurt and I were married and living in St. Louis, I rented a car and drove to Mountain View to find out more about what happened on that April day in 1996. Many things had never been resolved in my mind, including why Dad had been alive and no one had done anything to help him. All Kim and I knew was that Mom and Dad were found in the empty lot next door. We didn't know if they'd been running or gotten blown over there or what.

I took a tape recorder and a notebook and started asking questions. I would introduce myself to someone and we'd talk, and that conversation would lead me to someone else.

I spent time at the local newspaper office and saw all the articles and pictures that had been written at the time. In one of those articles I read an account of the man who had found Mom and Dad, so I tracked him down. Turned out he was a friendly local who had been fishing near their house. He'd spent the entire storm under a bridge with his son.

"We were under the bridge when the storm came up. There was a black cloud that grew bigger and darker. Then out of that cloud came first one tornado and then a second one." He described how the tornado sounded like a train passing on the bridge over the top of them.

"After the tornado passed, a hard rain came down," he said. "I wanted to see if I could find anybody who needed some help." He explained that he was trained as an emergency medical technician (EMT). "I saw your dad's hand hanging out of the ditch. I knew it was him because he had hammered his thumb earlier that week, and he had this big bandage wrapped around it. I looked down, and I couldn't tell by looking at him whether he was alive or not. I felt a pulse and that's how I knew he was unconscious, not dead. He looked like he was hurt real bad. But then I thought, *Where's Jenny Jo?* Because those two were inseparable."

He was right. I felt the tears building as I thought about how close they'd always been.

"So I rushed around, looking for Jenny. I found her in the back field, about twenty yards away. And the way she was lying, I knew she was dead." He teared up a bit.

"Was she on her stomach or on her back?" I asked.

He started weeping. He was reliving that night in his mind. "The way her head was turned, I knew she was dead."

I could tell he didn't want me to have a visual of what happened, so

I didn't press him further. He was only trying to protect me from seeing whatever he was seeing inside his mind. He brushed his tears away with the back of his hand.

"So I hurried back to your dad, and he wasn't breathing, and he didn't have a pulse no more."

"Oh, wow," I said.

I had always wondered why no one had done CPR on Dad, and I had wrongfully assumed that no one in those parts knew how. But now I knew it was because the man wanted to find my mom.

"You have to understand, it was chaos that night," the man said. "It started raining again after the storm. We were still looking for survivors, and the sun was going down. The electricity was out, so there were no street-lights. We were just trying to find anyone who was hurt. Cars couldn't make it down the street—not an ambulance, not a hearse, nothing."

I thanked him for his time and for helping my parents the night it happened. His words helped answer some of my questions. But even after a week in Mountain View, questions remained.

Today, almost a decade and a half later, the questions still sneak up on me. I'll be flipping channels on the TV and come across shows about storm watching and storm tracking. Often I stop and watch them just so I can learn more.

I marvel that there is so much footage of flying debris, but there is never footage of people flying through the debris. After watching count-less hours of tornado footage, I've never seen a body fly. Why? Do people get sucked into the middle? Do they get trapped on the inside or whipped around the outside? Or do they just get lifted and dropped?

Recently a news station ran a weather special, and as part of it, they went out to local schools and taught weather science in the classrooms. The kids made dioramas to show what they had learned about storms and other weather phenomena. One kid had a cow up in the cloud, which of course is like that scene from the movie *Twister* that opened the week after my parents died.

Almost fifteen years later, just seeing that stupid plastic cow on the news program brought back the tragedy of my parents' death.

———————

Before leaving Mountain View, I stopped by the gas station near my parents' home to fill up my car with gas. When I went inside to pay, I saw a picture of a sixth-grade girl taped above the register. "Why's this here?" I asked the clerk.

"We found that in the tornado of '96," he said. "We always wondered who it belonged to."

"That's me," I said.

I was so stunned at seeing that picture that I didn't ask him any other questions about when or where he had found it. But it made me feel good to know that someone at that gas station cared enough to hang on to a stranger's picture for so many years. The clerk let me take the picture—a reminder of everything I had lost, but also a sweet reminder of the childhood God had once blessed me with. Somehow, walking into a gas station and finding it reminded me that God hadn't abandoned me.

I won't deny that I was angry with God for a long time after my parents' death. Not because I had lost my faith in him, but because I had put my faith in him and been disappointed. I knew he could have redirected the tornado or protected my parents in some way, and he hadn't.

For a long time I called out to God for answers to all of my questions. When I finally accepted that not every question I had would be answered and that not having answers wouldn't be a deal breaker for my faith, I started to see God in new ways.

God was—and is—bigger than all of my questions.

And he is with me, even when the questions remain.

26

Commitment

Kickers on a football team are notoriously ritualistic and superstitious when it comes to doing their job. They have to repeat the same steps over and over again, so they're dependable when it comes time to kick a field goal or an extra point.

I know that now. I didn't know it when I moved in with Kurt and his roommate, who was a kicker for the Barnstormers. And even if I had known it, I never would have guessed that kickers can be just as compulsive when they are at home.

Kurt's roommate liked everything very neat and clean. He liked straight lines in the carpet. Every morning he would get up at six and vacuum. He was always kind to me and the kids while we were living there, and he tried his best to work around us, but I could tell we "messed with his flow." Whatever that was.

I was just doing what I had to do. I needed to be with Kurt. So did the kids. I got a job in an ob-gyn's office. I got the kids enrolled in school. We settled in and did our best to get along.

During his second season of arena football, Kurt joined a Bible study held by some of the arena players. At the meetings, he heard some of the same things I'd been telling him—like how he needed to say a prayer acknowledging that Jesus died on the cross for his sins and asking Jesus to be Lord of his life.

He came home from Bible study one night in June and said, "I did it. I said the prayer."

"What?"

"I said the prayer, but I didn't feel anything." Then he changed the subject and started talking about something else.

I had been waiting nearly four years to hear him say those words, but when it happened, it seemed rather anticlimactic. Maybe he still wasn't ready to commit his life. I decided to wait and see if anything changed in the way he was living.

It didn't take long. A few weeks later, he left with some of the guys in his Bible study. When he got home, he told me he had been baptized in a lake near our house.

"In that nasty water?" I asked, surprised.

"Yep."

Well, okay. Maybe this is the real thing.

I saw other changes too. Kurt started reading his Bible regularly. And although he hadn't actually proposed, he started talking about marriage as if his mind was made up.

The living arrangement—the kicker, me, the kids—didn't work for any of us. So when I received money from Mom and Dad's life insurance company, Kurt and I decided it was time to buy a place of our own. We hired a Realtor, who found us a brand-new house in a little suburb of Des Moines called Johnston.

Although we still weren't engaged, it wasn't a hard decision for me to buy a house with Kurt. He already had my heart, and with his new talk of marriage, I knew it was only a matter of time.

On September 18, we signed the papers on the house, making it officially ours. After the closing, Kurt ran out to do a few errands while I picked up the kids from school. We met back at the house a few hours later. It was so exciting to have a key to *our* house. We walked through the empty rooms, talking about what we would put in each space.

When we got to the master bedroom, we saw three outfits hanging from the door. Kurt had brought clothes from the condo for Zack, Jesse Jo, and me. He told us to get dressed, that we were going out for a nice dinner to celebrate the new house.

That's what he *said*, but I just knew there was another reason for us to go out. Kurt was going to propose.

A few minutes later, a limo pulled up outside the house. I was in a great mood as I climbed in and slid over the leather seats. *This is it. This is finally it!*

When we got to the restaurant, the maître d' said, "We have a very special table for you tonight, Mr. Warner."

We followed him to our table, and I looked at the diners who were seated near us. *You're all going to be a part of this. You don't know it yet, but you're going to see me get engaged tonight.* I couldn't help but smile throughout dinner. But I was also nervous. I remember thinking, *Let's get this done!*

When Kurt picked up his glass to make a toast, I thought for sure it was going to happen.

"To our new house!" he said.

Dinner arrived, and as soon as we finished, Kurt said, "Let's order dessert tonight."

We were always trying to save money, so we never ordered dessert. I thought, *They're going to bring a ring with the dessert!* But when the cake arrived, there was no ring that I could see. I took my fork and stabbed throughout my piece of cake, seeking what had to be hidden inside. Still no ring—just a plate of mashed cake.

My mood started to change. *He's not really doing all of this to celebrate the house, is he?*

The check came and Kurt paid it. Then he got up, and we followed him. *We're walking out of the restaurant? This is not happening!*

By the time we were back in the limo, I was furious. I sat with my arms crossed, not saying much. I was trying not to cry. Kurt seemed totally oblivious. He was too busy asking Zack and Jesse Jo questions.

"Wasn't that fun? Don't you love the limo? Do you like the new house?"

Unbelievable! He really is celebrating the house. That's why we went to dinner—to celebrate the house we could only afford because my parents died. I was so angry by the time we pulled into the driveway that I threw open the door and stormed off toward the house, leaving the kids with Kurt, who was paying the driver.

I opened the front door and froze. I couldn't make sense of the sight in front of me. Obviously, someone had been in our house, and my first thought was that we'd had burglars. It took my mind a moment to realize that burglars usually *take* stuff, not leave it behind.

Rose petals and lit candles lined the hall. I followed the path of petals and candles as it led to the back door and onto our patio. The kids followed me, picking up the rose petals as they walked.

What had been just an empty patio a couple of hours earlier now contained a new set of patio furniture. The table held flowers and a bucket of ice. Inside were cans of Sprite and a bottle of champagne.

A boom box sat on the patio next to the table. Of course, Zachary saw that right away and went to check it out. He was on all fours, looking at all the buttons, when Kurt kneeled next to him and pressed Play.

Our song, "Fishing in the Dark," came on; then Kurt reached over and flipped the light switch. The privacy fence along the back of the yard lit up with Christmas lights. The lights spelled out: "Will you marry me?"

Before Kurt said anything to me, he called Jesse Jo and Zack over. Zack was still interested in the boom box, but Jesse Jo came.

"Can I be your daddy?" Kurt asked.

"Yes, Daddy! Yes!" Jesse Jo said excitedly.

I smiled at his question. I knew he had to be careful, because Jesse Jo had recently been arguing with me that Kurt was going to marry *her* instead of me.

Then Kurt stood up, holding a single rose. "Brenda," he said, "will you marry me?"

I smiled, thinking of him standing with a rose at that sliding glass door almost four years ago. Then of course I said yes. I had known for a long time that Kurt was the man I wanted. I had chosen him, and now he had chosen me.

We danced to "Fishing in the Dark," and I looked up at the stars and thanked God for Kurt. *I placed my trust in you, and you sent me not only the man I wanted, but a man who wants you too. Thank you!* Then we had Sprite and champagne toasts with the kids.

That night, we grabbed a blanket and pillows from the car and spent our first night in our new house. We spent it as the family we had been for a long time, but would soon be legally as well.

———

Ever since Mom and Dad had died in the tornado, I had worried what would happen to Zack and Jesse Jo if anything happened to me. Where would they go? Who would take care of them? Kurt was also worried. If something happened to me, he didn't want to lose the kids too. Although they still saw Neil for occasional visits, Neil didn't know them like Kurt did.

After Kurt's proposal, I sat down with Neil and had a frank conversation. "You cheated on me and you did this to our family, not just me. Now that I've lost my parents in a tornado, I want the assurance of knowing that if something happened to me, they would be raised by the person they know and love."

"What're you asking?" Neil said.

"I want you to give up your parental rights so that Kurt can officially adopt them."

It was a lot to ask, but I give Neil credit—he agreed to do it. Although he would have no legal rights, I promised him he could continue visiting the kids. He had to trust me on that, because he wouldn't be able to enforce it once he gave up his rights.

Fortunately, he did trust me. We started the paperwork that day for the kids to be legally adopted.

———

Kurt continued to grow spiritually and to learn more and more about his faith. I had always wanted that, but suddenly it affected me in a way I never expected. One October day, just weeks after we got engaged, Kurt told me about something he'd just read in the Bible. "It says we should reserve sex for marriage."

"Yeah," I said. "What's your point?"

"I think we should stop having sex."

I just looked at him for a few moments. "Are you kidding me?"

"No. That's what the Bible says, and you always say that I should do what the Bible says, right?"

"You found *that*? Out of all the things you could find, out of all the things we could work on, you found *that*? No premarital sex?"

But it didn't surprise me, really. Ever since Kurt became a Christian, he had made changes in his life based on what he read in the Bible.

From that day until our wedding day a whole year later, we stopped having sex. We still lived together. In fact, we still slept in the same bed. But we didn't have intercourse. Once Kurt made up his mind, there was no going back.

Until then, I had always been the spiritual teacher in our relationship. I could pick and choose the lessons I wanted him to learn, like how to love your wife and what forgiveness meant. But now I knew Kurt was willing to listen to God and take a hard stance, even if I disagreed. I was proud of the godly man he was becoming.

Although I wasn't happy about not having sex at the time, I'm now glad that we refrained. I want to be able to share with our kids that though we did have sex outside of marriage, once we became convinced that it was wrong, we stopped doing it. We did the right thing, even though it was very difficult.

I made it through all of the "firsts" without Mom and Dad—the first Mother's Day and Father's Day, the first Thanksgiving and Christmas, their anniversary and all our birthdays. And I found new outlets for my grief.

Although I had never considered myself a creative person, one day I drove to the art store and bought paints and a huge canvas. Kurt and the kids happened to be gone that day, so I spent nine hours in a room just painting.

It felt like therapy.

When I finished and stood back to look at the picture, I saw things I hadn't realized I was painting—like rain and tornadoes. The whole process had released a creative spirit in me that I didn't know I had. After that, I worked harder to find ways to tap into those creative impulses.

Ever since Mother's Day, when I told Kurt that his mom didn't bring good into my life, I hadn't spoken to Sue. Although I didn't mind if Kurt visited her, I refused to go. Right before Kurt proposed to me, he had tried once again to patch things up between us. "Once she gets to know you, she'll like you," he said for the hundredth time.

"Why would I give her a chance to get to know me after the way she's treated me? She's not good to me."

"The two of you are a lot alike."

That was the wrong thing to say. It made me livid. And yet, somewhere deep inside, I also knew Kurt was right. Sue and I were both strong-willed and opinionated, and we both wanted Kurt for ourselves.

Once we announced our engagement, there was a lot of talk about what church we would get married in. I wanted to get married at the Cedar Falls church where we'd had Mom and Dad's memorial service. But by the time of our wedding, I would've lived in Des Moines for eighteen months. And Kurt's mom wanted us to get married in a Catholic church. The location didn't matter to her as long as it was Catholic.

Kurt asked me about the possibility one day.

"I know I'm not Catholic anymore, but it would really mean a lot to Mom if we could do this. Will you just talk to the priest about it?"

I didn't want to be unreasonable. Now that we were officially engaged, I did want to find a way to get along with his mom, so I agreed. A call was arranged between Sue's parish priest, Father O'Conner, and me.

During that phone call, I remember pacing at the top of our steps, not believing what the priest was telling me. Father O'Conner said that I had to annul my first marriage if I wanted to get married in the Catholic church. An annulment essentially said the marriage had never existed. But if the marriage had never existed, where did that put my kids?

"How does this make sense to you?" I asked him. "How is it better for me to sign a paper saying I was never married—making my kids illegitimate— than it is for me to tell the truth, which is that I got married, had children, and it didn't work out?"

The more the priest tried to explain it to me, the less I understood it. My voice grew louder. "My husband cheated on *me*. *I* didn't do anything wrong, and the kids didn't do anything wrong, but it sounds like we're the ones being punished by the Catholic Church."

I was pacing faster, talking even louder. Kurt took a few steps up the stairs; then he heard me yelling at the priest and retreated back downstairs.

I hung up the phone and stomped down to see him. "I am not doing this," I said.

"Okay, okay, I get it that you tried."

On Mother's Day 1997, Kurt called Sue to wish her a happy Mother's Day, but he said we wouldn't be coming to see her that day. The memories of the previous year at the restaurant were still too fresh for me. "I will come and see you tomorrow," Kurt continued. "But Brenda is the woman in my life now, and her kids are *my* kids. So on Mother's Day I'll be spending it with the mother of my children."

It was the first time Kurt had chosen me over his mother. It also convinced me that he would step up to honor and protect our family above all else.

It was a huge moment for me.

To honor and protect us in this way was the best wedding gift he could have given me. And I am thankful that it's a gift he continues to give our family each and every day.

27

Mrs. Kurt Warner

Our wedding day was cold—oh, was it cold! Although it was only October 11, the Iowa winter had already settled in. At the church, I took Jesse Jo with me to the bridal room, and Kurt took Zack to the groom's room so we could get them—and ourselves—dressed. Jesse Jo would be wearing a dress similar to mine, and Zack, once again, would be wearing a tux—a bigger one this time.

As I fixed Jesse Jo's hair, my bridesmaids were also in the room getting ready. They were dressed in our wedding colors, red and purple. Kim was there, of course. So were Desia and Lynn, my best friend since middle school. There was also a girlfriend I had worked with at the nursing home and one from the ob-gyn clinic where I currently worked in Des Moines.

But someone was missing: Mom. She wasn't there to help me get ready or to tell me how beautiful I looked. She would've been so happy to know that Kurt finally loved Jesus as much as I did. And that this time, I was marrying a man who deserved me and the kids.

The wedding was being held at my old church in Cedar Falls. It was good to be back. I had enjoyed seeing my pastor and some of my church friends during the rehearsal and dinner the previous evening. But Mom and Dad's memorial service had also been held at this church, and the dress rehearsal had marked the first time I'd been back since then. So the day held a lot of bittersweet memories. It was hard not to think about the past.

Kim's husband, John, had kindly offered to escort me down the aisle during the ceremony. But I wanted to honor Dad and to acknowledge that he should have been there with me. So I decided to walk the aisle alone, leaving an empty space by my side.

Thinking about that made me sad, and several times during the day, I got more emotional than I wanted to. I felt an incredible heaviness in my chest that wouldn't go away, no matter what I did. The girls around me were happy, and I didn't want to bring anyone else down, so I tried to be happy too. But I needed a moment to myself, and I just couldn't get one. The videographer had me miked, and every time I tried to be alone, he showed up and stuck a camera in my face.

When it was time for the ceremony, I was the last to leave the bridal room. I paused a moment, lowered my head, and closed my eyes. I thought about how many times I had pictured marrying Kurt. But in all those fantasies, I had also pictured Mom and Dad by my side. I could feel the tears forming, but I held them back so they wouldn't ruin my makeup.

When I got to the lobby of the church, Jesse Jo and Zack were already there with my cousin, Chris, who served as my personal attendant. She had them lined up and ready to go, and I took my place behind them. On cue, Jesse Jo stepped off with her little flower basket, taking short steps just like we'd practiced. But then Zack also grabbed hold of her basket and tried to run down the aisle, yanking on her basket and dragging her with him. Jesse Jo still tried to do what she'd been told, but what she probably wanted to do was club her brother. Everyone laughed, and it put a much-needed smile on my face too. They made it to the end of the aisle and, as instructed, stopped and stood by Kurt.

The "Wedding March" began, and everyone in the church stood. "I miss you, Dad," I whispered. Marrying Neil had been just a legal arrangement in a courthouse; we'd never had a wedding. So this was my wedding day, and Dad should have been there with me.

I took my first steps. The aisle looked like it was a mile long.

Hold it together! This is supposed to be the best day of your life.

I focused on Kurt, so handsome in his tux. I couldn't wait to make it to the end of the aisle and be with him. Now that Mom and Dad were gone, he was the one I turned to, the one who held me up when I couldn't hold myself up.

Just a few more steps. If I can just get to him, then I'm gonna make it.

Finally, I made it to Kurt. I breathed easier just standing next to him. Kurt and I said the traditional vows. There wasn't anything especially remarkable about the ceremony—until the end, that is. We kissed, we turned around, and my pastor said, "Let me present to you Mr. and Mrs. Meoni."

"No, no, no!" Kurt said, turning to the pastor.

He quickly corrected himself. "My apologies. Mr. and Mrs. Warner!"

Our guests laughed. So did we. I may have walked down the aisle with some sadness in my heart, but I went back up it with a big smile on my face.

That mistake with our last name still makes me chuckle. I've spent our entire married life being addressed as "Kurt Warner's wife," but that was the only time Kurt's *ever* been called by my name.

———

We used some of the insurance money from Mom and Dad to pay for the reception—and we did it up right. After a nice meal, it was time for music and dancing, but first I had a little surprise for Kurt.

Jesse Jo and I walked to the center of the dance floor and I handed her the microphone. She turned toward Kurt and said, "Daddy, may I have this dance?"

The whole crowd responded in unison. "Awwww."

Kurt came over and picked Jesse Jo up, and together they danced to "Butterfly Kisses." I watched the smiles on people's faces as they came up and snapped pictures, and I loved seeing how much that dance meant to Kurt. When the song finished, he was crying hard, and everyone in the room was giving them a standing ovation. There wasn't anything better I could have given him, but there was more coming.

Next I led Zack to the center of the dance floor where Kurt was still standing. "Stay there," I said to Kurt. I handed Zack the mic, and he blew on it and made funny noises. Everybody laughed, which made Zack say, "Ha-ha," into the microphone, getting an even bigger reaction from the crowd.

I pulled up a chair and told Kurt to sit down.

Kurt was still crying, and when I glanced across the dance floor, I saw that his brother, Matt, was sobbing. Zack stood in front of Kurt, and Kurt pulled on Zack's tux jacket, straightening him out just like any dad would do before his son takes the stage. Kurt was so proud, and it made me happy to see the smile on his face. Then the DJ started the music. It was "Thanks to the Keeper of the Stars," a country song by Tracy Byrd that thanked God for bringing a special person into his life. Zack held the microphone too close to his mouth, but he sang out every word.

For weeks prior to the wedding, every time I was in the car with Zack, I'd play that song over and over so it would stick in Zack's head. But I never played it around Kurt. He looked completely surprised as he watched Zack sing. I could see he just wanted to scoop Zack up and love on him.

Kurt had completely lost it by the time the song ended. Zack handed him the microphone, and Kurt, his voice cracking, said, "Now what?" When I said that was all, he replied, "Well, let's get this party started!"

The DJ played "Fishing in the Dark," and the two of us danced. There was nothing dark about that moment for me. I had hooked the prize catch.

After our first dance, Kurt danced with his mother, and I danced with his father, Gene. Then we switched so Kurt's stepmom, Mimi, could dance with Kurt, and I danced with his grandfather. After that, I was never without a partner. All night long, people stepped up to fill any empty spaces left by my parents' death. I felt very blessed and very loved to have them all in my life.

We had a great party. It was one of those wedding receptions where everybody was out of their seats and dancing the whole time. Even today, people still tell me it was the best wedding reception they've ever been to. I don't remember what time it ended, but it felt like it was much too soon.

Back at the hotel, Kurt and I celebrated our vows, and afterward we opened our wedding cards. We were surprised that we kept finding money inside of them.

Kurt would open one card and say, "Look at this!" then hand me a ten-dollar bill.

I'd open another card. "Oh my gosh. Aunt Loie and Uncle Francis gave us fifty bucks. Fifty bucks!"

We took the money out of the cards and made a big pile of it on the bed. After a few more cards, we couldn't stand it any longer, so we had to stop and count it. Then we opened more cards and counted up the new total.

"It can't be that much," Kurt said. "Count it again just to make sure!"

By the end of the night, we were in shock to see we had nearly a thousand dollars. We were humbled by these expressions of love—and enormously grateful.

Later, some friends, who were also staying at the hotel, called our room and asked if we wanted to meet them at the bar to watch the late football game. I told Kurt to go ahead. Instead of joining them, I went to bed and fell asleep instantly.

Thinking about that night now makes me chuckle. It was our first night as husband and wife, and already I was sleeping alone because of football. If I had only known then how many nights I'd spend as a football widow, I might have asked Kurt to stay.

———

Kurt and I enjoyed a weeklong honeymoon in Jamaica. It was nice to get away and have some alone time for just the two of us. We hadn't had time like that since we went to Las Vegas right before my parents died.

I lay in the sun while Kurt entered every competitive beach game offered. He signed me up to sing in a talent competition, and even though I can't sing, I couldn't let the dare pass and hear about it from him all week. So I got up and sang an old song I'd known from childhood. It was no surprise that I didn't win.

We had a great time, but when the week was up, we were both ready to get home and see the kids.

———

The videographer sent us raw footage of the wedding so we could decide what we wanted in the final cut. After the kids went to bed one night, Kurt and I snuggled up to watch it and relive that special day.

About an hour before the wedding, the videographer had taped Kurt and his mom getting their pictures taken outside. On the tape, after they finished posing, Sue looked Kurt in the eyes and asked, "Are you happy?"

"Yes, Mom," Kurt said.

Then she started to cry. "Are you really sure you're happy?"

I looked at Kurt. "It's an hour before the wedding. Doesn't she know you're happy by now?"

"Brenda, who cares? It's done. It's over with. She's my mom. She just wants to make sure we're happy!"

But I was annoyed.

Sure, we didn't like each other, but I had thought maybe she had warmed up a degree or two before the wedding. But watching her on tape, questioning Kurt as if she didn't think he was happy—that angered me.

As my boys have grown older and I've thought about having to give them up one day, I have come to understand what Sue was going through. She had attended every single game or event Kurt ever participated in, and she had worked three jobs in order for him to do those things. Kurt was her boy. And from the outside looking in, he was taking on a lot of responsibility by marrying an older woman with young children at a time when his dreams had just started to come true.

Although Sue obviously questioned whether I was a good thing for her son, eventually we were able to get past our disagreements. Today, we have a wonderful relationship. If I had it all to do over again, I wouldn't take everything she said so personally. I would try to understand where she was coming from.

Now I know that asking your son about his happiness is just one of those things moms do. But I also know I'll try to be more careful and not ask my son that while he's miked.

———

About a month after our wedding, we went to court and signed the papers for Kurt to adopt Zack and Jesse Jo. It was the first time I had been in court since my divorce. I couldn't help but reflect on how that sad ending had made this happy new beginning possible. The kids were excited, but I also wondered how changing their last name would affect them.

Apparently, I need not have worried.

We were riding the elevator up to the courtroom. It stopped on another floor and an older man got in. "Hi!" said Jesse Jo.

"Well, hi!" said the man. "What's your name?"

"My name is Jesse Jo, but someday I want to change it to Jessica."

"Well, maybe someday you can," he said with a smile as he stepped off the elevator.

We made it to the courtroom and sat waiting for the judge to come in. When he did, we saw that he was the same man who had been on the elevator with us. "Well, hello there, Jessica," he said as he opened the file.

When the proceedings were finished, the judge invited us to come up and get our picture taken with him. As we all posed for the camera, I saw Zack out of the corner of my eye. He was feeling around on the judge's desk for something.

I soon figured out what it was. Zack had located the judge's gavel and started pounding it. He'd heard the judge use the "hammer," as Zack called it, and he wanted to try it for himself.

It was a fun and memorable day for all of us, including the judge.

For years Zack and Jesse Jo had Kurt's heart, but now they had something else—his name.

———————

I finally had the life I'd dreamed of. I was happily married to a Christian man who loved me, and we lived in our new little house with our two beautiful kids.

But the dream didn't last more than a few months.

NFL Europe chose Kurt to play for one of their teams. Out of all the teams he could have played for, he was selected to play for the Amsterdam Admirals. That meant I had to send my newly wed and recently baptized husband to the sin city of Europe. I knew that Amsterdam's red-light district offered every conceivable kind of temptation to a virile young man— brothels, strip clubs, sex shops, sex shows, prostitution, and marijuana.

The only thing that didn't worry me was the marijuana.

I didn't want to start my marriage this way, but we knew this could be a great opportunity for Kurt. We talked a lot before he left, and I knew he was a different person than the guy who'd gone to that bachelor party years before. So I did my best to trust him despite the lions' den he was walking into.

Then, just as I came to terms with Kurt leaving, I got another surprise.

I was pregnant. And that kind of freaked me out.

My dream had my husband going to a nine-to-five job and returning home for dinner, not going to Europe and returning home months later. I wasn't expecting this kind of life. Saying "I do" and then saying good-bye was not normal. I had naively thought we'd have a marriage like my parents' marriage, and now I was learning it would look quite different.

For the first time since my parents died, I had someone to take care of me. But now he was leaving me alone to do what I'd been doing for so long—handling everything on my own. As with my first marriage, however, I was in. Unless Kurt cheated on me, there was no turning back. I would make the best of it.

So every day while Kurt was in Amsterdam, I got up and took the kids to school. I worked all day, then picked the kids up, came home, and made dinner. I gave them a bath. I read them a book. I kissed them good night. I didn't spend any time sitting around and whining, "This isn't what I planned." I just stepped up and did what had to be done.

While I was pregnant, I visited the doctor for regular checkups and tests. During one examination, the doctor noticed some irregularly shaped cells. He did a Pap smear, and it tested positive for precancerous cells. The cells were growing slowly, so the plan was to monitor them and see what happened.

But I knew what could happen if the growth accelerated. There was a chance I wouldn't be able to carry the baby to term or that they would want me to terminate the pregnancy so they could aggressively treat the cancer. Or I might be able to carry the baby to term but then need a hysterectomy and be unable to have any more children. None of those possibilities sounded good.

I didn't want to tell Kurt about the possibility of cancer over the phone. But I did tell the members of our couples' Bible study, and I asked them to pray. The next week, when we got back together for our regular meeting, they gave me a card with some cash in it. They had collected enough money to buy three tickets to Amsterdam so the kids and I could go see Kurt. It was an amazing gift, one I'll never forget.

We flew to the Netherlands and stayed with Kurt in his hotel room. It was an emotional moment for both Kurt and me as I tried to explain the test results. Kurt was upset at the possibility of not only losing the baby, but losing me too. Once again, it seemed, we were fishing in the dark. Neither of us knew how fast the cancer might grow.

Kurt wondered if he should come home, but I told him to finish out the season. Together, we prayed and trusted that God would take care of me and our growing baby.

And he did.

Although we worried throughout my pregnancy, after I delivered Kade, the doctors removed a part of my cervix and tested it. It was cancer-free.

Was it an inaccurate test due to the pregnancy or an answered prayer? We'll never know for sure. But God does answer prayers—of that I have no doubt.

I can see lots of answered prayers when I think about that period in my life. Somehow, I had made it through all those years of being a single mom. Although no one ever tapped me on the shoulder and handed me a Ben Franklin, somehow I always had enough to feed my children and keep a roof over their heads. When I needed a place to fall, my parents provided one. I had a sister who had my back and supported me in whatever I chose to do. God gave me friends who lifted me up and a job at the nursing home where I could lift up sick friends during their final days.

I learned through it all that God did have a plan, even if I didn't always like his timing. I had talked to God a lot about the right man for me and my kids, and many times I had asked, "Are you sure it's Kurt?" When God didn't give me quick and easy answers, I learned to be patient. I learned to forgive, and I learned to be strong, and I learned to be strong enough to lean on someone else.

It wasn't easy to learn all those lessons, but I needed them. And I would need them even more in the years to come.

Part Three

THE GOOD, THE BAD, AND THE UGLY

1998–2005

28

Firsts

Kurt's season in Amsterdam went well, and the St. Louis Rams invited him to their training camp. He flew home from Amsterdam, and just two short days later, he left the kids and me to report to camp. It was good to have him back in the States, but it would have been even better if he could've stayed home.

Training camp was five weeks long, but Kurt had no idea how long he'd be there. He hoped to go all the way through the camp and make the team, but every few days players would get cut. Some days Kurt doubted his chances. "I don't know if I am going to make it," he'd say when he called home. But he had good days, too, and those lifted his spirits. It was a roller coaster.

Tuesday was the last day of camp, and if he hadn't been cut by then, he would make the team. I couldn't wait for the day—mostly because, either way, camp would be over and he could come home. When the phone rang Tuesday night, I ran to answer it, ready to hear the good or bad news and very ready to see my husband again.

"Brenda, I made it! I made the team!" Kurt was thrilled, and I was thrilled for him. But then he said, "Can you pack up the house and meet me in St. Louis by the end of the week?"

"You're not coming home first?"

"No, I'm taking the bus back to St. Louis with the team. We have our last preseason game in a few days, and I want you here by then. I've missed you. Can you do it?"

I was nine months pregnant, with a disabled nine-year-old and a six-year-old, and he wanted me to pack the entire house and move us in three days. Was he crazy?

"Um . . . sure, I can do that," I said. "I'm so proud of you. Can't wait to see you in St. Louis!"

As I hung up the phone, I realized that this NFL thing was never going to give us a normal life and that as a wife I would be responsible for a lot of the details. But I did what I always did—the next thing on the list. I called the movers and arranged for a truck to come. I spent Wednesday organizing our stuff, Thursday they loaded the truck, and on Friday the three of us left for St. Louis. I liked to complain about how much work it took to organize the move all by myself, but I was secretly proud that Kurt knew he could count on me to make it happen.

Although Kurt now made only the league minimum salary, it was still more money than we had ever seen. But we didn't feel that rich. The rent on our little St. Louis apartment was as much as the mortgage on our house in Iowa. With the equivalent of two mortgages, we would still be on a tight budget.

We moved in on Saturday and school started on Tuesday, so I spent Monday enrolling them. Jesse Jo was no problem, but Zack's special needs called for a lot of meetings and paperwork.

I also had to find an obstetrician—quickly. Kurt helped me out with that one. He overheard another player mentioning that he and his wife were having a baby, and Kurt asked him the name of the doctor. I called and made an appointment, hoping the baby would hold out long enough for me to keep it.

I had never been to an NFL game until I went to Kurt's first game in St. Louis. My family hadn't watched football when I was growing up, and I had never been to a sports bar. So I had never seen banners, signed memorabilia, and jerseys hung as sacred art in homage to the local team. I didn't know there were people who screamed unintelligible directions at the coaches and players from their seats in the nosebleed sections. Until I walked into the Rams stadium for that first game, I'd never seen grown men paint the letters of the team on their naked chests or wear blue-and-gold clown wigs, or cover their faces in blue makeup and blow sheep horns.

Sure, I'd been to high school games as a cheerleader. And I'd been to Kurt's arena games and gotten a glimpse of how crazy fans there could be. But this was like the arena fans on steroids. It was a huge culture shock.

The Rams provided game-day child care, so when I arrived at the stadium, I was directed to the underground playground. As I checked in Zack and Jesse Jo, the other kids all ran around like crazy. It seemed like chaos, yet they also seemed well cared for.

I noticed how well dressed the kids were. They were dressed far better than my kids. For that matter, they were dressed far better than *I* was. They wore brand-new white athletic shoes, designer jeans, and in some cases, miniature jerseys just like their fathers'. I looked down at Jesse Jo's and Zack's garage sale finds and realized these other kids were in a different league than we were. Kurt was now making more money than we ever had before, but we hadn't seen a paycheck yet, and it would be a long time before we could upgrade our wardrobe to their standards.

The babysitters were kind, and I liked them immediately. They promised to take good care of my kids, and then one of the girls handed me a beeper. "I am sure they'll both be fine, but if we have a problem, this will go off."

Everything felt so different from what I was used to. During arena games, the kids had just sat with me. I inspected the beeper as I walked off to look for my seat. I had no idea how it worked. Maybe when they needed me, it would just announce, "Come here now."

I got lost trying to find my seat. I wandered around different levels of that enormous stadium, studying my ticket and reading the signs. I definitely wasn't in Iowa anymore. I finally found the correct section and walked out through the passage. The noise hit me immediately.

As I headed toward my row, I saw a familiar face—Tina Wilkins. A few days earlier, head coach Dick Vermeil's wife had hosted a catered welcome dinner for wives and girlfriends of players at the Rams facility, and I had sat next to Tina. It was a relief now to see someone I knew, and her presence confirmed that I was in the right place.

"Hey, Tina. How are you?" I asked.

"Good, but I'm so mad! My tickets are way over there." She pointed off to another section. "They're supposed to be here. I can't believe they put me way over there."

"I'm just thrilled to be here," I said. And I meant it. It was a huge thing for Kurt to be playing in the NFL. Plus, I had actually found my seat before game time. I thought I was doing well!

I couldn't believe how loud it was in the stadium. When the team exited from the tunnel and ran onto the field, the announcer called out some of the players' names, and the fans went crazy. Kurt's name wasn't announced. He'd said he was third string and warned me not to expect much. After the players stretched and warmed up, Kurt ran over to a table and grabbed a clipboard. He held on to it the whole game.

The wives around me cheered for their husbands, but I couldn't exactly do that. I kind of jokingly cheered inside my head. *Way to hold that clipboard! Yay!*

I felt old compared to the other wives. Most of them looked to be in their early twenties, and a few were pregnant, probably with their first baby. I was in my thirties, had already served my country for several years, and had two school-age kids.

The women were of different races, but they had one thing in common—they were beautiful. Many of them had long, silky hair, very different from my short, spiky cut. They wore their husbands' jerseys with tight jeans and high heels. Some had altered their jerseys so they were cut lower and fit tighter to emphasize their cleavage. I was dressed in normal clothes—jeans, a plain top, and sensible momma shoes.

When I asked how I could get one of Kurt's jerseys, one wife told me as politely as she could that they didn't make one with Kurt's name and number on it. She didn't exactly say it, but I got the message: Kurt just wasn't important enough yet. As she spoke, I noticed how much jewelry she wore. In fact, all of the wives seemed to be dripping in bling. They had diamonds and gold jewelry around their necks, on their ears, on their fingers, and wrapped around their wrists.

I was confident in who I was, yet I also felt like I didn't belong there. I wasn't about to leave, though. I would hold my own and not show my embarrassment, just as I had done years before when I had to buy groceries with food stamps.

My new doctor induced labor on a Tuesday because that was Kurt's day off. Baby boy Warner was a healthy eight pounds, twelve ounces, and twenty-three and a half inches long. A big boy! When it came time to name him, I had a few names in mind, but Kurt said no. "You got to name the other two, and I didn't get any input, so I am naming this one."

I probably should have laughed at how ridiculous that sounded, but instead I was once again touched by the depth of love he had for our kids.

We took Kade Eugene Warner home to our apartment, and Kurt got to rock and feed him. It was a bittersweet experience for him. He had met Zack when he was three and Jesse Jo when she was nine months old, and until Kade came, Kurt had never felt like he'd missed out on anything. But bonding with baby Kade made him realize what he'd missed in those early days with the other two.

Not long after Kade was born, I was invited to a baby shower for Cynthia, one of the players' wives. I still didn't know a lot of the wives, so I thought this was a good opportunity to hang out and get to know them.

The baby shower was held at a restaurant, and I was nervous just walking in. It was obviously a *very* nice restaurant. Some of the other women were already there, sitting at a long table. Again, I was struck by how beautiful everyone was. In fact, they were hot. They all wore heels and had young, beautiful bodies. I had just given birth to Kade, and let's just say my body still needed some work. I wore those horrible in-between clothes that women wear when they no longer need maternity clothes but they don't yet fit into their normal-size clothes.

I sat in an empty seat at the end of the table and opened my menu. And gulped. The prices were higher than on any menu I had ever seen. About that time, the waiters came over and took drink orders. "I'll take a water, please," I said, just as I always did at restaurants.

"Sparkling or mineral?" asked the waiter.

"Um . . . just regular. With ice, please."

The other women gave their orders. "I'll have a glass of Chardonnay." "What kind of martinis do you have?"

A few minutes later, the waiter asked if I wanted an appetizer. "No, thanks. I'll just take the house salad."

"Did you want an entrée, too, or just the salad?"

"The salad will be fine. Thank you." The salad alone was eighteen dollars and cost more than any entrée I'd ever eaten!

The other women ordered appetizers, salads, and entrées. Throughout the meal, they ordered more drinks, while I just had my water refilled. When it came time for dessert, someone had specially ordered a small cake for the mom-to-be, but the rest of the women ordered dessert off of the menu.

"What would you like?" the waiter asked me.

"Oh, I don't want anything," I lied.

Cynthia started opening gifts, beginning with the one from the person to her right. Since I was on her left, it would be a while before she got to mine.

The first present was a huge gift bag filled with lots of little baby things. I thought it must be from a group of people. But when she just thanked the woman next to her, I realized it was just from one person. The next woman handed her a bag equally large, and so did the woman after her. Each woman had filled her bag with hundreds of dollars' worth of gifts.

For my gift, I had gone to the local Dillard's and bought a cute little onesie with a matching bib and socks. I had it in the Dillard's box next to my chair. Cynthia still had a long way to go before she got around to mine, so I tried not to freak out. I kept hoping someone would give her something just as low budget as mine.

No one did. All the presents were equally lavish and expensive. The closer she got to me, the more the thought of handing her my little box scared me. But when I did, Cynthia was very gracious. She opened the gift and said, "This is so sweet! Thank you so much!"

All I could think was, *I want out of here.* I was so embarrassed.

Finally the bill came, and Cynthia's friend Shima, who had organized the party, asked that the bill be given to her. Then she said, "What do you all say we just split it?" She did the math in her head and announced the number everyone was to pay—more than three times what I had counted on.

I was horrified. They'd all had drinks, appetizers, entrées, and desserts. I'd had a salad and tap water. But there was no way I could raise my hand and say, "Excuse me; I just had a salad." *That would look dumber than my gift!* I laid my credit card on the silver tray and prayed it wasn't maxed out. That would have been the perfect ending to a thoroughly awkward luncheon.

When I got home, Kurt wanted to hear all about it. "How was it? Did you get to know anyone?"

I told him the whole embarrassing story.

"Oh, darlin', I am so sorry," he said. "But who cares? It was nice of you to go."

That was my first experience getting to know some of the other wives. I wasn't sure there would ever be a second.

One day while I was feeding Kade, I saw an interesting commercial on TV. A young man wearing casual clothes and sitting in an empty room spoke to the camera. "I don't want to make you go to church. I don't want to tell you about religion. I just love Jesus, and that's what we're about." The words "St. Louis Family Church" appeared at the bottom of the screen.

When Kurt got home that night, I said, "I saw this commercial for a new church. Let's just go try it." I was attracted to the fact that it didn't seem too "religious" and was different from what both Kurt and I were used to. Best of all, they offered Friday night services, which meant Kurt and I could attend together.

When I heard the preacher on our first visit, I was drawn to him. He seemed authentic and not at all showy. We went back the next Friday, and soon we were attending regularly, so I set up a meeting with Pastor Jeff to introduce ourselves.

"We're newlyweds and new to the area," I told him. "I saw your commercial, and we've been coming here for a few weeks now." I also let him in on something I had been praying about for a while. "Kurt plays for the Rams, and I just feel like God is taking us somewhere big. But I have no idea what that means or what we're supposed to be doing about that."

Now I realize how stupid that must have sounded. The NFL *was* big, and Pastor Jeff obviously knew that. But at that time, I still didn't understand the opportunities Kurt's position would bring us.

"It sounds to me like you need to prepare yourselves," said Pastor Jeff. "We'll start praying and really seeking God together."

Over time, Kurt and I became good friends with Pastor Jeff and his wife, Patsy, who was also a pastor at the church. We invited them over, they invited us over, and if Kurt had a late game on Sunday, we invited them to join us at the game. They introduced us to other couples at the church, like Rusty and Kim Maple and Lee and Cindy Georges. As life got crazy in St. Louis, they helped make things normal. These friends would pray with us and stay with us through all of our ups and downs in St. Louis. We're still friends with them today.

29

QB1

Though Kurt was very proficient at carrying that clipboard, the Rams won just four games that first year, and Kurt wasn't sure if he would be back on the team the following year. There were talks of bringing in a new quarterback, and if that happened, they wouldn't need the three they had. Someone would have to go. But none of that talk stopped him from doing everything he could both on and off the field.

Training camp was five weeks long and was held in Macomb, Illinois, a three-hour drive from St. Louis. Kurt hated being away from home. He called me every day, and after we talked, he asked to talk with the kids. But after a few days, that wasn't enough. "Do you think you can bring the kids here for a few days?" he asked.

Why not? The older kids were out of school for the summer. Kade was still a baby, so he would sleep in the car. To Zachary it would be another chance to listen to the radio, and Jesse Jo just wanted to see Daddy. So I loaded the three kids in the minivan and drove to Macomb to see Kurt.

We made that trip several times over the five weeks, and it was such a comfort for Kurt to have his family around. But as the end of camp neared, the stress grew. I could hear it in Kurt's voice when he called. Although he still missed us, he sounded distracted. I knew he was spending a lot of time thinking about his future with the Rams.

One day when he called, he asked, "You remember that guy I liked so much?"

"Yeah, the one with the new wife and baby?"

"They told him to turn in his playbook today."

"What does that mean?"

"It means he won't be playing for the Rams anymore."

Kurt felt fairly confident he would be the backup quarterback, but I wasn't so sure. Every time he called, he said something like, "They're making more decisions, and they just cut another guy," or, "After practice, they told another guy to turn in his playbook." I worried constantly. I still remembered the day he'd called from Green Bay and said, "I'm on my way home." Then, at least, we could both live in my parents' basement. What would we do now with three kids, a mortgage, and no income?

Two days later Kurt called and said, "Practice didn't go so well. I missed a few passes."

We were both stressed, and I wanted to say, "Well, don't do that!" But I bit my tongue and tried to build him up and encourage him. At the same time, life had to go on. I still had three kids to care for by myself. "Okay, well, call me tomorrow."

Finally, on the last night of camp, Kurt called me with good news. "I made it!" he said. "I'm going to be the backup!"

He told me the Rams had brought in Trent Green as their starting quarterback, and it would be Kurt's job to back Green up if for any reason he couldn't play. And that wasn't all the good news. Because it was his second year in the NFL, the league minimum was higher. This year he would be making more than $250,000.

Later, I naïvely asked, "What do the other players make?" I was shocked to learn that in some cases they made millions of dollars. No wonder their wives could afford to order dessert at nice restaurants!

Although we were no longer poor, we still watched every penny carefully and tried to put away a lot into savings. Because of the uncertainty of Kurt's career, we were never sure what would happen. Still, with the new contract and salary, Kurt felt we could go ahead and buy a house.

I wanted to buy a house within the same school district where the kids were already enrolled because I'd already done so much work getting them established there, but the houses were very expensive in that area. Fortunately, our friends Cindy and Lee told us about a new neighborhood not far from them where they were building homes on spec at reasonable prices.

Kurt and I made an appointment with the Realtor and sat down in his office in the model home. Of course, the model home was decked out with top-of-the-line everything, and we quickly learned that anything more than the basic plan would increase the price significantly.

To figure out the total price, the Realtor had to determine what amenities we wanted. He asked us lots of questions. "Do you want siding, half brick, or all brick? All brick is the most elegant, but it's also the most expensive."

"Can we see the prices?" I asked. He showed us the numbers. "We'll take the siding," I said.

"Do you want a three-car garage or a two-car garage?" he asked.

When he showed us the numbers, there was no question. "We'll stick with the two-car garage," Kurt said.

"The basic lights package is this price." He pointed to a number on his paper. "But everyone adds the overhead lights. For those, there is an additional cost."

"We'll go with the basic package," Kurt said.

"There won't be any lights in the room," said the Realtor.

"We'll use lamps," I said.

"What about ceiling fans?"

I looked up at the gorgeous fan in the model home and thought about how nice it would be to have one like that in our new house.

"No, thank you," I said.

For every decision the Realtor presented, we took the cheapest option. But when we finished, the house still came to three hundred thousand dollars. Kurt and I looked at each other. That was more than his annual contract. We really wanted the house, but we were worried about the money. We had to be. Kurt had only signed a one-year contract, and we weren't sure what would happen the following year. He could be with the Rams, or maybe another

NFL team. If things didn't go well or he got injured, he could be back in arena football or not playing at all. But we decided to go ahead with the house and promised each other we would watch our money carefully.

Despite the uncertain future, we were thrilled the day we moved in to that house. It was the largest one either of us had ever lived in. It was brand-new. And it was ours.

––––––––––

One game changed everything for Kurt and me that season, and I was in the stands when it happened. It was the second-to-last preseason game of the 1999 season, and Kurt expected to get a fair amount of playing time. "They won't want to leave Trent in too long and risk him getting hurt." It would be a great opportunity for me to see Kurt play and for Kurt to show the coaches what he could do.

But apparently the coaches did leave Trent Green in too long. I watched from the stands as he got hit and went down with a bad knee injury. He was definitely out for the game and potentially much longer than that— possibly the entire season. Kurt then went in and played a few series, but now they didn't want *him* getting hurt, so he didn't play much either.

We talked about the injury later that night. "Trent looked like he was in so much pain," Kurt told me. "I felt horrible for him."

"It didn't look good even from where I was sitting," I said.

Even though Trent's injury could benefit Kurt, he wasn't the type of guy to celebrate someone's misfortune. He genuinely felt terrible about Trent's injury. I don't remember him talking at all that night about what would happen to him, only what would happen to Green.

But during the next few days, he talked me through several possible scenarios. The team could bring in someone else who they thought knew the game better, or they could give Kurt a shot at starting quarterback. Kurt really hoped he would get a chance to prove himself.

A few days later, he called me from work to tell me their decision. I could hear it in his voice before I heard it in his words. "I'm in!" he said. He would finally have the chance he always dreamed of.

I was excited for Kurt, but I was also excited for me. I hoped that perhaps with Kurt *playing* in the game, I wouldn't be as bored watching it. I had discovered that I didn't like watching football, but maybe this would change things for me. Also, I was pretty sure that now the announcer would introduce Kurt at the beginning of the game with the other players, and that would be pretty cool.

Those were my only two thoughts when I heard that Kurt would start. I really didn't expect life to change more than that.

As Kurt took on a new role and new challenges, I was facing a challenge of my own. Unfortunately, it was nothing new for me.

I had always put Zack in public schools. They had a lot of resources for special-needs students, and I'd never had money for private schools anyway. But to get the public-school resources, I'd learned, you always had to fight the system.

That was just one reason why I hated those IEP meetings. They were always a battle—a battle for money and services. School systems have a fixed amount of money for services, and if one student requires a lot of services, there will be less for the other kids. So the people in charge are always trying to provide the minimum amount of help necessary for each child so that the money will go further.

I get it. It's their job. But my job is to be an advocate for my child. So very early in Zack's school career, I had learned I had a choice. I could go into those meetings, listen to what the experts told me my child needed, and sign off on that. Or I could fight for what *I* thought he needed.

I chose to fight.

Years earlier during an IEP meeting, a specialist had wanted me to sign a piece of paper stating that Zack was "mentally retarded." I refused. I knew he had brain damage that caused some intellectual disabilities, but I didn't want him labeled as "retarded."

"You have to sign it," the specialist told me.

"That's not a diagnosis I want in his records," I said.

"Well, we need to put something down so that when we grab his chart, we'll know who he is and how to work with him."

"That's exactly my point," I said. "I don't want you to label him. I want you to get to know him. That's the only way you'll know how to work with him best." I refused to sign the paper then, and I refused every time after that. Today, seventeen years later, I am a part of the Special Olympics R-word campaign to get rid of the word *retarded* because it is hurtful and dehumanizing to those with intellectual disabilities.

But at that time in St. Louis, I was fighting a different battle. Zack's new school was much bigger and more crowded than any school he had attended before, and I felt Zack needed a one-on-one assistant to help him safely navigate the corridors. But the school administration, and ultimately the school board, didn't believe Zack needed the assistance.

One day I walked into Zack's school without advance warning, and I found him sitting in a classroom with one teacher who had her back to him. "Zack, c'mon," I whispered. "You're coming home with me." I took him home without telling anyone.

When he turned up missing, the school searched for him until they finally called me and admitted they didn't know where he was. I told them he was home with me—and *why* he was home with me.

They got the message. And Zack got the assistant.

Kurt was happy. He was getting to play, he was performing well, and his team was winning. The Rams had only had four wins total the previous season, but now they had six straight.

Kurt even made the cover of *Sports Illustrated*. The caption beneath his picture read, "Who is this guy?" I had the cover blown up and clipped it to my painting easel.

For Kurt, that was a defining moment. Finally he felt that people were recognizing and appreciating his talents. To me, however, the defining moment came when he was featured in *People*. My mom had read that magazine when I was growing up, and it seemed huge to me that now Kurt was featured in it. I wished Mom could have been alive to see it.

At some point during the middle of the season, Kurt suggested that I fly out for one of their away games.

I hesitated. "I don't know. What about the kids?"

"Come on! It'll be fun."

So I did it. One of my girlfriends from church generously agreed to watch the kids. And I actually had a lot of fun hanging out with the other wives. So I started going to other away games, and eventually I went to them all. Later, when we moved to Phoenix (and by then had seven kids), I was always looking for ways to spend individual time with each child, so I made the away games into special Mommy-and-me trips. Each child got to pick the game he or she wanted to attend, and I would plan special individualized activities and surprises for him or her.

When Kurt had played third-string quarterback, family members had come for an occasional game. But now that Kurt was starting, family members wanted tickets *every* weekend. It added up quickly.

Kurt wanted everyone who wanted to come to be there, but he also knew that most of them couldn't afford an eighty-dollar ticket to every game and a hotel room every weekend. So in the beginning, our guests would stay with us. But we didn't have room for everybody, so eventually we started putting them in hotel rooms. The Rams offered a special phone number for friends and family to call, and they would help set up lodging and tickets for each game.

On a typical weekend, we might host Kurt's dad and stepmom, Gene and Mimi, coming with another couple, so that would mean two hotel rooms and four tickets. Sue might bring Kurt's brother, Matt, who would bring a couple of friends—two more rooms and four more tickets. Kim and John and Ali and Tor would occupy another room and require four more tickets. Uncle Francis and Aunt Loie often came—two more tickets and yet another room. Then Kurt's best friend and his girlfriend might show up, for a total of seven hotel rooms and sixteen tickets.

The trouble was, the cost for all of that came out of Kurt's paycheck. The Rams got reduced rates for family members at a special hotel downtown, but the cost of the rooms was deducted from his pay. So was the cost of tickets. Each player got two free tickets per game, and after that we had to pay standard ticket prices—again, deducted from his check. Since Kurt was paid by the game, we never knew until his paycheck arrived exactly how much of it would be left.

The uncertainty and, yes, the expense stressed me out. Later I would learn how to handle those kinds of awkward situations better. But at the time, it was all new to me, and I didn't do such a great job of it.

———

Since our phone number and address were still listed in the phone book, fans seemed to think they could call or come by anytime. It was weird.

The phone would ring late at night, and I would answer it.

"Is Kurt there?"

"Who is this?"

"I'm a fan."

"It's a fan on the phone." I'd hand the phone to Kurt.

The calls came more and more often. I quickly learned to take messages or to tell the callers, "No, Kurt cannot call you back." But that didn't stop them. People would just show up at our house, knock on the door, and introduce themselves. "Hi, my name is John. I live in the area, and I just wanted to stop over and introduce myself and tell you what a big fan I am."

"Nice to meet you," Kurt would say and then try to graciously shut the door.

People stopped by all the time. We didn't have a home security system. We lived in a new neighborhood with only one way in and out, so everyone had to go by our house. And we hadn't paid extra for a privacy fence, so our yard was wide-open. People would follow us home, and cars would slowly drive by, filled with people looking for Kurt. I started to feel like a prisoner in my own home. I didn't want to pick up the phone, answer the door, or even leave the house.

People even started dropping food off at our door—cookies or brownies or, if Kurt sounded like he had a cold at a press conference, chicken soup. Often Kurt would eat the offerings without even thinking about it. That horrified me. "Don't eat that!" I would tell him. "You don't know who those are from. What if they poisoned it?"

After games, we would leave the stadium and find hundreds of fans waiting for Kurt. They held out items they wanted him to sign or they reached out to touch Kurt as he passed. He enjoyed this new popularity, but I didn't. The children and I would follow Kurt as we tried to work our way through the crowd. I'd hold Kade tightly in my arms, grab Zack with one hand, and pray that Jesse Jo would stick with us.

The police would surround Kurt and walk with him, so he was always safe. But one time the crowd pushed the children and me further and further back until they cut us off completely. By the time I reached the car that night, I was furious. "We can't do this. We're completely unprotected."

I became very afraid for my safety and the safety of my children. Things were changing fast, and I didn't like it. And for the first time since our marriage, I felt that Kurt and I weren't on the same team. He warmly embraced the same public that frightened me. He welcomed them into his life and ate their brownies while I went into protection mode. The marine in me came out. I was willing to fight to keep my family safe, even if my husband didn't see the need.

Some of my fighting decisions did protect us.

It would take me a while to learn that, in some cases, they could also hurt other people.

30

Fighting for Normal

The more the Rams kept winning, the crazier life got. Honestly, I didn't understand it. Why did people want to have a picture taken with Kurt? Why did they all want something that was signed by him? And why did they want to *touch* him when he walked by?

Kurt said it wasn't fair for me to judge them because I wasn't a fan. But just because I wasn't a football fan didn't mean I had never been a fan at all. Growing up, I had adored Melissa Gilbert. I'd loved watching her play "Half Pint" on *Little House on the Prairie*. But I couldn't imagine running into Melissa Gilbert on the street today and saying, "Oh my goodness, it's so good to meet you. I am such a big fan. I watched you when I was little, and I really want your autograph. Can we take a picture?"

It was my personality, I guess. I had been a marine. I was awed by people who did truly heroic things, not by celebrities. So right or wrong, people wanting those things from Kurt just seemed odd—and eventually very annoying.

I would send Kurt to the grocery store to get something for dinner. It should have taken him half an hour, but he'd be gone for more than an hour.

"What took you so long?" I would ask when he got home.

"I got stopped by this guy who wanted to ask me a question, and then he went on talking, so I couldn't just walk away."

I was like, "Walk away! We have kids to feed." I wanted Kurt to care more about us than about offending someone who didn't respect his time.

One day I sent him to the grocery store, and as he was leaving, a woman asked him to sign something for her.

"Sure," Kurt said.

The woman looked through her purse, but she couldn't find anything for him to sign, so she said, "I just live down the street. Will you follow me home? My son has a poster in his room, and you can sign that."

Kurt politely declined. He was always polite. I would have said, "Are you crazy, lady?"

I got most annoyed when we went out to eat. People would ask Kurt to sign something, and that would only take a few seconds. But each person would then have to tell his or her story, and that took five minutes. When the eighth person in an hour came up, I would lose it. It took me several years before I finally understood it wasn't the eighth person's fault. He or she didn't know that seven other people had been there first.

My resentment was growing. It felt as if everyone took from Kurt and no one gave back, and these dynamics started to affect our family. He would come home, having been pulled in all of these different directions, and there was less of him left. Less time. Less patience. Less energy. So much had changed in a year.

Kurt and I had enjoyed a normal life when he was third-string quarterback. We'd had normal family meals and normal conversations. It had actually been the best year of our married life because the hours were somewhat regular and he was home a lot. But now that he was starting, his responsibilities increased. He spent more time watching film and consulting with the coaches.

As the Rams continued to win and Kurt's popularity continued to soar, the closest thing we had to normal was when our families visited us. But soon, even they treated us differently.

When our families came to the games the previous year, Kurt and I and the kids would go to their hotel to hang out by the pool and eat pizza on Friday night. (Kurt was always off-limits from Saturday morning on.) We all loved doing that. But once Kurt became the starter, everything changed. Instead of just enjoying hanging out with us, they all seemed to want something.

One weekend, for example, I invited my mom's extended family—the whole Woodyard clan—down for the game. We got them tickets and set them up in a hotel. I was excited to have them in town. When we got to the hotel, there were hugs and kisses, but then they started pulling stuff out. "Can you sign this?" and "I brought this for my friend. Can you sign it 'To Dave'?" My family members were now acting like fans too.

At the time I hadn't developed any rules for things like that, so I didn't know how to handle it. We would come to the hotel expecting to hang out at the pool and eat pizza and be normal people for once, but instead we were treated like celebrities. And that's the way everyone else treated us. I wanted family to treat us like *normal* people.

Then one week, when Kurt and I were back in Iowa, we visited Gene and Mimi. I was in the basement, and the door to their home office was open. Inside the office, all I could see was blue and gold. There were piles of Rams banners, jerseys, and balls. *Why do they have all that stuff?* I wondered.

Before we left that day, I found out why.

Gene took Kurt inside his office and asked him to sign stuff. "Hey, I saw John, and he said he would love to have a signed football," Gene said. "And you remember Suzie that you went to school with? Well, she sent over this jersey. She thinks this is all so cool." And suddenly, instead of visiting with family, Kurt was back at work in a little room, signing things.

Every relative we visited had a stash of merchandise they wanted signed. And with every request, I felt the life I wanted slipping away.

All I wanted was to be normal—to live a quiet and happy life like my parents had. I wanted to protect what I knew to be healthy and comfortable for my kids. But all this newfound fame seemed to be pushing me outside of normal. I now stood outside, looking in its windows, hoping one day I could return to the familiarity that I treasured.

I missed normal.

To this day, I miss normal.

Trying to find that balance between public and private life, I circled the wagons and put up a perimeter to keep people out. I did that with both family and friends. Mike was one of Kurt's friends from UNI, and he lived in Des Moines when we did. He and his wife, Mary Pat, were good friends of ours, and I liked them a lot. In fact, Mike and his wife were two of the people who had decorated the backyard the night Kurt proposed to me. They were good people.

One day while I was home alone in St. Louis, Mike called. "How are you doing?" he asked.

"Fine," I said. "How's Mary Pat?"

We chatted for a minute. Then he said, "Hey, I've got a radio station on the line with me. Do you mind doing an interview real quick?"

"Do you mean they're on the line right now?"

Then a smooth-talking radio voice spoke up. "Hey, Brenda, how are you doing?"

"Mike," I said, "you called me at home to ask for an interview without getting it okayed beforehand? This is totally inappropriate." I hung up.

I'm sure Mike didn't mean to offend me. He probably thought I'd enjoy the interview. But at the time, that call felt like just another invasion of our privacy, just one more attack on what little normality was left inside our home.

I was simply overwhelmed by all the demands on us. So, in response, I started putting up walls. I kicked people out of our circle, letting them know they were no longer welcome in our lives. I hoped that by eliminating the number of people close to us, I could reduce the number of demands on our time and attention. The fewer people, I thought, the better.

Everything was black-and-white to me in those days, and every intrusion was the same. I didn't see a difference between someone who wanted an autograph for a charity auction and someone who wanted Kurt to come home with her and sign her son's bedroom poster. My job as I saw it was to defend my family, and I was willing to do whatever it took to do that.

Ultimately my actions would earn me a negative reputation. At the time, I didn't care. But now, looking back, I do have some regrets.

I regret treating close family members who loved me and only wanted the best for me the same way I treated distant acquaintances. Their only offense was that, like me, they didn't know how to handle Kurt's newfound fame. I wish I had been more tactful.

I am not sorry I did it, in other words; but I am sorry for the *way* I did it. I still don't handle every situation well, but I'm not as quick to label everything as an invasion.

It helps that we now have rules and procedures in place to help us graciously hold the line on our privacy. For example, Kurt doesn't sign autographs when he is with the kids and me, but he does it happily when he's working. If someone needs something signed for a charity, that person can go through the foundation to have it done.

When we lived in St. Louis, I didn't feel like I had any choices. I didn't know that choices existed. I just thought, *If you stay away, we can do our thing, and you can do your thing, and nobody feels intruded upon.* Although separating myself from people had some benefits, in the case of my closest friends and family, it also brought some consequences that I'm still dealing with today.

———

One of the craziest things I learned as Kurt's celebrity grew was that the rich really do get richer. Kurt got lots of free clothing and shoes from sportswear manufacturers, and when we went out to eat, people would buy our meals or restaurant managers would comp them. I couldn't help wishing they had done that when I was a single mom and couldn't even afford a Happy Meal.

In one interview, Kurt mentioned that I had always driven beat-up, unreliable cars, but that after my parents died I'd been able to buy a new Pontiac Bonneville. Well, apparently somebody at Pontiac read that story, and he or she sent us a brand-new Bonneville at no charge. We gave our old one to Kurt's mom, but the idea that someone would just *give* us a new car just blew me away.

I took notice of how sometimes people and corporations just wanted to be associated with winners, and that later influenced how we ran our First Things First Foundation. We found we could leverage Kurt's "winner" reputation to influence like-minded businesses to support some of our community-oriented projects.

———

The Rams finished the season with thirteen wins and only three losses, and Kurt was named the league MVP. Then the team went on to win their next two playoff games, and before we knew it the unthinkable had happened. The Rams were headed to the Super Bowl!

One night during that period, Kurt and I sat in bed, talking. Everything had happened so fast, and it had been such a crazy season, that we hadn't had time to take it all in. That night Kurt looked at me and said, "We're in the Super Bowl."

Looking back at him, I smiled and said, "We're in the Super Bowl."

He shook his head in disbelief and said it again. "We're in the Super Bowl. We're really in the Super Bowl!"

It was the ultimate dream come true for him. In one year, he had accomplished what most players spent a lifetime pursuing.

———

Not only did the Rams win that Super Bowl, but Kurt was named the MVP.

Before leaving the field, Kurt ran over to where I was sitting and kissed me. Several photographers caught the moment. I was wearing a bright blue sweater with blue feathers around the neckline. It was a sweet and memorable moment, but more than ten years later, I still can't forget it because I see that picture everywhere.

In the locker room after the game, Kurt borrowed a phone and called Zack and Jesse Jo to tell them he'd just won the Super Bowl. But Zack apparently had more important things on his mind. Kurt could hear VeggieTales playing in the background, and Zack actually hung up on him.

I couldn't help smiling when Kurt got out of the locker room and told me what Zack had done. A lot in our world was changing. So I was glad to see our kids were still acting normal.

31

Super Expectations

After Kurt's Super Bowl kiss, the picture of me in the blue boa sweater showed up everywhere—sometimes with unflattering captions like: "Why is Kurt kissing his mom on the lips?" It was hard for me to read those things. I had built part of my identity around the fact that I was considered the "pretty one." So I was shocked when people started talking about how ugly I was or saying that I looked old enough to be Kurt's mom.

When I lived in Cedar Falls, I shopped at Walmart and bought Kathie Lee Gifford's line of clothes. They were sharp-looking and priced right. On rare, special occasions when I really splurged, I purchased clothes from JCPenney's. But now that I was in St. Louis and had discovered the NFL games were such a fashion show—at least for all the young and beautiful NFL wives—I knew I needed to upgrade my wardrobe a bit.

I still couldn't bring myself to spend thousands of dollars on designer clothes, so I went to Chico's—"clothier for the sophisticated woman"—and bought my wardrobe there. Chico's had the most beautiful clothes I'd ever seen. I didn't have to be skinny to fit into them because many of them had elastic waistbands. Though they cost more than I was used to paying, they weren't terribly expensive. Best of all, they had their own style—just like me. I thought I looked great.

But as soon as I started wearing my new wardrobe, people criticized me for looking older than I was. When Kurt and I made hospital visits, sometimes the kids would say, "Are you Kurt's mom?" I could forgive them;

they were children, after all. But when the media started asking the same question, my confidence really took a hit.

My hair was just like it had been when Kurt and I met eight years earlier—short and spiky, although maybe a little grayer. From the time Kurt first saw me across the crowded dance floor at Wild E. Coyote's, he had loved my hair and my unique style. But when I read comments about my looks in the opinion pages of the sports section or in the online chat rooms, I quickly learned that some people had an entirely different opinion about me and my hair. They thought, since Kurt was "so good-looking," that it was crazy for me to wear a short, spiky hairstyle. Then there were the jokes about how football players who got married before they were rich and famous married uglier wives than those who married afterward.

Even those who tried to support me weren't always helpful. I would read comments like, "Don't say mean things about her hair. She's still recovering from cancer treatments, and it's just taking a while for her hair to grow back in."

Huh? I'd never been treated for cancer, and I'd never lost my hair. I *chose* to wear it that way.

The first time I ever spoke at church, Pastor Patsy introduced me. I was standing backstage, listening to her talk to the crowd. There was lots of clapping and lively interaction until she mentioned my appearance. "Don't you guys like her hair?" Patsy said. The clapping faded off. But she continued, "I love it. Any woman that can carry herself with a cute, short cut like that is great in my eyes."

As she continued her introduction, I thought, *Wow*. I loved my spiky, short, natural-colored hair, and so did Kurt. "You're beautiful darlin'," he told me all the time. So I was always surprised when I found out others felt differently. I knew I didn't look like everybody else, but I thought that was a good thing. I wasn't insecure about how I looked. I had my own sense of style, and I was proud of it.

Of course, I wasn't delusional either. I knew that in a room of NFL wives, it wasn't me people stared at. I was thirty-three, a stay-at-home mom, and married to arguably one of the handsomest guys in the NFL. But I wasn't ugly—although some of the comments on the Internet sure were. After the Super Bowl, I remember reading, "Why would a Christian woman get a Jewish nose job?" That comment was just wrong on so many levels. I was speechless.

After the Super Bowl there seemed to be hundreds of articles online that talked about my looks, and I spent days reading them. Kurt came in one afternoon and said, "Why do you read all that stuff? You never know what you're going to get. It could be good, it could be bad, but either way, it's going to draw your attention away from the rest of your life because you're just going to worry about it."

He was right, but I couldn't help myself. I kept reading and found myself compared to a troll, Cloris Leachman, a postmenopausal Susan Powter, and Ivan Drago from *Rocky IV*. But one post was especially grating.

"Kurt, you have got to see this," I said, pointing to the computer.

"Are you still looking at the stuff?"

"Just look at this!" Kurt looked at the monitor and saw the picture of me next to a still from that old show *The Brady Bunch*. "They're saying I look like Alice. You know. The maid."

Kurt studied the two pictures side by side. Then he said, "Hm, I can see that."

I wanted to be mad at him, but all I could do was laugh. He was right. I did look a bit like Alice.

"So what?" he said. "Some people won't like what you look like, and some people will. But a lot of people are going to comment just because you're getting so much media attention."

He was more right about that last part than he knew.

As Kurt became more successful on the field, I got more media attention in the stands. That wasn't something I had any control over, and I never did anything to encourage it. The cameras were so far away and there are so many of them, I never knew if they were filming me or not. But I would find out how much coverage I'd received by reading the comments in the chat rooms the next day. There I'd find comments like, "If they show Brenda Warner's ugly mug on the game one more time, I'm going to puke."

But the networks continued to air pictures of me, and soon, people started recognizing me in public places. The funny thing was, they didn't always recognize Kurt. He wore a helmet during the game, and I didn't. People would see my face and come up and say, "I saw you on TV!" Only then would they also recognize Kurt.

Sometimes I felt awkward and self-conscious about all the attention. I hadn't asked for it, and I wasn't sure how to handle it. Of course, some good things came out of being recognized. I liked getting the VIP treatment at restaurants. But I just didn't like the whole celebrity thing. It felt phony and strange, like I was being recognized for something I wasn't.

But who was I anyway, now that I was no longer a marine or a nurse or even the "pretty one"? My only job now was to stay home and take care of the kids. Although that was a noble calling, and one I took seriously, it wasn't respected in the same way my previous roles had been. And until now, I hadn't realized how much appearances had shaped who I thought I was.

Neil had chosen a younger woman, and I'd had to rebuild my confidence after that rejection. Now, in the world where Kurt and I lived, all of the women seemed to be younger and often prettier. My confidence wavered once again.

Although Kurt was supportive and told me I was beautiful, he was often preoccupied with his own career. And as a man, he just couldn't understand what I was going through. No one questioned his behavior or analyzed his looks the way they did mine. Everything he did was loved on and off the field. So he just didn't always get it. And now that my biggest cheerleader—my mom—was gone, there was no one to help me navigate the waters of my identity. I would have to figure this one out on my own.

My first red-carpet experience was for Celebrity Fight Night in Phoenix, Arizona. This elite, star-studded annual charity event, presented in honor of Muhammad Ali, draws large numbers of sports stars and Hollywood celebrities. To get ready for the annual event, Kurt had to put a suit on and comb his hair. Then he was ready to go—and he looked gorgeous.

I had to work a lot harder to prepare for the same event. While getting dressed at the hotel, I had to worry about my hair, nails, makeup, clothes, jewelry, shoes, and the undergarments that would help to hold it all in place. As every woman knows, you can be assured that at least one of those things won't work with another, but until you get everything on, you never know which one it's going to be.

That night, it was my shoes.

I already felt like I didn't belong at the event. And after a season of people criticizing my looks—well, I just wanted everything to be perfect. But after getting dressed, I realized that my pantyhose made my foot slide inside my new shoes.

A girlfriend of mine suggested I stick some tape on the instep of the shoe to keep my foot from sliding forward. The front desk fortunately had some duct tape, and I put it inside my shoes in an *X* shape so the ball of my foot would catch on it and not slide. When my foot was in the shoe, the *X* was completely covered, and no one would ever know. And better yet, I got the shoe fixed without making us late. Disaster averted!

When we arrived at the Arizona Biltmore Resort, the noise and commotion made it hard to see what was happening. But I did see the woman in front of me, and I couldn't take my eyes off her. Bo Derek! She was a "perfect 10" in a movie a number of years ago. Just my luck to follow *her* on the red carpet. Then a little farther ahead of us, I spotted Steven Seagal and Reba McEntire.

I was totally unprepared for the chaos as we moved ahead. Photographers screamed, "Kurt! Kurt! This way." Then, "To the right, to the right." And then, "To the left, to the left!" Every cameraperson behind the velvet ropes wanted to capture his or her own perfect shot, so they shouted directions at the celebrities until they got what they needed. I smiled and turned as Kurt turned. Inside I was freaking out, but I was trying my best to smile and dote on him like the perfect loving and supportive wife.

Then someone said, "Now just Kurt. Just Kurt." Well, what was I supposed to do? I wasn't going in without him, yet they didn't want me in the picture. So I stood off to the side as the media fawned over Kurt, telling him how good-looking he was and snapping pictures. I froze a smile on my face—not that anybody cared. They didn't want me in the frame anyway.

I'm sure it was only minutes, but I felt as if I stood there for an eternity, trying to act as if I knew what I was doing. Finally Kurt finished, and we moved farther along.

Now it was time for the interviews. Kurt had to step up to the camera and answer a few questions. I didn't know whether I was on camera too, so just in case, I sucked in my belly and held it while I smiled as big as I possibly could. I nodded and smiled like, "Kurt, you're so brilliant," but I didn't hear a word the interviewer or Kurt said. For all I knew, they were discussing how much I looked like Alice from *The Brady Bunch*.

Because I didn't hear what they said, I didn't realize Kurt had finished the interview. So when he turned to leave, I didn't know to move out of his way, and he stepped on my foot. I backed up to get out of his way, but because he was standing on my shoe, my foot released, and suddenly I was behind him with one shoe missing. The shoe stayed on the red carpet, right next to the media section, where everyone could see the duct-taped X.

By then, Kurt was three steps ahead of me, and I had to hobble back, grab my shoe, and put it on while trying to catch up with him. I was horrified. I pictured the captions I'd read in the chat rooms the next day: "Brenda Warner's alien feet had to be taped to her shoes." Or, "Warner sports a new designer in shoes—duct tape. Is that French or Goodwill?" And since the TV cameras were right there, I could also hear the prime announcement, followed by, "Film at eleven."

"I can't believe you stepped on my shoe!" I said to Kurt later as we got ready for bed and I told him the whole embarrassing story. Of course, he didn't think it was a big deal. Easy for him to say. He woke up looking pretty, and he went to bed looking pretty. If he had to work as hard at pretty as I did, I bet he'd care more.

Kurt fell asleep, but I lay there thinking about the night. I'd never been a part of such a glamorous event. As I tried to fall asleep in the luxury hotel room, I kept waiting for someone to tap me on the shoulder and say, "You don't belong here. You must go now."

32

First Things First

Training camp in 2000 was very different from the previous two years. Then, we'd been on pins and needles, waiting to hear if Kurt had made the team. Now, his position as starting quarterback was secure. The only question was how much they would pay him.

The previous year Kurt had led his team to the Super Bowl while being paid the league minimum of $250,000. We knew that number would change. We just didn't know by how much.

During the off-season, I'd felt God encouraging me to pray on the number 747. I didn't know why or what it meant, but all summer I'd found myself thinking about that number or doodling it. I would see a 747 plane and feel God nudging me to pray. I didn't see any significance behind the number, but I was obedient. Whenever prompted, I prayed.

Of course, I had also prayed for Kurt's contract, my mind still boggling as I became more aware of what star NFL players made. The agent would show us a number and say, "We're going to ask for this." I would nod, but inside I was thinking, *There's no way they'll pay that!*

When players are in contract negotiations, the team and the player usually resolve their issues before training camp. Obviously, the team needs the players to be at camp, so the first day of camp usually serves as a deadline for getting the contract done. If negotiations drag on, not showing up at camp can help to tip negotiations in the player's favor. A team is likely to pay a little more to avoid missing crucial training days.

When it looked as if Kurt's contract wouldn't be completed before the start of camp, Kurt's agent advised him not to attend. But Kurt didn't want to miss a day with the team. He thought that would set a bad example. So the returning Super Bowl MVP, still making league minimum, went to camp anyway.

Fortunately, it only took a couple of days to get the details settled. Once the contract was worked out, I drove to the training facility in Macomb so I could be with Kurt when he signed it. Kurt had been offered a seven-year, $47 million contract.

When I heard that number, I was blown away. I'd had no idea when I was praying about 747 that I was praying for Kurt's contract. Neither of us could ever have imagined such a staggering figure. It seemed a little ridiculous, actually. Kurt would get paid this huge sum of money to do the same job he'd done the year before for significantly less.

I thought about how hard my dad worked for so many years, and how little he had made in comparison. I wished he could have been there to see this.

I had also been praying for a new house. We needed a house where I could feel safe from prying strangers. We needed more privacy and more security. And I didn't want to have to build. After all the cheap choices we had to make with our present home, neither Kurt nor I ever wanted to pick out cabinet knobs and wallpaper again, even if we had more money to buy them.

When I got home from training camp, my friend Cindy, who was watching the kids, told me there was a house I needed to look at. I woke up the next day and went to see it. Built by a baseball player who had a lot of kids, it had five bedrooms on the top floor. We only had three kids at the time, but Kurt and I both knew we wanted more, so the extra rooms would allow us to expand our family. There was a big game room downstairs and a pool out back. Best of all, it was situated on five acres of land. We wouldn't even see another house until midwinter when the leaves fell off the trees. The extra land would provide the privacy we'd been lacking in our current house, and there were security features, like a gated driveway.

It was perfect for us, so I bought it *that day*—the day after Kurt's contract was signed. It was the craziest thing I'd ever done.

Kurt and I had skimped on ceiling lights, doorknobs, and windowpanes to afford the house we lived in then. We'd had to use my parents' insurance money for a down payment on the house before that—without it, we wouldn't have been able to buy a house at all. Prior to that, I had lived in a hundred-year-old rental home with crooked floors. And now I was signing papers on a five-bedroom house without caring about the price.

I couldn't believe how much our lives had changed.

We moved in as soon as possible so the kids could start their new schools in August. Of course, new schools meant more meetings with school personnel to make sure Zack could get what he needed. But I hoped this would be the last time I would ever have to prepare Zack for a new school.

I loved the house so much I didn't plan to ever move again.

––––––––

Moving to the new house allowed me to put up physical walls in addition to the emotional walls I had used to separate myself from friends and family. My marine instincts had kicked in big-time. Our new house was basically a five-acre foxhole.

When we moved, I gave our new address and phone number to only a very few people. My sister, Kim, was one of them. I trusted Kim to protect that information and to be a buffer between me and other people. I just didn't realize how difficult that would be for her.

Now that Kurt and I were essentially celebrities, people who knew that Kim was my sister wanted things from her involving Kurt and me. Sometimes it was stupid stuff, like the woman I had only met once who wanted Kim to ask me to invest in her business. But sometimes Kim's friends had legitimate requests. They didn't think it'd be hard to get a signed jersey for a school auction or other fund-raiser. But Kim knew better than to ask. She knew I would say no, so she had to tell them no. And when they were offended, she or her kids would pay the price.

Other times, family members just wanted to connect with Kurt and me, but I had Kim shut them out too. I even put Kim in the middle between the Woodyards and myself.

Kim called one day and said, "Can I give Aunt Cheryl your new number?"

"No," I said. "If she needs anything, just have her ask you, and then you can ask me."

"But Brenda, it's not my job to be a buffer between you and Aunt Cheryl."

She was right, although at the time I didn't see it that way. I had assumed that since she got some nice perks from being my sister—like free tickets to the Super Bowl, shopping trips with me, and gifts for her family—she would be glad to protect me from outsiders wanting to get inside or family members wanting to be fans. But the thrill of shopping trips and nice gifts quickly disappeared for Kim, and the burden of people asking for stuff never did.

I didn't realize it, but I had set up Kim to be my "no" person. It never should have happened that way. And worse, I hadn't asked Kim if she minded being in that position. She had to run interference for me, and when she got tired of saying no or when she let someone through whom I didn't want through, I would get upset with her. Kim quite reasonably started to resent the position I put her in.

Kim got frustrated with me, and I couldn't figure out why she seemed so ungrateful when I'd given her so much. Instead of thinking the best about Kim's actions, I assumed the worst. As a result, I pushed her away too. I didn't stop to think about how she felt or how much I hurt her when I did that. Even today, we're still working to overcome some of the damage I did to our relationship during those years.

If I could do that time period over again, I would consider Kim's feelings more. I would sit down with her and say, "I don't know what I am doing, but I know you have my back, and I can't deal with all these requests. Can you help me figure something out?" Or at a minimum, I would ask, "Would you be willing to run interference on this for me?" At least then she would have had a choice in the matter and some control over the situation.

What I didn't understand at the time was that Kurt and I were not the only ones struggling to deal with our new income and celebrity. The people close to us were struggling too. Not only did they have to tell their neighbors, teachers, and relatives that they couldn't get autographed merchandise for them—at least not if they wanted to remain in good standing with us—they also had to figure out how to have a relationship with us.

When our friends and family were still struggling to pay their bills—just as I had for so many years—they didn't know how to be emotionally supportive to a multimillionaire. And I didn't know how to be supportive of them. So I ended up hurting a lot of people.

But I also hurt myself. The Woodyards, for example, had been good to me, and I should have found a way to talk to them myself. When I physically and emotionally separated myself from those who knew me best and loved me the most, there was no one to keep me grounded when I felt vulnerable.

After months of building walls and separating myself from people, I had convinced myself I had done the right thing. And to some extent, I had. Many of the threats to our security and the uninvited "asks" did go away. But many of them didn't. Now that people thought I was someone who could get them what they wanted—whether it was a loan, signed memorabilia, or a meet-and-greet—the more they wanted to connect with me for what I could *do* for them. That made me feel more alone and isolated than I ever had in my life.

One day my friend Patsy and I went shopping, and I saw a really cute pair of boots. I tried them on and loved them. Then I found out they cost three hundred dollars.

"Get them," Patsy said.

"Well, I guess I could," I said, but I wasn't sure. I wasn't used to having that kind of money, so I was still pretty frugal when it came to shopping. "But I like the red ones too."

"Get them both."

"I can't get them both! I was just trying to choose between them."

She looked at me and said, "I want you to listen to me and then answer me honestly: Why can't you get them both?"

It was a moment I'll never forget. We were making more money than we ever had before in our lives. But at that point I hadn't yet stopped to think about how I was going to use it and how I was going to make decisions about it.

Patsy continued. "Are you worried about what people will say if you buy two pairs of boots? That's not right. Do you think you don't deserve two pairs of boots? Well, what makes you feel that way? Are you worried that Kurt will say you shouldn't do that? You should have the kind of marriage where you can decide how you want to spend some of the money—and I know that's the kind of marriage you and Kurt have. So tell me again why you don't want to buy the boots."

As she went through the reasons and knocked them down one by one, I realized that I hadn't yet given myself permission to enjoy the money we were making. I needed to free myself from the grip of worrying about money for so many years and realize that what I had now was a blessing. It was okay to enjoy it and have some fun too.

"Receive the blessing," Patsy urged me. "Buy both."

So I did. But I still struggled with how to relate to all that money.

Once Kurt got a fifty-thousand-dollar check for a speaking engagement. He brought it home and showed it to me.

"Get out of here!" I said. "Are you kidding me?"

"Do you know how long it would've taken your dad to earn that at John Deere?"

"More than a year—and you got that for talking for twenty minutes? Seriously? Nobody has anything worth that to say!"

"I know," he said. "I feel like I just stole this money!"

Having a lot of money could be fun, but it also introduced new problems. People asked us to lend them money, invest in their businesses, or pay their medical bills. We wanted to help legitimate causes that we felt strongly about, and we did. We also supported our church—Kurt gave 10 percent of everything he earned. But as more requests came in, we knew we needed a plan. We had to be more intentional about how we spent our money.

Around that time, Kurt told me he wanted to start a foundation.

"What's that?" I asked.

"It's a way for us to support the causes we believe in."

"We already give a lot of money to causes. Why do you want to give more away?"

Kurt explained that if we set up a foundation, not only could we contribute our money to deserving people and causes, but others could donate to it too. Plus, requests for money from strangers could be vetted by the foundation staff so we'd know which ones were legitimate.

I would like to say my first reaction was, "That's a beautiful idea, sweetheart. How quickly can we get one started?" But honestly, I wasn't sure I wanted any part of it. I hadn't grown up doing charity work. If anything, I had been the girl who *needed* the charity. It took Kurt weeks of discussing it before I began to understand what he had in mind.

In the meantime, I talked to some of the other NFL players and their wives who had set up charities and learned there were lots of different reasons for doing it. Some set up foundations to enhance their reputations. Others did it for tax purposes. Some seemed to do it to alleviate their guilt about their wealth, and many genuinely wanted to help those less fortunate. But most of the people I talked to said they spent very little time with their foundations. They just cut a check once a year.

That wasn't at all what Kurt had in mind. (He would never do anything the easy way.) His vision for the foundation included our active participation. While I admired him for that vision, I wasn't sure I shared it.

Eventually, though, Kurt won me over, and we started the foundation. We called it First Things First because of a television interview that took place after Kurt won the Super Bowl.

Immediately after the game, an interviewer had asked Kurt about the remarkable 73-yard pass that had turned the game around. "First things first," the interviewer said, "tell me about the final touchdown pass to Isaac [Bruce]."

"Well, first things first," Kurt answered, "I've got to thank my Lord and Savior up above. Thank you, Jesus!"

And that was the driving purpose behind our foundation. It's founded on the belief that all things are possible when we put first things first. Starting First Things First was one of the best decisions we've ever made. It has allowed me to help develop programs that otherwise would never have existed.

For example, after seeing a little boy at a bus stop wearing nothing but a Windbreaker during a cold Missouri winter, I suggested we start a coat drive. Now, ten years later, we've collected and dispersed more than a hundred thousand coats. Other projects have included furnishing new homes for single moms; taking children with life-threatening illnesses, and their families, to Disney World; and serving at children's hospitals.

Marci and Jen, who currently work with us, can tell you countless stories about how the foundation's work has changed lives. But I can also tell you that working through the foundation has changed my life more than I ever could have imagined.

33

Call-ins

Although Kurt started the 2000 season with a fabulous new contract, not everything went his way. Coach Dick Vermeil retired, and Mike Martz, the former offensive coordinator, was named the new head coach. Vermeil had been one of Kurt's biggest supporters, so Kurt hated losing him. But he was happy to have Martz as the replacement because that meant the offensive strategy would probably remain the same.

Kurt started the year off great, winning his first six games. But in the middle of the season, he broke his hand and missed several games before returning at the end of the season. The defense also struggled, and ultimately eleven players were let go at the end of the season. They finished with a 10–6 record but lost to the New Orleans Saints in the playoffs.

After the season, Kurt played in the Pro Bowl in Hawaii, and I attended even though I was nine months pregnant. Why not? I had left my cheating husband when I was eight months pregnant with Jesse Jo, and I had moved my household goods and kids to St. Louis when I was nine months pregnant with Kade. How bad could it be to give birth in Hawaii?

I did take precautions, though. My obstetrician traveled with me, and she got hospital credentials to treat me in Hawaii if needed. It was a great bargain. I got peace of mind and medical attention, and she got a Hawaiian vacation.

I wore a bikini on the beach. Of course, during the Pro Bowl there were lots of these athletes with stunning bodies hanging out in the sun and sand, but it didn't bother me. At one point, a young couple walked by and stared at my belly. The girl smiled as if she were thinking, *Isn't that cute?* but I heard the guy say, "That's gross."

I didn't let him bother me either. I was proud of how I looked, and I was confident and comfortable in who I was. I even thought about the pastor's wife who had suggested I look into plus-size modeling and wondered what she'd think now. Kurt's winning the Super Bowl had validated something inside of me. There were still bad days when I read every online comment, but there were also good days, when I liked how I looked and felt good in my own skin.

Fortunately, other than being uncomfortable during the flight, everything went fine, and Jada Jo waited until we got back to St. Louis to be born. We now had four kids ages eleven and under, and we had established a bit of a gender pattern—boy, girl, boy, girl. So although Kurt's team lost the Pro Bowl, we still had a good finish to the season. Kurt wasn't a Pro Bowl champion, but he would always be a Super Bowl champion—and of course he'd always prefer the latter.

In my bikini, nine months pregnant with Jada Jo at the Pro Bowl in Hawaii

During the off-season, I threw Kurt a big thirtieth birthday party at a local hotel. I tricked him into thinking he was getting a massage in our suite. But I let his offensive linemen sneak into the room, and they held him down and duct-taped him to the massage board. He was completely naked except for his lower half, which was covered by a sheet. The guys held him down while they duct-taped over the sheet and then taped his arms together. I took a black Sharpie and wrote "30" on his chest; then I put a crazy wig on him and blindfolded him. The guys stood the board upright and loaded it onto a dolly so they could wheel him downstairs.

We arranged to take him through the back halls of the hotel so people wouldn't see him, but Kurt had no idea where we were going. As his teammates rolled him through the corridors, a fire truck with sirens blaring passed outside of the hotel.

"I hear a fire truck," Kurt said. "What are we doing?"

"You're fine, Kurt. You're fine," one of the guys answered.

"Seriously, this isn't funny! You're not strapping me to a fire truck and driving me around, are you?"

We had a good laugh about that, but we stuck with the original plan. We wheeled Kurt into the hotel banquet room where we were having the party. The invited guests all remained quiet until we pulled off his blindfold. Then they all gathered around him—family, friends, players, and coaches.

We told him that in order to get off the board, he had to sing "Play That Funky Music, White Boy." So the band started playing, and Kurt started singing. Everyone laughed and clapped, and then the guys untaped him. He left the room with the sheet still wrapped around his dignity and got dressed, returning in his clothes a few minutes later to enjoy a good laugh and a very happy birthday.

To me the most important thing about that party was that I could give Kurt a special gift. I spent money on it, but it wasn't about the money. Instead it was an opportunity to create happy memories together.

The year 2001 was a much better year for Kurt than the previous one had been. Unfortunately, on January 6, during the last regular-season game against the Atlanta Falcons, Kurt took either a knee or an elbow to the throat. Although it happened early in the game, he continued to play.

After the game, Kurt's voice was raspy, and the team doctors decided he needed to be checked out. One of them came with us to the hospital, where Kurt was diagnosed with a throat bruise and bleeding of the vocal cords. The hospital specialist told us that he shouldn't talk for two weeks to avoid further injury to his throat.

He had a playoff game in two weeks.

"I think you can go ahead and practice," the Rams doctor told Kurt. "Just don't use your voice until game time."

"Wait a second," I said. "The specialist just told us he was hit so hard that he shouldn't talk at all, but you think he should play? What if he were a construction worker? Would he be allowed to go back to work so soon?"

"Well, that's a different type of occupation. There's no way he could do that," the doctor admitted. "But don't worry. They won't hit him until game time."

I couldn't believe what I was hearing. Kurt was at risk for permanently injuring himself if he talked for the next two weeks, and if he worked in construction, it would be considered too dangerous for him to go back to work, but if a bunch of three-hundred-pound linemen accidentally fell on him, that was okay.

Seeing my shock, the doctor tried to comfort me. "If it'll make you feel better, we can have emergency tracheotomy equipment on the sideline."

"That's supposed to comfort me? That he needs emergency equipment so that he's okay to play? Does that make sense to you?"

In my opinion, the doctor wasn't looking out for Kurt. He was representing the Rams organization. But Kurt wasn't helping matters. He wanted to play too. This was the weak point in the whole system. If a player was needed on the field, everyone involved—the player, coach, and doctors—was willing to do whatever it took to get him back out there. Who would look out for the player's long-term health and survival when everyone was just focused on winning the next playoff game?

I left the hospital believing that nobody except me had Kurt's best interests in mind, not even Kurt. To me, that was just more proof that I needed to protect my family, because no one else would.

Kurt did go back to practice. I was nervous those entire two weeks, but fortunately he didn't get reinjured. And of course, he played in the playoff game.

The Rams went on to the Super Bowl that year. They lost to the New England Patriots on the final play, but Kurt was once again named league MVP. Despite the injury scare, it had been another great season for him.

The highs of the 2001 season were quickly forgotten once the 2002 season got under way. The team started out badly, losing their first five games. Some of the fans at the games would yell at Kurt and berate him. One man near my seat thought he knew everything. He would scream that there was an open player when Kurt threw an incomplete pass. He'd yell that Kurt should have passed when he ran with the ball. And after a play was completed, the guy would announce which play Kurt should have called instead of the one he did.

Finally, I couldn't take it any longer.

"Who are you?" I asked.

"What do you mean?" the man said.

"You are an overweight man with a ponytail, yelling at my husband because you think you know more about what he's doing than he does. So who are you?"

I knew I shouldn't get into stuff like that with fans, but people like that made me so mad. Kurt *always* did the best he could. I was lucky; this time the guy quieted down and watched the rest of the game, but other times I wasn't so fortunate. Often my comments just fueled their fire.

Things got bad after the third loss. Losing so many games after a winning season irritated the fans and media, so they questioned everything about the Rams. Was Kurt past his prime? Was the coach making poor decisions? Were there problems in the locker room? Needless to say, things were tense at work for Kurt. But they were about to get worse.

In the fourth game, against Dallas, Kurt injured his right hand. Later, it was discovered he had actually broken the pinkie finger on his throwing hand, and he'd be out for several weeks.

Second-string quarterback Jamie Martin started the next game, and the Rams lost again. Then, in the sixth game, Jamie got injured, requiring the third-string quarterback, Marc Bulger, to lead the team.

Under Marc, the Rams won the next five games—and suddenly the media had another "Who is this guy?" story. At that point, Kurt was healthy enough to return, but many of the fans and the media had taken a liking to

Bulger and wanted him to remain as the starter. The same adulation that St. Louis had heaped on Kurt in 1999, when he took over for an injured Trent Green and did so well, was now being heaped on Bulger.

Nonetheless, Kurt started the next game against the Washington Redskins. Unfortunately, he hurt his throwing hand again in the first quarter. At the time, he thought it was only a bruise. He continued to play, and the team lost a close game. By the time he finished the game, his right hand was swelling, and it was huge by the time he got home that night.

"Oh no, Kurt!" I said when I looked at it. "What did the trainer say?"

"He said to ice it."

"Ice it? That's it?" After the throat injury, I was suspicious of the team's medical advice. "I can't believe it! You've been in the NFL for five years, and every time you have an injury, they just tell you to ice or stim it." *Stim* was shorthand for electrical stimulation, and trainers seemed to think that, like ice, it was a cure-all for many injuries.

"That's all they've got?" I ranted. "Who are these trainers anyway? Have they ever gone to medical school?"

But Kurt also thought the hand was just bruised, so he iced it and continued to practice. "They keep saying, just rub it out," Kurt said one day after practice, "but it's really hurting."

"Did they do X-rays?" I asked.

"No," Kurt said.

"I am telling you, as a nurse, that you need to have an X-ray."

Kurt's hand didn't get better. Every day, he let the trainers and coaches know he was in pain. They adjusted the practices so Kurt wouldn't have to take any snaps, but they still insisted the injury was just bruising. In the meantime, I worried that Kurt would believe them and potentially be overlooking a real injury.

Kurt started the game the following Sunday against Philadelphia, and of course he didn't play well. How could a quarterback with an injured throwing hand expect to do well? Kurt was in pain, and the pain affected every throw. They lost the game.

On the bus ride home, Kurt arranged with the team doctor to get an

X-ray the following day. When he told me he had scheduled an X-ray, I said he should consider an outside doctor.

In a meeting with Coach Martz on Monday morning, Kurt told Martz that he was getting the X-ray done that afternoon.

"Okay," said Martz. "Let me know what you find out."

Kurt returned a few hours later with bad news. He had a hairline fracture on the knuckle of his previously injured pinkie. Martz put Kurt on the injured reserve list, effectively ending his season.

Kurt was very disappointed. He wanted to play. But he also knew how much the injury affected his ability to throw, so he expected and understood Martz's decision. What he didn't expect was the way Martz would explain the story to the media. He basically said that the Rams had insisted on the X-ray and that Kurt had refused to tell them he was hurt.

The next day, newspaper articles and television sports reporters implied that Kurt had lied to his coaches, saying he was fine when he knew he wasn't. They went on to say that Martz was the one who had wanted Kurt to have the X-ray.

I read one of those articles before I left the house that morning. It had been written by a local reporter, and it made me livid because he basically called Kurt a liar.

I grabbed my keys and headed out to my kickboxing class, which I really needed at the moment to burn off some of my anger. Kurt had taken my car and left me with his truck, which rarely happened. When I started up the truck, sports talk radio was on, and they were talking about Kurt. As I listened, I realized the guest on the show was the same reporter who had written the newspaper story I had just read.

The host was trying to get something started. "Can players trust another player who lies about an injury? Can a coach trust a player who doesn't tell the truth about his injuries? That's our topic today. Call in if you want to talk about it."

I couldn't stand it any longer. I picked up my cell phone, and when the station answered, I said, "This is Brenda Warner, and I would like to speak."

"Hold on a second," said the guy who had answered.

My heart was racing. I had never done anything like this before. But I couldn't help it. I was just so angry.

The host of the show, Bryan Burwell, came on. "Brenda Warner, what's happening?"

"This is ridiculous! Martz had nothing to do with it. All week long I said, 'Kurt, I'm a nurse. You should get your hand x-rayed.' The team doctors never once said he should get an X-ray. They said, 'No, it's only bruised.'"

Kurt hadn't lied about his injury, I went on to say. He had told the Rams coaches all along what was going on with his hand. They knew because they saw it, and they were the ones who told him to reduce his snaps in practice. It was the Rams doctors and trainers who didn't think his injury was serious. Both Kurt and I did. I was the one who insisted he get the X-ray.

It was a brief call, but I hoped my point had been made. But during the kickboxing class, I began to wonder if I should have made the call. After class, I called Kurt and said, "I made a phone call to a radio station."

"What?"

"I made a phone call to a radio station."

"About what?"

"Well, they were calling you a liar."

"I didn't lie."

"I know. I told them that."

"All right."

That was the end of it as far as we were concerned, but not as far as the media were concerned. All day long, my call was replayed on St. Louis radio and TV stations. Although my intention had been to show that Kurt wasn't a liar, the media slanted it to say, "Brenda Warner calls *Martz* a liar." By the time the local evening news came on, that was the headline. And by late that night, it was a headline on ESPN.

And it didn't stop there. Sports reporters were like a dog with a new bone, and they wouldn't let go of the story. When Kurt got to work the next day, they were waiting for him and his teammates to comment on the story.

"None of this is really an issue, so I'm not worried about it," Kurt told them. "There's nothing I need to comment on." But still they wouldn't let it go. They accused me of meddling in team business. Print and television reporters dug up every bad photo of me they could find. They especially loved photos of me cheering for Kurt at the games because my face was usually distorted and my mouth was always wide-open.

The reporters wanted Kurt to say I was wrong and that he'd told me to never do that again. But the truth was, Kurt agreed with everything I said. He may not have liked the aftermath of my call to the radio station, but he knew I had spoken the truth.

He didn't want to create any more trouble for the team, though, so he told the reporters, "Of course we talked about it. We discussed it, and we know how we're going to handle it. As I said, it's not an issue. It's not anything that needs to be any kind of big deal at all."

But the story wouldn't die down. Kurt's teammates were questioned about whether they had ever lied about injuries, whether the Rams ever tried to hide injuries, and whether or not they trusted the coach. In a year when the team already wasn't playing well, those kinds of distractions weren't helpful.

I had already dealt with the "Brenda Warner is ugly" crowd for years, but now the comments got even more personal and nasty. No one defended me or considered I might be telling the truth. Instead they questioned my sexuality and made gross comments about my anatomy. But to me the most hurtful comments were the ones that said I was the one who wore the pants in the family and that I was interfering with Kurt's career.

It wasn't just a public battle. It was also a private one. Close family members called and said, "What have you done now?" They made me feel even guiltier for something I wasn't sure I should even feel guilty about. When family members came to watch the game that week, I felt like they were smirking at me, thinking, *You blew it.*

The whole situation was a big mess. The team wasn't doing well, and everyone was trying to defend themselves to keep their jobs. Any accusations against the team or the coaches were blown out of proportion by the media and vehemently argued by those who were accused.

Kurt and I had a hard talk about it all one night, and for the umpteenth time that week, I apologized to him. "I am so sorry. I've created a problem for you, and I don't know what to do to make it better."

"You've done nothing wrong," Kurt said, also for the umpteenth time.

"Do you want me to do an interview to apologize and explain what I was trying to say?"

Kurt thought it would be better to let it pass. "I'll handle it."

"I am so sorry I did this to you."

"You did nothing wrong," he repeated. "You just told the truth."

But somehow having the truth on my side didn't make me feel much better.

It was a painful lesson, and I learned it the hard way—that even when I had good intentions, even when my cause was right, I shouldn't act in anger. I still believe I did nothing wrong by making that call, but I should never have called while I was so mad. I wasn't as articulate as I could have been. My words didn't come out as clearly as they could have.

And for that, we all had to pay a price.

34

Personal Attacks

I vowed to make up for my mistake by following the advice so many people had already been giving me online. I would "shut my ugly trap." For the first time in our marriage, I became the stereotypical submissive wife. I couldn't think of any other way to make it up to him.

Unfortunately, my new role didn't last as long as I would have liked.

After a Super Bowl season the previous year, the Rams ended the 2002 season with only seven wins and nine losses. They had zero wins and six losses for the games Kurt started, but when Marc Bulger both started and finished the game, they had six wins and zero losses. Heading into the off-season, the media tried to start a quarterback controversy, saying next year's quarterback should be Bulger instead of Kurt.

The comments about me continued and in some cases grew even nastier. One commenter said, "Kurt is such a good man and a man of honor that he would stay with his wife no matter what. Poor guy." And then one night I read, "Kurt should tell his wife that he wears the balls in the family." That hurt more than any other comment because I wondered if it made Kurt feel like less of a man.

Although Kurt reassured me that he never felt that way, I worried he was just saying that to be kind. I worried about a lot of things during that time. More than ever before, I needed people to jump into my foxhole with me—people I could trust, people who had my back. Little did anybody know I was now pregnant with our *fifth* child.

Fortunately, I did have friends I could call on. Three team wives—Tina Wilkins, the kicker's wife; Kelly Proehl; and Andrea Conwell—would protect me by getting me out of the stands when fans got nasty or started calling me vile names. They would also yell back because I no longer could take any chances by yelling back myself. I don't know what I would have done without them. I also relied on my pastors, Jeff and Patsy, and our friends from church. They provided me with real community, and when I needed them, they rose up and fought for me.

One friend told me, "I just yelled at my mother-in-law and told her that she doesn't know what she's talking about. She said you have a big mouth. But I said, 'You don't even know her. Leave her alone.'"

Although I was thankful for her support, I felt miserable that people who cared for me had to take sides against their families. It just didn't seem fair.

I had always thought that journalists had to double- and triple-check their facts before printing anything. But I was now learning that they could basically say whatever they wanted to say. And if the traditional media was bad, the Internet was the Wild West. Online, people were accountable to no one. It was like I had this dark shadow over me that gave people a distorted impression of who I was. And when they found something about me they didn't like, they felt that gave them permission to attack me however they wanted. It was vile and vicious.

Kurt would call home from work. "What are you doing?"

"Nothing."

"Get off the computer. Get off! I think you're beautiful, and you did nothing wrong."

He always knew I was looking at the comments even when I didn't tell him.

But I wasn't the only one they attacked. Some fans who were upset about the season blamed Kurt, which angered me more than the comments about me.

The world of professional football had become a scary place.

During the off-season the controversies finally died down. Kurt did so well during training camp and the preseason games that there was no question he would once again be the starting quarterback for the 2003 season.

The first game of the season was an away game against the New York Giants. As I watched from the stands, I noticed that Kurt kept hitting his helmet as if the communications system inside it wasn't working and he couldn't receive the next play from the coaches.

The first half was horrible. Kurt fumbled the ball a lot and made some bad mistakes in judgment, things that weren't typical of him. I felt helpless as I watched him struggle, occasionally hitting the side of his helmet with the palm of his hand as if he was trying to make it work. I prayed they would get it fixed during halftime.

Kurt did play better in the second half and looked more like himself, but with six sacks the Rams lost 23–13. I knew he wasn't going to be happy with his performance.

By then, I needed security at all the games. A security guard would escort me from the stands down to the players' area. While most of the family members stayed in a roped-in area to wait for their player to come out, I waited in a different area with the guard.

As I stood there, Martz walked by. When he saw me, he said, "It was a tough game."

"Yeah. What's going on? Is Kurt okay?"

I meant, Is Kurt upset with his performance? But Martz's answer was something unexpected. "Well, they're looking at him right now."

"What do you mean, they're looking at him?"

"I'm sorry. He just wasn't acting right," Martz said. "I should have just pulled him, but he kept saying it was the headset in his helmet. Nothing was wrong with the headset, but something just wasn't right."

"Where is he?"

"They're looking at him in the locker room. They think he might have a concussion."

Martz let me follow him to the locker room, where Kurt lay on a bench. He had a headache and felt nauseous—both symptoms of a concussion. He was leaning over a trash can, but he wasn't vomiting.

"What's going on?" I asked.

"I was feeling kind of queasy, so they're watching me."

"What's the plan?"

"They think I should get checked at the hospital."

I rode in the ambulance with Kurt, and one of the team trainers came with us. They checked him in and said they would run some tests. They planned to keep him overnight for observation.

Doctors kept coming in and doing various neurological tests, but Kurt said he was feeling fine. He seemed fine, so we started talking about the game.

"Martz says you just weren't acting right, and you thought it was your headset."

"My headset *wasn't* working."

I thought that was weird. Was it true that his headset wasn't working, or had the concussion somehow affected his ability to hear?

Kurt was released the next morning. I flew home on my regularly scheduled flight, and Kurt and the Rams trainer got on another flight. After we got back to St. Louis, Kurt told me he had been checked out by the Rams doctors during halftime and cleared to go back into the game. I believed that Martz suspected a concussion despite those tests, because he had apologized to me after the game for leaving Kurt in.

Kurt had toughed it out while the Rams medical professionals missed signs of his injury. While I knew concussions are difficult to diagnose, I also didn't think it was right to leave it up to a player to report his own symptoms. If someone suspected a head injury, Kurt should have been kept out of the rest of the game regardless of what the sideline tests showed. Once again, my distrust of the Rams leadership grew.

But Kurt felt fine. He showed no sign of a concussion, and his tests were all negative. So on Wednesday he returned to practice ready to prepare for Sunday's game. But now Martz was concerned about Kurt's health and decided for safety reasons to play Bulger instead. When Bulger won the game on Sunday, suddenly Kurt was no longer the starting quarterback for the Rams.

While in St. Louis, I received many offers to do different kinds of projects, but I was careful about the opportunities I chose. I spent a lot of time working with our foundation, so I wanted anything else I did to complement my work there.

At one point, a local country music station wanted me to do a ten-minute call-in radio show on Monday mornings to give a behind-the-scenes look at life in the NFL. In return, one of the radio station's advertisers would give us free furniture whenever we needed it to help furnish homes for single moms.

That sounded like the perfect fit for me. I could talk about our life and what we did as a family, and I could also get out the word about our charitable activities, like the coat drive we organized every winter.

The show was fun. Steve and D.C., the two hosts, would ask me questions like, "What did Kurt do yesterday before the game?" I would joke about how crabby he'd been or how he'd fed the kids cereal but hadn't put the dishes in the dishwasher when he was done. Then I would invite people out to the coat drive or other activities the foundation had going on. It was a good opportunity for me to shine a positive light on what we were doing and, frankly, on me. The show received great feedback, and I looked forward to doing it every week.

On September 29, I called in to do my regular show. Kurt had not played in a game in three weeks. Although Martz hadn't said the change was permanent, Kurt was frustrated. He was healthy, and he wasn't playing.

So the conversation started with one of the hosts asking, "How is Kurt handling being the backup? Isn't that hard?"

"Of course it's hard. He'd rather be playing," I said. "Anybody would rather play. Nobody likes being a backup."

"So would he like to be traded? To play somewhere else and be able to play somewhere else as the starter?"

"Probably, just from the point that we want to play." Realizing that I'd just said "we," I corrected myself. "*He* wants to play, plain and simple. So, if he's not going to play here, then he wants to play somewhere."

The point I was trying to make was that Kurt was a competitor and he wanted to be on the field, not sitting on a bench. "You just want to be wanted, like anybody, whether you're a DJ or whatever you do," I added.

I wanted them to know that no matter what Kurt did on or off the field, we were going to be okay because we believed in things bigger than football. "So you know what?" I said. "We're open for anything. We've always said we trust God in everything that happens for us. This is one of those situations where we again have to put our trust in him and know he'll take care of us."

I went about my day and didn't think about the interview again until Kurt got home. "Everybody wants an interview from me today," he said, puzzled. "What happened on the radio this morning?"

It wasn't like he was saying, "What did you do now?" It was more like he was curious. I thought back to my conversation that morning. I had mentioned that Kurt would be willing to play somewhere else, but he had signed a seven-year contract, so it wasn't like he could leave anyway. I couldn't think of anything I would have said that would have upset anyone.

I told him about my conversation, and I could see from his expression that, once again, I'd stuck my foot in my mouth. Apparently the wife of a quarterback doesn't say, "He wants to play, even if it means he has to play somewhere else." To normal people that sounds logical. Of course he wants to play. But to the sports media, fans, and his fellow players, apparently that sounded like the ultimate betrayal.

The fact that I originally misspoke and said, "We want to play" instead of, "He wants to play," only made the sound bite more delicious. And once again, the reaction took on a life of its own. The new headline? "Brenda calls a radio station and asks for a trade."

Of course, that's not what I did. But it was a great excuse to remind everyone of my call to a radio station the previous year. The press started calling me Brenda Ono after John Lennon's opinionated wife, Yoko Ono, who was accused of contributing to the Beatles' breakup. Somehow it was my fault that the Rams were having trouble.

That was ridiculous, of course. The Rams had been successful, and then they didn't have success, and people needed someone to blame. Although I agreed that my comments on the radio probably sent a few more reporters to the Rams locker rooms looking for quotes, I refused to accept blame for the team's performance.

I realized that I had been naïve about how things worked in the sports world. I'd thought that if you had a seven-year contract, you played for seven years. But that's not true. Contracts are broken all the time, as I would soon learn.

I also became aware that certain reporters always put a "Rams-approved" spin on their stories because it bought them access to players and coaches. That meant that no matter what I said, or how I said it, they would write their story with the spin they wanted. And the spin they wanted was that I was the root cause of the Rams' troubles.

I immediately stopped doing the radio show, which prevented more trouble but also left me no way to clear my name. And although plenty of reporters wanted interviews, I knew they didn't want to understand my side; they just wanted a controversial quote to keep the story going. I turned them all down.

Some people in the media felt that now the Rams *had* to release Kurt because of what I said. And some Christians were mad at me because I wasn't being the submissive wife they thought I was called to be. I was catching it from all sides.

I knew I shouldn't have been reading the articles and Internet posts. But I wanted to know what they were saying before I left the house. I felt I needed to read it before I heard it in public. To me, it was like fighting in a war. If I knew how big the battle was going to be, I could better prepare to fight. I wanted to know how many different lies were being told, and I wanted to be ready to counterattack with the truth if I had a chance to defend myself.

But just as Kurt had warned, reading all that garbage overwhelmed me. I finally called Patsy and told her about the things I read. "What have I done?" I asked her.

Patsy was a very calming influence. "You are not going to fight this battle. God is going to fight it for you. And we are going to believe that you'll find favor with God and the truth will be known."

Patsy's wisdom calmed me down. Did I believe in God enough to trust he could and would fight this battle for me? I was the kind of person who took action to protect herself and others. Could I step back and trust God to do it for me? It was a scary thought, and I wasn't sure I could do it. But frankly, what choice did I have? I had tried it my way, and so far that had been a disaster.

That night I told Kurt what Patsy had said. He agreed with her. "You know who you are. You know what your motive was. Stand on that, and let God take care of the rest."

It was much easier said than done.

―――――――

At one time we had been the toast of the town. But football fame is fleeting, and it didn't take long for us to become burned toast. Kurt was let go by the Rams and picked up by the New York Giants.

Although many people in St. Louis were glad to see us go and to officially have Bulger as the quarterback, many others felt as we did—that we hadn't been treated fairly. But what's fair? We were paid millions while my dad had once worked the line at John Deere for a few thousand. Was that fair? We had our pick of the best restaurants, and we attended red-carpet movie premieres while single moms in St. Louis couldn't afford Happy Meals and video rentals. Was that fair?

Our six years in St. Louis taught me that every opportunity comes with blessings and burdens. It was up to us to make the most of what we'd been given. Kurt and I left St. Louis the same way we entered: with our shoulders back and our heads held high.

35

Giant Letdowns

Within days of the Rams letting Kurt go, we flew to New York to sign a contract with the Giants and to buy a house. There was a big press conference. And I was there again, but you wouldn't have known it. Instead of standing by Kurt's side as I had when he signed in St. Louis, I stood in the back of the room. Because of everything that had happened, I had decided to make sure things would be very different in New York.

To be honest, I couldn't believe we were leaving St. Louis. After the Cinderella story of Kurt being league MVP and going to the Super Bowl in his first year as the starter, we had both thought he would spend his whole career there. We'd never dreamed he'd play anywhere else. But now here we were, in New York, signing a two-year contract with no guarantee that he would play more than one year. The Giants had just signed Eli Manning, a promising new quarterback who would probably start the following year. Kurt was just there to fill in until the new guy was ready to go.

We had no idea what would happen after that. Would this be his last year playing football? Would he have a great year and be kept on with the Giants, or would another team want him as a starter? Would he be relegated to a backup position here or somewhere else, and would Kurt even want that?

We couldn't look that far into the future. Instead we looked for homes. We found one in New Jersey and bought it that day so we could get the whole gang moved in and settled before school started in the fall. Then we flew back to St. Louis to get the house and the kids packed up.

There were five of them now. Our son, Elijah Storm, was nine months old. He had been born in November and was the best thing to come out of those last few months in St. Louis.

———————

I spent the first few weeks in the new house decorating and, once again, figuring out the school situation for the kids. Meetings, paperwork, and placement issues filled those first days. Jesse Jo had just finished the sixth grade in St. Louis, but we and the educators in New Jersey decided she was ready for eighth grade. It was the right step for her educationally, but I worried about her making the transition emotionally. It was a big jump.

But Jesse Jo wasn't the only one with transition issues. Kurt and I both had trouble accepting our new life. Everything had happened so fast.

"Who releases a two-time NFL MVP?" Kurt asked at one point.

"No one unless they're crazy," I answered. And I did think they were crazy for letting Kurt go.

We found ourselves asking a lot of questions in those days. "What is God doing?" "Why are we in this situation?" "What does our future look like?" "Is it all coming to an end?" We felt like we'd done the right things and given God the credit for the blessings we had enjoyed. Had we not done enough? Was this a punishment of some sort?

For the first time, Kurt had to deal with a negative reputation he couldn't seem to shake. He felt like people had the wrong impression of him. "They keep saying I am injury prone, but I'm not. With the spread offense, I just take more hits than other quarterbacks because I have less protection."

If somebody brought up the name Brenda Warner during that time, especially in St. Louis, they would probably get the wrong impression of who I was too. Stories come and go in the sports world, and I knew that eventually people would forget what had happened, but I sensed that would take time. Once you were labeled with a certain reputation, you were more or less stuck until the moment passed, and living with that could be difficult.

But as time passed and we settled in, we came to realize that many of the decisions that affected our lives weren't personal. Football was a business run by people who made decisions based on things outside our control—drafts, politics, money, marketing, and sometimes just who they liked best. All Kurt could do, all we needed to do, was honor God in whatever situation he put us in.

We had always believed that God was in charge and that he would take care of us. But now we needed to trust God to keep us safe from whomever or whatever threatened to destroy us—public opinion, media, bloggers, coaches, or even undeserved bad reputations. We decided we weren't going to fight for our reputations. Instead we trusted that one day we would see how God had used these misimpressions for good.

I decided that I would give Kurt more space in New York. It wasn't that our relationship had changed. It was as strong as ever. But I wanted him to shine, to earn his reputation back, without my doing anything knowingly or unknowingly to hurt him. So when I attended the Giants games, I just showed up, watched him play, and tried to stay out of the way. No one knew who I was or cared, and I didn't ask for any special treatment.

It was like a do-over for me. Because New York was such a large media market, I knew that if I messed up, the mistake would take on an even bigger life than anything I'd done in St. Louis. It was wise just to keep quiet.

I had attended a Bible study for Rams wives while I was in St. Louis, but in New Jersey, Kurt and I decided to host a study for couples. It was nice to meet with some of the players and their wives and study God's Word together, but I didn't really make any new close friends.

Shortly after we moved in to our New Jersey home, I discovered I was pregnant. So yet again, I had to find a new ob-gyn. At the first appointment, the doctor asked me when my last period had been. I gave him a date, but the size of the baby on the monitor didn't match with that date. I wasn't worried, however. I never really kept close track of my periods. "I'm probably wrong."

"Come back in four weeks," he said. "We'll check it again, and that should tell us for sure," he said.

Four weeks later, I was back in the office, and Kurt was with me. The doctor said he saw the sac, but he didn't see a heartbeat. "What does that mean?" I asked.

"Well, it could mean I'm simply missing it. Since you aren't sure about your last period, let's have you come back in a week, and we'll check it again."

A week later we returned, and this time after checking me, the doctor had bad news. "You have a blighted ovum," he said. "Essentially that means the embryo isn't developing, and you will soon miscarry."

Miscarry? I've already had five successful pregnancies. How could I miscarry?

He offered to do a D and C, which would involve opening up my cervix, scraping the uterine wall, and removing the contents. But I said no. If the baby wasn't going to make it, I wanted my pregnancy to end naturally.

I went home, and within a day or two I started bleeding heavily. I remember Kurt walking through the double doors into our bedroom as I walked out of the bathroom. "It's happening," I said. I'll never forget the sadness on his face.

He immediately tried to comfort me. "You go to bed. I'll take care of the kids. Just let me know if you need a heating pad or anything." Then he was gone, and I was by myself.

The nurse had given me instructions before I left the office. She said there could be a lot of blood, but I didn't have to worry about keeping what came out—I could "just flush it." That bothered me. I couldn't process where the baby would be. Would I see human tissue in the toilet? Would that be my baby?

In the bathroom, I sat on the toilet and felt the gush. When it finished, I stood up, but I hesitated before I flushed. It just seemed wrong to treat a human life that way. But what could I do? The experience was already horrible, and anything more would just make it worse. Fortunately for me, I never saw any human tissue, only heavy bleeding.

That afternoon, Kurt sent the kids upstairs, one by one, to love on me and to let me explain what happened. I did my best to tell them, in whatever way they could comprehend.

Jesse Jo sat next to me and immediately asked, "Why are you so sad?" It reminded me of the night Kim called to tell me Mom and Dad had died in a tornado. Jesse Jo had asked the same question eight years earlier while she danced around in her little nightgown. While Jesse Jo understood, it was much harder to know how to explain it to the youngest ones. I did the best I could.

"I had a baby growing inside of me, and it died. I am sad because I never got to hold that baby," I said. "But now that baby is up in heaven with Grandma and Papa, and Grandma is happy because now she gets to hold it."

I never saw a baby. I never even saw expelled tissue, yet I believed there had been a life and a soul within me. It was hard to process it all.

The hardest part about grieving a miscarriage was that there was nothing there to grieve. I lay in bed, feeling the gushes, and went to the bathroom every hour or so. There was nothing to hold or touch. I just waited to finish bleeding.

The medical community says the contents of a miscarriage are not a big deal, and you should just flush them. But it *is* a big deal, and you feel the miscarriage and the loss. I just didn't know what to do with those feelings of loss. So during the next few days, I continued to explain it to the kids as I tried to understand it for myself. Some days I explained it to them one way, and other days I explained it totally differently. But that's the way my mind was working. Some days I comprehended it one way, and other days it was harder to understand.

I knew Kurt grieved, but I think the experience was much more personal for me. He had to get up and go to work the next day, but I kept bleeding. It made me feel connected to the loss in a way that I don't think he ever felt. I know he was preoccupied with football and physically didn't feel the same loss, yet I still found myself getting mad at him for not reacting the same way I did.

I felt alone in my grief. Some friends and family members seemed to imply that I shouldn't grieve because I had five healthy children. That reminded me of Mom's and Dad's deaths, when people said things like, "At least you had twenty-eight good years with them." But I would rather have had them, period. And although I *was* thankful for my five healthy children, that didn't lessen the loss I felt over the one I didn't have. I'd rather have my baby in my arms than flush tissue down a toilet.

Maybe it was the New Jersey winter, or maybe it was just the city smog, but it felt as if a gray cloud hung over us. I remained sad about the miscarriage, and perhaps my mood spilled over onto the kids, because they didn't seem their usual bouncy selves either.

I knew it was an awkward age for Jesse Jo and that skipping a grade added new challenges. But she became more emotional than we'd ever seen, and she started spending a lot of time in her room, alone. I worried whether we had done the right thing by moving her up a grade. I also missed her. We had been through so much together through the years, and now she seemed to be withdrawing. Was this normal for middle school? We weren't sure because Zack's development had been so different.

But Zack had his own way of acting out. One day I told him I was going to take him to the doctor later that morning. When it came time to leave and I went out to get in the minivan, I saw that all four tires were flat. That little stinker had unscrewed the caps on the tires, let the air out, and then screwed the caps back on! But I couldn't be mad at him. Zack may not have been highly verbal, but moments like that revealed just how smart he was.

On the field, Kurt was doing pretty well. He knew he probably wouldn't be there longer than a year, so it was important for him to help the Giants win so that other teams would be interested in him or possibly the Giants would keep him. And he was well on his way. The Giants had won only four games the previous year, and already Kurt had helped them win five of the first seven. Then they lost their eighth game of the season to the Chicago Bears at home. The following week they were playing Arizona on the road.

I left for the Arizona game a day before Kurt, and when I arrived, I called him. "We have to move here. People live on the very tip-tops of mountains. This is absolutely the most beautiful place I've ever seen in my life." When we were there for Celebrity Fight Night a few years earlier, we'd gone straight from the airport to the resort in a limo, and I hadn't really seen the place. Now that I'd gotten a good look, I liked what I saw.

"I'm the Giants' quarterback, Brenda. The Cardinals have a quarterback."

"I'm serious. You've got to figure this out. It's beautiful here."

"It's not going to happen."

Apparently a win wasn't happening either. The Giants lost to the Cardinals, bringing their season total to five wins and four losses. When Kurt got back to New York, the Giants' head coach, Tom Coughlin, called him in and said they weren't going to start him anymore. They wanted to give Eli Manning, their new draft pick, a chance to grow before the next season.

When Kurt told me that, I was angry. "Why would they do that?" I asked. "They brought you in, said you're their guy, and now nine games in, they're saying you're not the guy and they're just done with you. That's screwy."

"They're looking to the future. They think if they just give up on this year and get the new guy some experience, they'll be better off for their future."

That hurt. As Kurt said, "It's a terrible position to be in when you're not the guy the team is committed to."

The gray cloud seemed to be spreading. We prayed and asked God harder questions: "Are our lives not right?" "Are you trying to teach us something we're not getting?" "Are we not in line with your will?"

But we didn't hear any easy answers.

After the miscarriage, the doctor told me to wait three months before we tried to get pregnant again.

I didn't listen.

I had been an ob-gyn nurse when we lived in Johnston, Iowa. I knew the chances of having five healthy kids and then having a miscarriage were low. It had probably just been a fluke that I had miscarried at all, so I didn't think I needed to wait that long. We tried right away to have another baby, trusting that everything would turn out okay.

I got pregnant immediately. But almost immediately something felt different.

Up until the miscarriage, every time I had gotten pregnant and told Kurt about it, he'd had the same reaction—tears. He'd always been happy and excited, and I had treasured the moments when I got to tell him we were expecting another one. But this time Kurt reacted differently. Although he tried his best to hide it, I could tell that he was scared to get his hopes up. He smiled and acted happy, but his typical exuberant joy was missing. He didn't call his mom and dad and brother as he had before. He didn't call anyone.

Unlike many women, I had never waited until I was three months pregnant before telling people about my pregnancies. For me, waiting seemed like a sign that I didn't trust God. So as soon as the pregnancy test registered positive, I told my friends and family. And although Kurt's reaction disappointed me, I wasn't going to use it as some sort of litmus test for his faith. I would let him feel his feelings, and if I had to, I would believe for both of us.

It was too early for an ultrasound, but my blood test numbers came back looking good. We scheduled a date for the ultrasound a few weeks out.

More than once during those weeks I said to Kurt, "You just have to believe that everything is going to be okay this time."

Kurt came with me to the appointment. As they were doing the ultrasound, I looked into Kurt's eyes, and although I didn't say anything out loud, he knew what I was trying to communicate. "Believe with me. Just believe."

But the ultrasound showed another empty sac, and I would miscarry again. Kurt looked crushed as he took my hand. I could see the tears forming in his eyes. I took a deep breath to keep my own emotions under control.

This was not how things were supposed to go. I wasn't supposed to have one miscarriage, and now there would be two.

Everything around us seemed enveloped in that thick gray fog. Not only were these things happening to me, but Kurt was no longer starting either. Why did God have us here? Why were we going through all of this? Why did God want us to experience this profound sadness?

This time the bleeding wasn't as heavy, but the loss still was.

During the next few weeks and months, Kurt and I tried to figure out what the miscarriages meant. I'd had a positive pregnancy test. There had been a baby in me. But now it was gone. Were we not supposed to have any more kids? We both wanted a houseful of kids to fill it with light and laughter. Were we supposed to adopt? Nothing was clear.

I thought a lot about death in those gray days. Death was so final, and although I believed heaven was a real place and one day I would go there, I didn't really understand how it worked. Would I see Mom and Dad there? Would I see my babies?

When I thought about Mom and Dad in heaven, I pictured them looking like Mom and Dad. Although the Bible says we're spirits, I liked to picture them with their bodies in beautiful white robes. But what would a baby who doesn't have a body look like? How was I supposed to picture my babies in heaven, and how would I recognize them when I got there?

Those questions bothered me for a long time, and sometimes they still do. But eventually I came to the conclusion that I will recognize my babies immediately in heaven. I will *feel* them. I will know their *presence*. They're my children; of course I will know them!

Kurt's contract wasn't renewed at the end of the season. He was a free agent, which at the time seemed like a fancy way to say unemployed.

The nine months in New Jersey had brought with it a lot of loss—the loss of our St. Louis life, the loss of another quarterback job, and the loss of two babies. But we were also slowly gaining something: trust. We were learning to be faithful even during dark times. And we were learning to lean on our belief that God would be faithful to us.

In St. Louis, I had fought our battles using my own strength, but that hadn't worked very well. In New Jersey, I was learning to rely on God's strength. Kurt and I both still wrestled with questions and occasional doubts, but we hung in there. Privately, some friends told us they felt the impact of our faith more during those quiet months in New Jersey than during our vocal years in St. Louis.

We spent a lot of time talking about what we would do next. Kurt considered retiring, but he felt he still had it in him to play at the highest levels. And despite the negative things that had happened in his career, he still loved football. And we still wanted to have another child, although we weren't sure how that would happen.

I had prayed for a lot of things that hadn't always happened the way I thought they should. I had believed Zack would be healed completely, and although he had done amazingly well, he wasn't healed. I had believed God could keep Mom and Dad alive despite the tornado, and yet they'd died. And recently, I had believed I wouldn't miscarry a second time, and yet I had.

But I learned not to tell God how to do things. Instead I grew closer to him as I learned to accept that he was in control, that he loved me, and that I could trust him no matter what happened.

During this time, Kurt seriously studied the Bible to find answers to the questions that troubled him. As he read, he began to get excited about the idea of restoration. God is a God of restoration. And as we moved through those gray days in New Jersey, we began to believe that restoration could happen in our life.

Why not? We were in a situation where we didn't expect to find ourselves. Why couldn't we hope and pray for things to change? I didn't know what restoration might look like, though I believed it could happen.

But I knew that if things were to be restored, it would have to be God's doing, not ours.

We had done everything we knew to do.

Now it was time for God to take over.

Part Four

RESTORATION AND REFLECTION

2005–Present

36

Phoenix Rising

Who says God doesn't have a sense of humor?

Kurt's last game as a starter for the St. Louis Rams had been at Giants Stadium in New York. We'd often remarked at the coincidence of the Giants' picking him up when the Rams released him. But we were even more amazed when Kurt's last game as a starter for the Giants was against the Arizona Cardinals, and then the Cardinals picked him up after the Giants released him.

It was as if God had a plan. And that was fine with me. I was more than ready to put New York behind us. And I had dreamed of living in Arizona ever since the trip to Kurt's game a few months earlier.

But my inability to trust people in the football world still remained. When it came time to negotiate Kurt's contract, the fighter in me reemerged. "Don't believe anything they say," I told Kurt.

"They said they're going to—"

"Don't believe a word of it." I was fed up with promises from coaches and team owners. I hadn't met one yet who kept his word. Of course, I kept out of the negotiations; I certainly didn't want to start any trouble again. But on the day Kurt was supposed to sign his contract with the Cardinals, I still didn't feel quite right about everything. Was this what Kurt was supposed to be doing? Could we trust this coach? I desperately wanted him not to get burned again.

"Do you really think you should sign?" I asked Kurt.

"The coach said, 'You're our guy.'"

"I know, but you've heard that before."

"We don't really have another choice," Kurt reminded me.

Before the signing, Kurt took me to Denny Green's office to introduce me to his new head coach. We talked a lot, mostly just chitchat—I don't really remember what we said. But I do remember noticing that Coach Green collected John Deere tractors. He had them all over his office, and they reminded me of my dad. I took that as a sign from God that Arizona was where he wanted us.

That day Kurt signed a one-year, four-million-dollar contract with the Arizona Cardinals.

———

While Kurt was considering the Arizona contract, Jesse Jo and I had started looking at houses online. We thought we'd found the perfect one. But when Kurt saw it, he said it was too expensive. We didn't want to build, so instead we prayed that God would give us the house he'd already prepared for us. "Please make it the perfect house to fit the needs of our family," I prayed.

After the signing, Kurt and I went out to look at houses. We looked at fourteen different homes and found something wrong with each one. We were about to give up.

"Let's just go see the one Jesse Jo and I saw on the Internet," I said. Kurt must have been worn down, because he agreed.

Once we got there and saw the house, we knew it was the perfect fit for our family. From the locations of the bedrooms to the large kitchen where we could all have dinner together, it looked as if it had been built for us. "Look, it has an elevator," I said. "That's weird. Why would we ever need an elevator in a two-story house?"

Kurt also fell in love with the house, and we bought it that day. God had indeed prepared that house especially for us. Twice in the next two years I would be on bed rest, and that elevator would provide my only way to get between the upper and lower floors.

From the John Deere tractors to the perfectly suited house, this move felt right. Even the name of the city suggested that something bigger than us was going on. The phoenix was the mythical bird that was reborn out of its own ashes. Moving from the gray winter of New Jersey to the sunshine and warmth of Arizona felt like a rebirth for us.

On the day we moved into the house, I took a pregnancy test. It was positive.

I have often heard women who've been through infertility describe how each month they missed a period, they were sure that this time was it. I could understand that because that was the way I felt. I convinced myself that this time I was going to have a healthy baby.

I told Kurt I was pregnant, and once again, he got an ob-gyn referral from a player on the team whose wife was pregnant. I went in and saw the doctor right away. "I just tested positive, but I've had two miscarriages and I want to take every precaution," I told her.

"Here's our plan," she said. Her heels made a *click-clack* noise as she confidently strode down the tiled hall and I followed her to the examination room. She was not a warm and nurturing doctor, like some I'd gone to in the past. She was quick and professional, and I liked that.

"Let's go over your history, do some blood work, and get a urine test. Then we'll set up an appointment for an ultrasound," she said.

All right. We're doing the plan. I felt confident in her capable hands.

I returned to the doctor's office alone for the ultrasound. I wasn't trying to protect Kurt as much as I was trying to protect myself from any unwanted attention. Kurt had been on the local television sports reports a lot lately, and I didn't want anyone in the office to recognize him and know who I was. I had even filled out the paperwork at the first appointment using *Brenda Carney* as my name. I had already lost two babies. If there was more bad news, I didn't want it in the newspapers. It was hard enough to endure a miscarriage in private.

I sat in the little room and prayed silently. *God, please, a healthy pregnancy. A heartbeat. A healthy heartbeat, God.* That's how I prayed, just saying what I was asking for.

The doctor came in, and instead of having me lie on my back, she tilted me to a forty-five-degree angle and then turned the monitor away so I couldn't see it.

I had worked in an ob-gyn office, and I'd seen plenty of ultrasounds over the years. I had given birth to five children and had seen their healthy scans, and I'd had two miscarriages and seen the sacs where the heartbeat should have been. I wanted to see the monitor. Whatever it was, I could handle it. But ever since New York, I had tried not to be demanding. This was only my second visit to this doctor, and I didn't want to cause any trouble.

As she adjusted the wand, I lay there waiting. When she got it, she immediately turned the monitor so I could see it.

"Oh my God," I said. "Thank you. Thank you." Knowing that my baby was okay gave me such an enormous feeling of relief!

Then she said, "And here's the other heartbeat."

I sat up, startled. "Why does it have another heartbeat?"

She stopped moving the wand. "Lie back down," she said.

I reclined back to the forty-five-degree position where I'd started.

"No, no, no," I said as realization dawned.

She just looked at me.

"I am thirty-eight years old!"

She kept eye contact with me. "And you'll continue to be thirty-eight years old."

"No, no. I have five children." Of course, she already knew that because we'd discussed my history.

"Well," she said, "now you have seven."

"There's no history of twins in the family!"

"There is now."

I'm sure she thought, *This is the dumbest nurse and mother of five I've ever met!*

But I just couldn't believe it. "Okay, okay. And they're healthy?"

"Look." She turned the monitor back so I could see it again.

"Oh my gosh, oh my gosh, oh my gosh."

She printed a picture and ripped it off the machine. "Here's your picture. Congratulations. We'll need to do some more blood work, but then you're free to go."

I think I said, "Oh my gosh" a hundred more times on the way out of the office. I was completely in shock.

I got in the car and called Kurt. He was at home, and the kids were at school. "You want to meet me for lunch?"

"Is everything okay?"

"Everything's great!" We discussed where we were going to meet, and I couldn't help but chuckle to myself when I thought about telling him the news. As I drove into the parking lot, I had another laugh at the name of the restaurant: The Good Egg. *It should have been the Good Eggs.*

I met Kurt inside, and we got seated in a booth. I couldn't wait any longer to tell him. I slid the picture of the ultrasound across the table.

"There it is. There's the ultrasound."

"This is awesome."

My face must have been blank, because he said, "Aren't you happy?"

"What do you see?" I asked.

"Is that . . . ?" he asked, pointing.

"That's one of them," I said.

I waited for what I'd said to register. He looked up at me, stunned, his mouth hanging open. And then he asked, "What vehicle can hold nine people?"

"Does it matter? Two humans are coming out of my body in seven months, and you want to know what car they're going to ride in?"

"Okay, okay. Are they healthy?"

"They're great."

"What did she say about the miscarriages?"

"We're good. I'm healthy. They did some more blood work, but she's not worried."

I spent the rest of our lunch trying to reassure Kurt that I'd be fine carrying twins, when the truth was, I was still freaking out over the whole idea.

When the kids got home from school, we sat them down and told them I was having twins.

"No, you're not," Jesse Jo said.

"I am."

"You might be pregnant, but you're not having twins."

"I am. I really am."

"You're not fooling me twice." I had forgotten that when we learned I was pregnant with Elijah, I had taken Jesse Jo and Kade out for ice cream and said, "Guess what? I'm having triplets!" They'd been all excited until I asked them what the date was. It was April 1. April Fool's Day.

"Nope," Jesse Jo said, "you're not fooling me again."

I pulled out the ultrasound photo and tried to show her, but she still didn't believe me. I laughed, thinking how surprised she'd be when we brought two bundles home from the hospital.

Kurt was away at training camp when I had the ultrasound appointment that would determine the twins' sex. I knew he wanted to be there for the moment, but there was no way he could leave camp. So I played a little trick on him. I went to my appointment that morning as scheduled, and then I drove two and a half hours to surprise him at camp. Kurt tried to text and call me all morning long, but I didn't answer my phone. Instead I worked with the Cardinals media office to arrange a fake interview for Kurt after practice.

The interview was happening when I arrived, just as I had planned. I walked in and stood behind him. On my cue the reporter said, "I hear you're expecting twins. Do you know whether it's boys, girls, or a boy and a girl?"

"I don't know. We're supposed to find out today, but my wife isn't answering her phone."

"Well, how do you feel about pink? Lots and lots of pink?" asked the reporter.

The surprise on Kurt's face was priceless.

Kurt took the field in 2005 as the starting quarterback for the Cardinals. He lost the first three games and then injured his groin. Coach Green replaced Kurt with the previous year's starter, Josh McCown.

Once again, I felt the sting of betrayal. It was tough on Kurt too. He was often frustrated and easily distracted in those days, but he continued to do everything he could to earn back his spot. By the middle of the season, McCown wasn't doing as well as hoped, so Green put Kurt back in as a starter.

Four days before Thanksgiving, Kurt traveled to St. Louis as the starting quarterback for the Cardinals. Although the Cardinals had lost to St. Louis earlier that season in Phoenix, this would be the first time Kurt had been back in St. Louis since they released him.

I knew it was a big day for Kurt, and I wished I could have been there for him. He was 0–5 as a starter for the Cardinals, and he had a lot to prove to St. Louis. But the doctor had ordered me on mandatory bed rest, so I had to stay in Phoenix. As I watched the pregame show, I thought about how much goes on behind the scenes in an NFL player's life. Fans could get mad because their favorite fantasy player didn't do well in a certain game, but I wondered if they ever stop to think about how many NFL players may have lost someone close to them that week, had a mom who was diagnosed with cancer, or had a child who was sick. Just because they're paid millions of dollars doesn't mean players are exempt from the same kinds of human trials and tragedies that we all face. In some cases it's worse because they have to endure those trials under enormous public pressure.

Fans closely watched Kurt's performance on the field, but they didn't realize that he was coming home from work each day and taking care of five kids—giving them their baths, helping them with their homework, and basically being the dad and mom while I stayed in bed to keep the twins safe. We had a babysitter to help out, but she wasn't full-time, in-house care. That was Kurt's job. So in addition to his responsibilities on the field, Kurt was also overwhelmed by his responsibilities off the field. I was so pleased and proud to watch what happened during the pregame.

When Kurt took the field, the St. Louis Rams fans stood on their feet and applauded him. This was the team that had basically kicked him out of town a little more than a year earlier. I could see that he was so grateful to be welcomed back to a place where we both had so many fond memories. Even the announcers remarked what a rare sight it was to see fans cheering for the opposing team's quarterback.

I cheered Kurt on from my bed that day. He played well, and the Cardinals won by a score of 38–28. Kurt returned home that night.

Four days later, on Thanksgiving morning, the babysitter quit, making it even harder on Kurt and me.

A week later, I went to the hospital, where they put me on hospital bed rest until the twins were born.

37

Twins

I was thirty-eight years old—in medical terms, of "advanced maternal age." I was having twins, my last two children had been considered "rapid delivery," and I had miscarried twice. No wonder they considered my pregnancy to be high risk.

I had delivered Jada in an hour and forty-five minutes. Elijah had taken forty-five minutes. With twins, the doctor wanted to make sure I didn't go into labor too early. My mandatory bed rest started in October, which meant two months of lying on my back until I delivered.

My bedroom was upstairs and away from the main living areas. But since our house had glass walls and high ceilings, it had the acoustics of a cathedral. From my bed, I could hear everything that went on downstairs. I could hear the kids' games of hide-and-seek and their laughter as they sang songs and danced for the babysitter. During meals I could even hear the chatter of their conversation.

"Anybody down there?" I'd yell.

"What do you need?" Kurt or one of the older kids would yell back.

"Nothing." I never wanted to eat. It wasn't fun to eat while lying down. I just wanted to connect. I was miserable being upstairs alone, and I missed being with my family.

When I was first put on bed rest, I used the intercom button on our phone to beep them if I needed something. Each time I did it, someone would come running. "Are you okay?" "Do you need anything?"

Two weeks later, I would beep and, if there was no response, I'd beep again. Still nobody would show up. Then I would beep continuously. No matter how many times I pushed that button, nobody would come and check on me. Nobody! They got tired of helping me with all the little things I could no longer do.

But I was tired of it too. The only thing I could do was get up to use the restroom. That's it. Everything else I had to do lying down—eating, reading, and watching TV.

I wasn't hungry very often, but whenever I was, the snack I wanted seemed to be across the room. I'd see something sitting on the dresser, and I'd beep someone so they could get it for me. But they wouldn't answer that beep, or the next one, or the one after that. Finally, whatever was there would look so good that I would just get up and get it.

It never failed. As soon as I was safely back in bed, lying on my back and eating my snack, someone would walk in and say, "How'd you get that?" And then they'd be mad that I had gotten out of bed. I couldn't win.

Mostly, though, I did everything I could to follow the doctor's orders. I felt like I needed to earn the twins by doing the right things and by doing nothing to lose them. I had already lost two babies, and I couldn't stand the thought of losing two more. So I spent my days lying down. When I wasn't gaining enough weight, I forced myself to eat more. I beat myself up if I felt like I'd stood for too long brushing my teeth or if I'd walked across the room to get a snack. I even congratulated myself if I made fewer trips to the potty.

Bed rest gave me lots of time to read about all the risks inherent in having multiples. As a nurse, I already knew too much about what could go wrong. Now, lying in bed with my laptop, I researched the details.

Some websites indicated that twin pregnancies were much more common than historically believed. Until ultrasounds, no one knew if there'd been two babies inside but then something happened to one of them. Even with ultrasound, there were many situations where a strong twin survived and a weaker twin was either absorbed or expelled. Or if both made it to full term, often one of the twins had a problem. Sometimes both did. I already knew I was high risk, but my Internet reading just confirmed how great those risks actually were.

When Kurt came home after work, the first thing I wanted to do was unload on him all the scary things I had read. But I knew that was wrong, especially since he already had a lot on his mind dealing with football and helping the kids. So instead of laying all my fears on Kurt, I spent a lot of time praying.

"I will not believe this is going to happen," I would say out loud after reading scary medical news. "Please keep these babies healthy," I'd ask God. Or I'd rebuke the devil: "You will have no part in this pregnancy." After suffering two miscarriages and knowing the risks of carrying twins at my age, I had to fight that spirit of fear throughout my pregnancy, and the only way to fight it was through prayer.

I wanted to be the best mom possible for the twins growing inside me, but I also missed being a mom to my other five kids and being a supportive wife to Kurt. The whole family felt the tension, but the strain of the extra work fell on Kurt more than anyone else.

With less than a month left, I went to the hospital for one of my regular checkups, and the doctor decided to admit me. I wasn't expecting that, and it certainly wasn't convenient. Kurt was already juggling being starting quarterback and running the home. The kids were all scared I was never coming home. And Christmas was right around the corner.

On Sunday, December 18, Kurt was playing in Houston, the third-to-last game of the season. While lying on the hospital bed and watching him on TV, I couldn't help but think about the C-section we had scheduled for the next morning. I had made it through the pregnancy, and all tests indicated the twins would be born healthy. I just needed Kurt to play his game and get home. By this time tomorrow, I would be holding my babies.

Kurt played great at first. He completed ten of ten passes for 105 yards. It was fun to see his glory moments replayed in slow motion. I hadn't watched a lot of games on TV. If Kurt was playing, I'd been in the stadium, and if Kurt wasn't playing, I hadn't watched.

Suddenly something went wrong. Kurt got hit and didn't get up. The commentator kept saying, "Warner is down. Warner is down." I turned up the volume, but the louder the stupid hospital TV got, the more distorted the sound became. They kept showing the play over and over, in close-ups and in slow motion. I longed to jump up and help Kurt somehow, but I couldn't even sit up. His injury looked horrible and painful, and I winced at the thought of all the things that could be hurt.

After Kurt was helped to the sidelines, he borrowed someone's cell phone and called me. "It's just my knee—no big deal. It's not that bad. I'll be home tonight, and I'll be fine." He knew I was watching, and I guessed that he was worried I would go into labor.

The bad news was that the injury to his knee meant he was done for the season.

The good news was that he was done for the season.

The next day, I gave birth to twin girls we named Sienna and Sierra. I had only gained twenty-four pounds with them, but they were born healthy at five pounds and five pounds, one ounce.

And now their daddy would be staying home until the start of the next season to help take care of them.

During our time in New York, Kurt and I had prayed and believed for restoration. Who knew God would be so literal? We had lost two babies, and now we had two baby girls. When I get to heaven someday and meet the babies I miscarried, I won't be surprised to find that they are both girls.

We had never had a full-time nanny before, and I didn't really want one now. I loved being a mom; it was my calling. But with five children and now twin babies as well as Kurt's demanding job, we knew we needed help. Although our family was our top priority, Kurt and I also believed in doing things just for the two of us, whether it was working with our foundation or having an occasional date night. We tried using fickle teens, or having family and friends come and stay with us for short periods of time, but that didn't solve our ongoing problem. We needed to find long-term, reliable care for our children, and with twin babies, it was obvious that teenage babysitters would no longer cut it.

One night Kurt was on the phone with his friend Rory. They had met back in Des Moines when Kurt played arena football and Rory worked for the team. Rory and his wife, Betsy, had become close friends of ours. They'd had three little girls, and since no one else on the arena team had kids, we had hung out with them a lot.

Betsy taught gymnastics to special-needs kids, and she was a teacher who had knowledge about special education, so we had really connected. She'd been good with Zack and taught Zack and Jesse Jo to swim. Anyone who felt comfortable taking a blind kid into a pool and teaching him to swim had to be pretty special.

Rory and Betsy had moved to New York to work with an arena team while we were there. So occasionally, they'd come over to the house, and we'd all hang out.

Now Rory told Kurt that he wanted to get out of arena football and especially out of New York. The cost of living was too high, and they were tired of trying to make ends meet.

As a joke, Kurt said, "Well, we just had twins, and we're looking for some help. You and Betsy could always come and be our nannies."

A couple of days later Rory called back. "Were you serious? If so, we might be interested."

Kurt and I spent a lot of time talking about it. We knew hiring Rory and Betsy would change the dynamics of our family life. We would be adding another mother to the house, which was very different from having a teenage girl in the house. But we already knew Rory and Betsy loved our kids, that they were good people, and that we could trust them.

So we decided to ask them to work for us—Betsy as our full-time nanny, and Rory as a part-time house manager, to keep up with the landscaping, mow the lawn, and fix things that were broken. By then, their two oldest girls had already gone to college and moved out. Their youngest daughter was Jesse Jo's age, so she could go to school with Jesse Jo.

It was one of the best decisions we ever made. They live in a house near us, and Betsy works whatever hours we need her during the week. When we go out of town, Betsy just steps in and takes over. Betsy, Rory, and their daughter Andrea have become an intimate part of our family.

At first, it was a big step for me to have a nanny. Betsy did such a good job with the kids—and the kids loved her so much—that I had to work through some pride issues. The first time the girls ran to her with a scrape instead of me was difficult. But it was wonderful to be able to do charity work with our foundation or to travel with Kurt and not worry about the kids at home. And I realized Betsy was exactly who I wanted taking care of my kids—someone who loved them almost as much as I did.

I was making progress. In St. Louis, I had put my energy into building up walls and keeping people out. In New York, I had gone into seclusion. But now I was finding healthy and balanced ways to bring people back into my life and to trust them again.

———————

Then, on February 14, Kurt signed a three-year contract with the Cardinals for up to twenty-two million dollars. That, too, was a sign of restoration. The new contract meant they were investing in Kurt as their starting quarterback for the next three years, and he was restored the status he'd lost in St. Louis. We didn't know it at the time, but two years later, Kurt would lead the Cardinals back to the Super Bowl. If the last Super Bowl had been the beginning of his decline, the Super Bowl with the Cardinals would be the final evidence of God's restoration for our family.

But restorations don't always come neat and tidy. Kurt signed his contract with the Cardinals in February, but in April they used their first-round draft pick to select a young hotshot quarterback, Matt Leinart, the Heisman Trophy winner from USC. Of course, the media speculated that Kurt's days with the Cardinals were numbered. But that didn't make any sense to me. Why would they sign him to a three-year contract for that much money if they didn't plan on his being "the guy"?

Coach Green attempted to clear up the controversy by saying he hoped Leinart wouldn't have to play even one down of football in 2006, reassuring Kurt, the fans, and the media that Kurt was still their man for the upcoming year. But it didn't reassure me. My trust issues with football management hadn't gone away.

Kurt opened the 2006 season by throwing three touchdowns for more than three hundred yards in a win against San Francisco. He was named

NFC offensive player of the week for his performance. But during week four, while the Cardinals were in Atlanta and headed for their third loss, Coach Green took Kurt out in the fourth quarter, replacing him with Leinart. Although the Cardinals lost anyway, Green named Leinart the starting quarterback for the rest of the season. Once again, Kurt had been demoted.

No matter what Kurt did, it seemed he couldn't catch a break. I already had trust issues with football management, and Coach Green only reinforced my belief that most of them couldn't be trusted. When he got fired at the end of the season, I wasn't sorry to see him go—he could ride out on his John Deere tractor. But I didn't have any reason to think the next guy would be any better.

On Veterans Day, I was outside playing with the kids—Elijah and I were jumping on the trampoline—when an excruciating pain suddenly shot through my back. I crawled into the house and upstairs to my bed. When the pain didn't go away, I called a friend, who took me to the emergency room. An X-ray revealed a ruptured disc. They would have to do emergency surgery.

The surgery went well, and three days later, I was allowed to come home. But once again, I was told to limit my physical activity and rest in bed. Betsy watched the kids during the day and on the weekends when Kurt was gone. But from the time he got home in the afternoon until the next morning when he left for work, he once again had to be mom and dad. Only now there were seven kids, and two of them were less than a year old.

He was exhausted from all the work and emotionally drained from the ups and downs on the field. And I felt like I was locked in an upstairs dungeon. We couldn't support and help each other out. It was probably the toughest thing we'd been through in our marriage.

Before I left the hospital, I had called Stacy, a girlfriend of mine from nursing school, and asked her to spend a few days helping me. Three days after I came home, I got a small cramp in my left leg. Stacy and I looked at it, but other than the discomfort, the leg looked fine.

"How bad does it hurt?" Stacy asked.

"It doesn't even really hurt," I said. "It just feels like a cramp."

"Well, it looks okay."

But Kurt said, "I think you should call the doctor."

Stacy had her bachelor of science in nursing, and I was a registered nurse. Kurt, on the other hand, didn't understand medical things, and he didn't like to talk about them. Medical things just grossed Kurt out. If a Band-Aid couldn't fix it, all Kurt knew was to ice or stim. If that didn't work, then his next favorite treatment was to ignore it and hope it went away. For some reason, he was determined not to ignore this.

"I'm not calling the doctor," I said. "It's, like, five o'clock."

"I really don't think it's a big deal," Stacy said.

"Something's telling me you need to get it checked," Kurt said. "Call the doctor."

And we were like, "Seriously? No."

So Kurt called the doctor himself. "Something's wrong with Brenda's leg, and I want her to be seen."

"I can see her tomorrow at eight," the doctor told Kurt.

"I want her seen now."

How could he argue with Kurt Warner? "Bring her in," the doctor said.

The doctor found a blood clot. Had it gotten to my lungs, it would have killed me in seconds.

Both Stacy and I were shocked. I didn't have any of the classic symptoms of a blood clot. My leg wasn't red, swollen, irritated, or warm, and except for that mild cramp, it wasn't painful to the touch. I would never have had it checked if not for Kurt and his strong sense that something was wrong. I had emergency surgery again, they put in a filter to catch the clot so it wouldn't get to my lungs, and I was put on blood thinners for six months.

Despite all the craziness Kurt had going on, he had continued to listen to that still, small voice inside of him, and that may well have saved my life. I had spent so many years worrying about his medical issues and taking care of him that it was nice to have him doing the same for me.

A few months later, I went to my final appointment with the back doctor.

"You're healed," he said.

"What does that mean?" I asked. "Now that I am healed, what can I do? What can't I do?"

"Well, you still have to take it easy."

"Will I ever do a back flip again?" Although my cheerleader days were long gone, I had stayed in shape and could still do many of the moves, including back flips.

The doctor looked at me incredulously. "That's our goal?" he asked. "Back flips? That's really our goal?"

"Yeah, that's what I do."

I think he was trying to gently remind me that I was almost forty and maybe it was time to give up the back flips. But I had come to believe that God restored things that were taken away. Why not my back flips? I didn't think it was too much to ask.

Just so you know, it's been a few years since that back surgery. And I can still do a back flip.

38

Discoveries

During Kurt's first Super Bowl year in St. Louis, we often visited sick children in the hospital. One of the hospitals I visited was Ranken Jordan—a pediatric hospital for seriously ill and injured children. They needed people to help rock babies, and I wanted to help. The babies didn't care who I was, who my husband was, or how much money he made. Most of the people who worked there didn't even know my last name. To me, those hours in the hospital offered a respite from the whirlwind of that first Super Bowl season. Holding sick babies balanced out the craziness of my life, and I loved just being with them. I visited Ranken Jordan weekly, as my schedule allowed, until we moved to New Jersey.

After Betsy moved to Phoenix and became our nanny, I looked for somewhere nearby where I could rock sick babies again. I discovered Hacienda Healthcare, a local medical facility that provided specialized services for medically fragile and chronically ill children. They offered a place for babies who had been discharged from the hospital but either weren't ready to go home or had no home to go to. Many of them still had a trach, feeding tube, or oxygen tubes, and they just needed time to grow stronger. But some had been abused and taken away from their families, and they had nowhere else to go.

Hacienda, it turned out, was happy for me to come rock the babies, so I began going there on a regular basis. Whenever I arrived, I generally asked,

"How's everybody doing?" The nurses and other volunteers would fill me in, introducing me to the newest patients and letting me know who'd been released or who was having a bad day. "Who can I hold today?" I'd ask, and one of the nurses would name a child. "Bianca hasn't had anyone hold her all day." The next time, they might name another child or they might say, "Bianca would love to have you hold her again." It was possible to get the same baby three or four times. A bond would then form, and sometimes I would even request the same child by name.

Because of privacy laws, the nurses who worked at Hacienda couldn't reveal any information about the children. But when no one visited a child and he or she had a lot of injuries, it was easy to figure out that child suffered from abuse. Many showed signs of shaken-baby syndrome, including some of the same symptoms Zack had shown. Fortunately, Zack had beat the odds. Many of these babies wouldn't. As I held them or watched them loaded into wheelchairs, I felt newly grateful for Zack's recovery. Our situation could have been much worse.

When people learn that I hold sick babies, they say things like, "Oh, it's so nice that you do something for them." The truth is, they do more for me, but that's hard to explain. I've been holding babies for eight years now, and I've come in contact with hundreds of them. You would think it would be easy to forget the individual infants, yet their little faces come to mind more often than I ever dreamed possible. At home, one of my kids will be driving me crazy, but then I'll think about that baby with a cleft palate or the one with the trach and I'll think, *I am so grateful my child's healthy.* In that moment, I'm more patient and understanding, and I slow down to enjoy my child's personality, instead of letting his or her behavior annoy me.

Those sick little babies have made me a better mother just by being who they are. The world might say they are broken and useless. But I would say they are inspirational teachers, showing me how to love more deeply, parent more patiently, and serve more intimately. They make me want to be a better person, both at home and in my community.

A few years ago, I felt like this special gift needed to be shared, so I invited other players' and coaches' wives to join me. Now there are about ten of us who go to Hacienda each week. We sit in a circle of pink or blue rocking chairs, holding babies with tubes in their stomachs, noses, or throats, and just rock them and cuddle them. For some of those babies, it may be the only time all week that they are rocked to sleep.

And I'm not alone in feeling the impact of those babies. Throughout the week, I'll receive text messages from some of the other wives saying that they're better mothers because of the time they spent holding a sick child.

When I first started going to Hacienda, they were caring for a little baby named Daniel. He was probably six months old the first time I saw him. He had beautiful, long, black eyelashes. He also had that chubby-faced look babies get when they're given steroids—plus a trach, a feeding tube, and an oxygen tube. There was a sensor attached to his big toe, and his head had to always be elevated so the fluid wouldn't build up in his brain. Daniel reminded me of Zack at that age, except that he never interacted with any of us because he didn't react to stimuli. He was hard to hold because of all the medical devices attached to him, and harder still to love because he couldn't respond.

Although I knew about Daniel, I didn't get to hold him at first. But months went by, and while other babies were moved, went home, or died, he remained there. The nurses couldn't discuss his condition, but being a nurse and having gone through Zack's trauma, I could see his was a case of abuse. He had suffered neurological damage; his eyes didn't move together. Mom and Dad never came to visit, and although no one ever confirmed it, I was pretty sure Daniel had been shaken. His situation broke my heart. When my girlfriends came with me to hold babies, we would pray for him. And when we went separately, they'd text me. "I got to hold Daniel today. He is so sweet. I just prayed for him."

Through a combination of rumors, newspaper stories, and pure guess-work, we think we pieced together his story. Daniel had been abused by his dad and was brain-dead, with no hope for recovery. The state wanted to take custody of him so they could take him off life support, but the mother wouldn't give up her rights. It wasn't because she loved Daniel—she never once came to see him—but because once the state removed life support and Daniel died, then her boyfriend, whom she did love, would be charged with murder. Daniel didn't have much of a life, but to the woman who'd given birth to him, he held value as a pawn to keep her boyfriend out of prison.

We knew there were legal proceedings pending, so it wasn't a surprise when I got a text from my girlfriend Blake saying the hospital had taken Daniel off life support. The state now had custody of him. "They don't think he'll last long," she wrote. I said a prayer for him when I got the text.

The next time I went to hold babies, Daniel wasn't there anymore. Someone told me they had moved him to hospice. "It'll be anytime now." Again, I prayed for him as I rocked the other babies.

I hadn't spent a lot of time with Daniel, so I didn't think about him too much. But some of the wives, including Blake, felt a special bond with him, so they got special permission to go to hospice and hold him there. During the next few weeks, they would tell me that Daniel was still in hospice and still hanging on. Friends who visited him regularly would text me: "He's a strong little sucker" or "He's just holding on. I'm so sad for him." But other than those updates, Daniel still didn't occupy my thoughts much.

One night Zack and I were home alone. Kurt had taken the other kids to get some frozen yogurt. Around nine o'clock that night, I felt a small voice inside of me, telling me to hold Daniel. *But I don't even know where he is.* I had never even been to the hospice center, and I knew you needed special clearance to get inside. I didn't have clearance, and it was nine o'clock at night, way too late to get involved in something like that. I was already in my pajamas because I was typically in bed by then. It was hard to imagine getting dressed and going out at that time.

But the thought persisted.

After fifteen minutes of arguing with myself, I called Kurt and said, "I think I'm supposed to go hold Daniel."

"Go," he said.

"Zack's here alone."

"I'm on my way."

"But I don't even know where the hospice center is."

"Google it."

"But they have special security. They won't let me in. They don't know me from Adam."

"Your girlfriends go. Why don't you just call one of them?"

"It's nine thirty at night! I am not going to call them now."

"Well, see what you can do. I'm on my way home."

I hung up with Kurt, sat there for several minutes, then finally texted Blake: "Address of hospice?"

She texted it back right away. So I got dressed, and as soon as Kurt got home, I left, still thinking, *This is never going to work.* I just knew that they would stop me at the door. How would I convince them to let me in? I thought about using Kurt's name. "Hi, I'm Brenda Warner, Kurt Warner's wife." I hated doing that. But if there was no other way to get in, I was willing to try it.

When I pulled into the parking lot, I realized the hospice was less like a hospital and more like a house. As a result, the place seemed more inviting and less intimidating than I had expected.

I knocked on the door, trying to think through what to say. But before I could decide, the door opened. The person standing there was not a security guard, but a petite older lady with kind eyes.

"I'm here to hold Daniel," I said.

"Come on in."

I walked right in, no questions asked. *She could lose her job for this,* I thought, but I wasn't going to argue. Something (or Someone) much bigger was at work. The patients all seemed to be kept in separate bedrooms, and as I followed the woman, I could hear the beeping of their machines. In the center of the house, in what was probably once the kitchen, there was a nurses' station with monitors all lit up and a desk area for paperwork. A crib sat behind the work area.

"We have him back here because he doesn't have anybody," the lady told me. "He's so sweet, and if he's back here, we can give him lots of love."

"Can I go ahead and hold him?"

"Yes, that would be great. I have to go take care of another patient."

"You do what you need to do," I told her. "I know him, and I'm totally comfortable taking care of him."

When I picked Daniel up out of the crib, I realized it was the first time I'd ever seen him without tubes. For the past several weeks, that sweet boy had hung on to life without any extra medical intervention. He wasn't healed, he wasn't even responsive, but he wasn't dead either.

I picked him up and kissed his fat little cheeks. I hugged him and loved him and slowly danced with him. I took out my iPhone and turned on some praise music—FFH and Steven Curtis Chapman. While I held Daniel, nurses came and went from behind the desk.

"Thank you for doing this," one said.

"How do you know him?" another nurse asked. I explained that I'd held him at Hacienda. "Oh, that's so sweet."

They would stop at the station for a few minutes; then something would beep, and they would be off again. At one point, the older nurse came back and said, "We just had a patient die. We need to contact the family, the doctor, and the funeral home, so we're going to be busy for a while. Will you be okay?"

"I'm fine," I said. "You do your thing."

We could both hear Daniel's lungs starting to take on fluid. He was bubbling and gurgling. The nurse looked at me again. "Are you sure you're okay?"

"I'm fine."

"Do you want me to suction him before I go?"

As a nurse, I knew that suctioning him wouldn't make a difference to him. The only reason she would do that was to make it more comfortable for me, so I didn't have to hear his body shut down.

"No, I'm fine."

As time passed, Daniel began mottling. When someone starts to die, their blood pools, and they lose color. I knew it wouldn't be long, so I just started talking to him. "Daniel, my mom and dad are in heaven, and my mom would love to hold you. She looks just like me—she's got a long nose. When you see her, go give her a hug for me."

I didn't cry as I talked. I just tried to coach him through the next steps.

"And Jesus loves you. He did not plan on this happening to you. This can be an evil world, but you're going to leave it soon, and you're going to run and fly."

As I spoke, I watched his little chest as it rose and fell a little more slowly than when I had arrived.

One of the nurses came by and said, "Honey, it's not going to be long."

"I know. I'm fine."

"Are you sure?"

"Yeah, I'm fine." But inside I was thinking, *How am I fine? Why am I not crying? Am I that cold?*

I didn't know why I was okay, so I just kept kissing him and talking to him. "Sweetheart, they say there's a bright light. If you see a bright light, go to it, because that's Jesus. I don't know if you're seeing it, but just go on, hon. If you're trying to fight, don't fight anymore; just go."

His lungs continued to fill up as he worked so hard to breathe.

And then I started praying, "God, please take him out of his misery. Either heal him now, or take him out of his misery."

While I was praying, Daniel took his last breath. I expected it to come with a gasp or something, but instead he just took a breath and never took another.

Right then, a nurse walked in. I glanced at my watch and said, "Time of death, 11:10."

"Thank you."

"My privilege."

"Can you keep him for a second?"

"I'm fine."

I kissed him again. I was relieved for him, but also so sad.

The nurse returned and said, "I have to make the calls."

"Go ahead. I'll keep holding him while you do it."

The nurse notified the authorities. When she finished, I put Daniel back in his crib and covered him with the blanket—not over his face, but just up to his chest. I kissed him one last time.

"I don't know who you are," the nurse said. "But I just want you to know, he would have died alone if you hadn't been here tonight."

I picked up my iPhone and thought, *God, thank you for using me. You knew that I would listen to your call, and you needed me to help Daniel get to you.* It meant so much to me that I was the one who got to hold Daniel into heaven.

"I'm going to go now," I said as I headed to the front door.

"Thank you again," the nurse said. It seemed as if she wanted to say something else, but I could hear the monitor alerting her that she was needed. She waved as I left.

I got into my car and shut the door; then I drove home in silence. It was a dark night, but the sky was beautiful. I felt so privileged to be there. *Thank you, God, for letting me do that. I love you, God.*

By the time I got home, the kids were asleep and Kurt was already in bed. I crawled in next to him. "Are you okay?" he asked.

"Daniel died."

"It's wonderful that you were there," he said and snuggled up next to me.

But I didn't sleep. I lay there knowing that a child had just died in my arms, and knowing how much it would have crushed me if that child had been mine.

After Kurt left for work and the kids went to school, I got a little teary-eyed. They weren't tears of sadness that Daniel was gone, and they weren't tears of joy that he was in heaven. They were tears for the children in this world who have to bear such a horrible existence.

We later learned through news reports that Daniel's dad had abused him so badly that the poor baby's brain had completely shut down. Daniel had never really had a chance. All of the medical advances in the world couldn't undo what his dad had done. The father was sentenced to prison, but before he was incarcerated, he got his girlfriend pregnant again. All I could think was, *What kind of woman does that?*

But I already knew the answer. The kind of woman who thinks she needs a man at any cost.

The morning after I held Daniel, the hospice nurse called the volunteer coordinator at Hacienda and said, "An angel came by last night and held Daniel until he died." Blake heard about it and figured it was me. She sent me a text and said she was touched to hear the story.

Holding a sick baby who may not live through the night can rock your world. But that baby can also change your world for good, just by being himself. He doesn't need to do anything but just be who he is.

39

My Name Is Brenda

After Coach Green was let go, the Cardinals hired Ken Whisenhunt as the head coach, beginning with the 2007 season. At that point, I didn't care who they hired. I wouldn't believe anything the new coach said to Kurt anyway.

In the beginning, Whisenhunt started Leinart, but he substituted Kurt in for specific game situations. When Leinart broke his collarbone in October, Kurt was once again the starting quarterback. Kurt played well the whole season, but Whisenhunt said Leinart would begin the 2008 training camp as the starter. He wasn't going to punish him because of an injury. But he also said the starting position would go to the best-performing player, and he promised Kurt an opportunity to earn the spot.

"Whisenhunt says he's going to give me a fair shot," Kurt told me.

"Yeah, so did everybody else," I reminded him.

But Kurt worked hard during the off-season and headed to training camp with a lot of hope. During camp he would call me, and I'd ask him about the competition between him and Leinart.

"I'm looking good," Kurt would say, "but you never know."

"Has Coach Whisenhunt said anything?"

"No. He just tells me it's a fair competition."

I still didn't trust Whisenhunt until the decision was actually made. And when it was, honestly, I was stunned. For the first time I could remember since Coach Vermeil, a coach kept his promise, and Whisenhunt gave Kurt the starting job.

When I saw Coach Whisenhunt after the decision, I looked him in the eye and said, "I didn't trust you, just as I haven't trusted his other coaches. But thank you for sticking to your word and giving Kurt the starting position."

"I didn't give it to him," Whisenhunt said. "He earned it."

Not only did Kurt earn the spot, but he kept it throughout the season. By then, I had been around football long enough to know how much pressure Whisenhunt probably felt to play Leinart. It's possible that he risked his job by playing the "old man" instead of the "young hotshot." But he stuck to his promise, and the starting position stayed with the player who earned it. This was a big deal to Kurt because he got to play, but it was also a big deal to me because I regained some of the trust I'd lost in recent years.

Whisenhunt's decision paid off. Kurt stayed healthy all fall and delivered in a big way, leading the Cardinals to their first Super Bowl in franchise history.

Being at the Super Bowl for the third time gave me a chance to reflect on the previous two. The first Super Bowl had felt like a fairy tale or a movie, as if it was meant to be. The Rams were a come-from-behind team with a no-name quarterback who wouldn't have even played except for an injury. The community of St. Louis had come together and supported the team, and the team players and their wives had joined together in a type of sports family.

In the limo on the way to the Super Bowl that year, I said to my friends and family, "I feel as if today, my life is going to change forever." Little did I know how much and how often it would change from that point on.

For the second Super Bowl at the end of the 2001 season, the Rams were no longer the underdog. I just assumed we would win—that's all I knew from my previous experience. So when we lost, I was more surprised than anyone.

But by the time Kurt led the Cardinals—who also weren't expected to win—to the Super Bowl on January 18, 2009, I was a lot less naïve. I knew how many things had to come together, how many little things had to happen just right—like managing injuries—for such an accomplishment. I was aware of how many NFL players played for years and never made it to even one Super Bowl. So I just felt grateful that Kurt was going to the big game for the third time.

During the Cardinals Super Bowl we were better prepared to enjoy the blessings and cope with the burdens that came with the increased attention. We had systems in place to protect our family and create a healthy distance from aggressive fans, while also not viewing every request as an intrusion. But mostly, we were just grateful to still be on the journey.

Without the NFL, there was so much Kurt and I wouldn't have. I'm not talking about things like celebrity, fame, or money, though for the most part I enjoyed those privileges. More important to both of us, we would have never had the opportunity to touch so many lives, to tell our stories, or even as painful as it was, to learn from our own mistakes in such a public way. Best of all, the NFL gave my husband the opportunity to live out his boyhood dreams. For a wife, there was nothing better than being along for that ride—three times!

————————

For me, perhaps the most unexpected thing about the Cardinals' Super Bowl season was the reaction of the fans and media who hadn't seen me since St. Louis. They acted as if I had been on an extreme makeover show. Reading blogs and comments on the Internet was actually a lot of fun this time. Many of them described me as "hot" and tried to guess how much work I'd had done, although they could never quite figure it out.

I had to laugh. The truth was that, after nursing so many kids, I'd had some breast enhancement surgery years ago while I was still in St. Louis. But there had been no more plastic surgery since then. The biggest actual difference in my appearance was my hair. It had grown out so quickly during my pregnancy that I hadn't had time to get it cut, so I'd just decided to leave it long. And I had dyed it blonde at the suggestion of my stylist.

That was it. But if you read the posts online, you'd think I'd gone through years of plastic surgeries, injections, and hair extensions in some grand effort to make myself over. Nothing could have been further from the truth.

The renewed interest in my appearance amused me at first, but when every reporter of every magazine and news station that interviewed me asked the same question, I finally got a little irritated. "It's just hair," I told them.

But to tell the truth, I was enjoying my new look. Kurt had bought me a Lexus convertible, and one day I'd been driving down the road, my long, blonde hair flowing in the wind, just enjoying life. After a while, I noticed a red truck with a couple of young guys in it, driving erratically. It was as if they were trying to catch me. After a few stoplights, they did. They pulled up next to me, and the one on the passenger side leaned out the window and whistled. When I turned to look at him, he put his head back in the truck. "She's old!" I heard him say to his buddy.

I laughed at his disappointment, but in many ways I felt younger than I ever had before.

Another time Kurt, Jesse Jo, and I were flying somewhere together, and Kurt and I boarded the plane before Jesse Jo did. As she made her way down the aisle to where we sat, she overheard two guys talking.

"Do you know who that was?" the first guy said.

"Wasn't that Kurt Warner?"

"Yeah, but who was that woman with him?"

"I don't know. But it definitely wasn't his wife."

When Jesse Jo made it back to us, she told us about the conversation, and we all had a good laugh.

Although it was fun to once again be considered pretty, I'd learned a lot over the years. I didn't *need* to be pretty. There was a lot more to me than the little girl who had danced for attention, the teenager who tried all those hairstyles, or the young woman who'd been distraught about being compared to the maid on *The Brady Bunch*. I had found my true beauty, and it wasn't in how I looked.

———————

I didn't watch football to see the game. I watched football to see my husband play. Over the years, it became more painful for both of us. For me, it was difficult to watch his body take more violent hits and see how slowly he got up as compared to his early years in football. For him, the bruises lasted longer, the broken bones didn't heal as quickly, and when fresh injuries happened on top of old injuries, there were days when he couldn't even play with the kids because of the pain.

Kurt had another great season in 2009 and once again went to the playoffs. On January 16, 2010, the Cardinals were playing the New Orleans Saints in the Superdome. During the first half, Kurt took a hit that knocked him to the ground. I remember how still the entire dome became as seventy thousand people waited for Kurt to move. Everything was eerily silent as trainers ran onto the field. It felt as though everybody there—and probably the TV audience too—had united in their desire for Kurt to move.

In that moment I wanted to scream, "Kurt, get up! Just get up and let's go home—for good." But regardless of how many injuries he took, how I worried about him, I knew Kurt had to make the retirement decision on his own. I never wanted to be the one to push him, because I never wanted him to live with a moment of regret.

On his own, Kurt decided to retire from football at the end of the 2009 season. Although he misses the friends he made along the way and the game of football, I know he doesn't miss the physical punishment his body took. When I look into his eyes, I see that he knows he made the right decision. There is no regret, only peace that he did the right thing at the right time.

Reflecting back, I was annoyed by a lot of things that happened while Kurt was in the NFL. But time showed me I had a lot to be grateful for too. The biggest difference between the NFL and any other job Kurt might have had was how public the workplace was. Every employee has times when he doesn't get along with a boss or agree with the decisions his boss makes. Every employer has to make judgment calls and personnel decisions based on the bottom line. But when you're working in the NFL, those decisions play out in front of tens of thousands of fans in the stands and millions more watching at home, all of whom feel they have an investment in the relationship. That doesn't happen in many other places. Even movie stars make one, maybe two movies a year. But NFL players have their performance judged every weekend for an entire season, raising the stakes for everyone involved.

But overall, I am incredibly thankful for the experiences we've had because Kurt was called up to play in the pros. My life is very different than I expected it to be, but I wouldn't trade it for anything.

———————

Since Kurt's retirement, new opportunities have opened up for him in broadcasting. And for me, opportunities have come up to speak and to share my story on television and through other media. It's been exciting to see what the future has in store for both of us. And I've been surprised at how retirement has brought new opportunities that have expanded our influence.

One of the most unexpected opportunities came up shortly after Kurt retired. Although I had forgiven Kurt years ago about that bachelor party incident, from that time on, we had rules about our relationship. For years, it was hard for me to trust anyone, even Kurt. In our marriage, that lack of trust often came out as jealousy.

It's not that Kurt ever did anything. He didn't. It's that I feared he would. I didn't write a lot about it in this book because I discussed it so much in *First Things First: The Rules of Being a Warner*, the book Kurt and I cowrote about our marriage. I shared the rules we'd established in our marriage and the extraordinary steps Kurt had willingly taken to help me feel secure.

While we were involved with writing that book, a question came up about Kurt competing on a hit reality show called *Dancing with the Stars*, which paired celebrities with professional dancers in a dancing competition.

In no uncertain terms, I guaranteed that would never happen for Kurt. After all, I'd seen that show. Watch Kurt dance that close to a woman who was practically naked? Forget it!

After Kurt retired, he was indeed asked to be on the show. He laughed because he already knew what I would say. But to both of our surprise, I wasn't so sure. Despite my opinionated nature, I really do try not to make flippant decisions. I always want to pray about them. Of course, I assumed this would be an easy one. There was no way God would want Kurt on that show. Duh!

Apparently, I was wrong. After praying about it and discussing it with Kurt, I really did feel he should do the show. I had grown a lot in the eighteen years we'd been married, and he had proven faithful. And something told me *Dancing with the Stars* could be an important stepping-stone for him.

Although it was a scary step for both of us—we knew he'd be spending more time with his dance partner each day than with me—we felt like he could do it differently than it'd been done in the past. And he did. After his very first dance, he left his partner—Anna Trebunskaya—on the floor and walked over to kiss me. That was a sweet surprise and just one of many little things he did to honor our marriage during the show.

Dancing with the Stars was an unexpected thing for me to deal with, but like all the unexpected events in my life, I grew from it. Before I met Kurt, I prayed for an ugly man no one else wanted. Instead I got a gorgeous man everyone loved. But God was teaching me that I couldn't invent enough rules to reassure myself. I also couldn't guard my husband's heart. All I could do was guard my own heart and pray that Kurt would do the same with his. Learning to let go of what I couldn't control in this situation freed me and helped me release a lot of my fear.

———

Like many people, I've spent a lot of my life searching for my identity. When I was younger, I thought I was the pretty one. In high school I was a popular cheerleader but also a Jesus freak. I've been a gung-ho marine, a faithful wife and mother, a hardworking nurse, and, sadly, a grieving daughter. But of all my roles, I received the most attention for being an NFL player's wife—a sometimes outspoken one.

Having so many roles and sometimes receiving unwanted recognition for the wrong ones has occasionally caused me to question who I *really* was. But now I know who I am.

When people approach me, they often start the conversation in the same way. "Are you Kurt Warner's wife?"

These days, in answer, I hold out my hand and say, "My name is Brenda."

Those four words mean different things to different people. To some it appears as an overture of friendship, "Hey, we can be good friends, so let's just get rid of the formalities. Call me Brenda." To others, it might feel a little more aggressive, as in, "If you want to talk, then be courteous enough to use my name."

I mean it as neither.

What that phrase means to me is that I've figured out who I really am, and I want people to know me for just that. Although I love Kurt dearly and am proud to be his wife, the wife of an NFL quarterback isn't who I am. I don't walk behind Kurt and I don't walk before him. I walk alongside him.

I am a former marine. I have a nursing degree. I've lived on food stamps, and I've lived on millions of dollars. I have been divorced, and I've been married to the man of my dreams. I've watched my seven children grow and succeed beyond my wildest dreams. I've watched one baby suffer permanent brain damage and blindness and two babies die before they ever lived.

I am not immune to grief, and every day I miss my parents more than I think is possible. I am not a crier or a whiner, and I would rather control my world than be controlled by it. I've been mostly faithful and trustworthy, yet I've been betrayed and I've certainly had times when I let down those I loved. If you are in my inner circle, I will have your back, and I know some, but not all, I let in will have mine. I love babies with tracheotomies, seniors in hospice, and the homeless who ask nothing from me.

My original goal in writing a book was to help my children understand more about me and the experiences that shaped me. It's important that they see me as something more than the media has made me out to be—good or bad.

But I've also learned that when people hear my story, when they get to know the real Brenda, they find that we share a lot in common. Sometimes they can relate to the adversities I've faced, the mistakes I've made, or the dreams I have for my children. Maybe they're in a dark place and wondering if there is hope. Maybe they're feeling weak and vulnerable and badly in need of strength. I hope my experiences will help them understand their own experiences, inspire them to take a next step, and give them strength to make the hard choices in their lives.

Most of all, I want the people I encounter to know they don't have to be who people say they are . . . or who they were yesterday. We all have the ability to change and grow past our expectations and the limitations others try to impose on us.

In the end, only we get to decide who we will be tomorrow.

Unexpected Life

Her hand shook as she put the key into the lock and turned it. Then she hesitated just a second before pushing the door open.

I knew how much that moment meant to this young woman. It was the first time she was entering her new house, and she would remember it forever. But she didn't know the moment was going to be bigger and better than she had ever dreamed.

She stepped inside and stopped still, frozen in shock over what she saw. Furniture and decorations filled the house—the house that she expected to be empty.

The woman was in her thirties. She had dark hair and a fair complexion, and she worked hard in an administrative job to provide for her two growing boys. But she'd been fighting an uphill battle to make ends meet, and until a few months ago she'd never dreamed she'd own her own home. Now she just couldn't believe her eyes.

For a few seconds, she just stood there, staring. But her confusion turned to joy as comprehension dawned. "Is this for us? Is this all for us?" Her young boys followed her into the house, and then they erupted in screams of excitement

I didn't need to look at her face to know the emotion she was going through. I had already seen it many times during the past eight years, and each time it sent chills through me. This mom's joy turned to gratitude as she mentally checked off all the things she would no longer have to find a way to pay for—living-room furniture, beds, mattresses, curtains, and more. Her tears came hard and fast as she realized that her greatest dream—being a homeowner—had just been exceeded.

Since 2002, our First Things First Foundation has partnered with home-building organizations like Habitat for Humanity for a unique outreach. Volunteers and future homeowners build the houses according to the criteria of the home-building organization. Future owners must meet certain strict requirements, including financial counseling and hours of sweat equity. Then the houses are typically turned over empty to the new family, ready for them to move in. But the families have scrimped and saved to afford their first house, so even simple items like a mattress or curtains can severely challenge their monthly budget.

That's where we come in. Our Homes for the Holiday program works with these home-building organizations to find applicants who will be moving into their house around an upcoming holiday. Then we partner with corporate sponsors to help us turn the houses into homes. We help furnish the home so that when the family walks in, they have everything they need, right down to food in the fridge and laundry soap for the washing machine.

As I looked around this home, I felt gratitude for the items from our sponsors, including furniture and a computer donated from Aaron's and linens, decorations, and lawn and garden supplies provided through a grant from U-Haul.

The boys couldn't contain their excitement or their grins as they checked out each room of the house. "We've got new beds and a computer!"

Their mom looked on with tears streaming down her face. She turned to Kurt and me and said, "It's beautiful. It's the best Christmas present ever!"

There were many Christmases when I couldn't afford to buy presents for Zack and Jesse Jo. If it weren't for my parents helping me out, the kids wouldn't have had anything on Christmas morning. So I knew what having your own place meant to that family. As a single mother, I thought I was doing well when I rented a hundred-year-old house with crooked floors. At that time, I would never have dreamed big enough to think that one day I could have a fully furnished home, yet now I was the one helping that crazy big dream come true for this mom and her sons.

As I watched the family get used to their new residence, I thought about all the memories that would be made in that home, the stories around the dinner table, the game nights on the couch, the long talks before turning out the lights at bedtime.

"There's going to be a lot of laughter in this house," I said to her.

She grabbed my hand. "I never thought I'd have a house like this," she said. "You don't know what this means to the boys—to *me*."

"I do know. More than you think," I said, and then I handed her a check for two thousand dollars. "This will help you get started."

She cried as she hugged me. The furnishings may have been an unexpected gift to her, but if she only knew my whole story, she'd know it was even more unexpected that I was the one to offer it. Had a few things been different, it could have been me receiving instead of helping to give it.

Later that week, Kurt and I took our kids to visit Sunshine Acres, a long-term residential home for kids whose parents couldn't take care of them any longer. Since 1954, Sunshine Acres has been home to more than sixteen hundred children. The founders believed that they should never solicit money and that no child should ever be turned away for financial reasons. They completely trusted God to supply all their needs. He did—and he still does. Unsolicited donations fund almost all the facility's needs, and proceeds from their unique gift shop provide the rest.

Visiting Sunshine Acres is one of our family's favorite Christmas traditions. My kids get to play and interact with the kids who live there, and I get reminded about how God always supplies our needs, even when they seem as overwhelming as they always do at Sunshine Acres.

Typically we take gifts to the children and share a meal. But in recent years, we've also brought one of our favorite traditions. Snow!

When I was on bed rest and spending way too much time online, I found a place that would truck in snow for us. So every year on Christmas morning since then, we've had snow delivered to our front lawn in Phoenix. The kids go out and play in the seventy-degree sunshine, wearing sweaters and mittens so their hands don't get cold as they throw snowballs and build snowmen.

To kids living in the desert Southwest, snow is a rare treat. Our kids have always had so much fun with our Christmas snow that several years ago we started bringing it to Sunshine Acres as well. So that day I watched as kids made snowmen and forts and threw snowballs. Of course, the biggest kid of all had the best aim—Kurt.

Together, some of the children built a snowman complete with sunglasses and a baseball cap. Somebody stuck a football underneath its snowy arm. Then the kids gathered around the snowman for a picture—some posing, some making silly faces, and one boy licking the snowman. It looked like a little United Nations. Kids of all colors and cultures—African American, Asian, Caucasian, Hispanic—had one thing in common.

The smiles on their faces.

A few days later, on Christmas Day, our own snow arrived. It's one of our favorite Christmas traditions.

The night before, everyone in the family had received red footie pajamas with their names embroidered on them. Zack, the girls, and I still had ours on. We'd found that they were perfect for sliding down a mound of snow—unless you slid the wrong way. The pajamas had a flap in the back, and if you weren't careful, things could suddenly get cold! Elijah and Kade had on football jerseys—not Cardinals jerseys, but Dolphins jerseys, I think. Kurt wore white shorts with a dark blue First Things First sweatshirt.

It was a stunning sight—the bright blue Phoenix sky in the background, the leafy green and brown palm trees on either side, and in the middle, eight colorful personalities doing their own thing on a pile of brilliant white snow.

I smiled at the kids, but on the inside, I had mixed feelings. More than ten years had passed since Mom and Dad were killed. But this Christmas, for some reason, I missed them as much as I had the first Christmas they were gone. Standing in the driveway, watching the snow slowly start to melt, I wished more than anything that my mom and dad could be standing next to me, seeing these crazy kids playing with each other. At the same time, part of me wondered how long I would be witnessing scenes like this. Because our kids were growing up fast, and soon they'd be gone.

A lot of changes are coming for us in the next few years. Zack is now twenty-two and set to graduate from high school in May. He has taught his fellow students at Chaparral High School to be more open and loving to students with special needs, and his fellow students have responded in amazing ways.

Despite his challenges, Zack has had homecoming and prom dates. Students and teachers have befriended him. And he currently works on the air at a radio station. I know the doctor never expected *that* when he released my son from the hospital more than twenty years ago.

At some point, Zack will likely move to a group home or some other long-term living solution so he can be independent. For his sake I look forward to that, though I can't imagine my life without him in our house.

Jesse Jo turned nineteen in January. She's finished her first year and a half at New York University, where she has put together her own program of studies for music therapy. She has also been studying sign language. She plans to use her unique musical skill to help those with special needs not just in our community but around the world.

While growing up, Jesse Jo often served as Zack's eyes. Now she will use that same unique vision to serve countless others.

Neil stayed involved in Zack and Jesse Jo's lives, occasionally coming to St. Louis and even to Phoenix to visit. But time and distance have strained their ties. While Zack still regularly hears from Neil, Jesse Jo chooses not to. Now that they are older, I allow them to make decisions about this relationship on their own. They each need to decide how to handle their relationship with Neil. I stay out of it and just support them no matter what they decide.

As for me, I'm grateful for what happened. I've moved on and my life is better now, despite the anguish I went through at the time. And Neil is happy too. He married Sharon, and they have two beautiful children. I only want the best for them, and I hope that they live happily ever after.

Forgiveness has settled in my soul, and Neil feels the same way. We don't carry the past around, and we've both moved on, happy and loved.

Kade is in gifted classes at school, where his favorite subject is science. He is my gentle giant. At twelve, he is already bigger than me, but he is kind and has a gentle soul. He recently prayed over a hurt player on the opposing football team in his Pop Warner league. His coach wasn't happy. "We don't do that," he said. But Kade does that. Kurt and I were so proud of him and his compassion for the injured, even when they're on the other team.

At ten, Jada Jo is busy with musical theater, but she also loves math. And Jada Jo recently took on a very big project. Through educating her teachers and her peers—and a lot of signed petitions—Jada Jo helped make her elementary school a place where the word *retarded* will never again be said. Thanks to her hard work, her school is R-word free.

For her last birthday, Jada Jo invited the special-needs class from her school to our house for a party. We picked up all of the kids in a Hummer limousine and brought them over for cupcakes and Silly String fights. It was a birthday party none of us will ever forget.

Elijah's goal in life these days is to beat his big brother Kade at something. At anything. He is a tough competitor on the Pop Warner field, and we love to see how well he's doing. But we're even happier when his coaches and the other parents say, "He's such a nice kid and has great manners." Most of all, I love to see the sparkle in his eye and the confidence that lets this seven-year-old blond boy wear a Mohawk with pride. He's at that special age where none of us knows what lies ahead for him, and the possibilities are endless.

And although the baby girls aren't babies anymore—they turned five in December—I love that they are so connected. Every night I put them into separate beds to sleep, but somehow they always end up in the same bed anyway. I tease them by saying, "You're not conjoined twins; you know that, right?" There's a unique bond between those two girls that people notice and feel compelled to comment on.

As I sipped my coffee and tried to dodge the flying snow, I watched Jesse Jo take dozens of pictures. I knew what she was trying to do. She wanted to capture the moment so that when she is away at college, she could look at those pictures and remember details about us that she might otherwise forget.

I wanted to tell her that even if she's doing what she wants to do—or, more important, what she feels she has to do—it can still hurt to be away from those she loves. But as painful as those separation experiences are, they help us grow. They force us to make choices we wouldn't otherwise make and to find strength we never thought we had.

But I didn't say anything. I didn't want to distract her. I also wanted those moments captured in pictures, because when the moment is gone—and I knew it soon would be—the pictures would remind me of just how good I have it now.

With Jesse Jo in college, I realized the next big thing for our family would be to find a group home for Zack. While it's hard to imagine him not living in the same house with me, I also know that he needs to learn how to have a life without me. He deserves a chance to grow and stretch his wings just like the other kids. We're currently evaluating group homes and teaching Zack the life skills he'll need to be successful on his own—in preparation for the day that he, too, leaves our nest.

Between the flying snowballs, I caught a glimpse of my handsome husband across the yard. After earlier pelting unsuspecting neighbors with snowballs, Kurt had been intently focused on building a snowman. But now he was posing for pictures with a woman in a floppy hat and a bikini top. Even when I'm deep in thought, missing my parents and wondering about the future, that man has a way of making me smile.

"Hey Brenda," Kurt called to me. "Get a look at her!"

Apparently, the snowman was a *snowwoman*. And she was wearing my bikini.

Just one more unexpected call, in a very unexpected life.

And I thank God for the love, strength, and humor that helped me handle every one of them.

Acknowledgments

Kurt: If I had to choose again, I'd still choose you. My true-life story continues to be an unbelievable fairy-tale romance because of the way you love me. You are the balance in my life. Thank you for believing I had a story worth sharing, for covering for me with our crazy clan while I worked on this book, and for praying me through to the end. Your support, and knowing you had my back, made this book possible.

Zack, Jesse Jo, Kade, Jada Jo, Elijah, Sienna, and Sierra: This story is my truth and I wrote it down for you. I want you to know why I am the way I am—the good, bad, and ugly. I'm flawed and as you all know better than anyone else, I'm not perfect. But I am loved by a mighty God who loves you mightily. I hope you will learn from my life, grow to be better than me, and despite my faults, love me like I love you.

A special thanks to Jesse Jo: You amaze me every day; you are so much smarter than I am. I needed you so much. Thank you for your help when I couldn't get it all done. This book wouldn't have been done if it weren't for you—yours was the heart I wrote for.

Kim: My sister and my friend, thank you for allowing me to share our life with the world. You didn't ask for a sister like me but you supported my calling anyway. Thank you.

Jennifer: My writer friend who knows me better than I know myself but still seems to like me. I appreciate your ability to "get me" when my life has been so unexplainable. You worked so hard, hand in hand, call after call, tears and laughter. What a ride this has been with you. Thank you for giving my stories the words to touch a heart.

Creative Trust: I called and you answered with excitement. Thanks for representing me.

To everyone at Thomas Nelson who worked to make this book happen, especially Jenn, Anne, Julie, and Matt: Thanks for your passion for my story and for your hard work to make this happen so quickly. You are my home team.

Finally, to all the family and friends who have truly loved me over the years: I appreciate your support through the highs and the lows. You encouraged me to keep sharing my life story, telling me it would touch hearts and change lives. A special thank you to Kim, Rusty, Kim, Rachael, Peter, Marci, Mark, Chrissy, and Jen who all read the first draft and called me excited, but mad that you couldn't put it down. That's when I knew all the hard work was worth it.

About Brenda Warner

Brenda Warner is a speaker, philanthropist, and *New York Times* best-selling author. She is the mother of seven children, a registered nurse, and a marine. But most of all, she is a storyteller who candidly shares her struggles in hopes that her life experiences can help other women. Through her message of hope and faith and her charitable work, she inspires others during their own dark days.

As a much-sought-after speaker, Brenda encourages her audiences to take responsibility for their choices and to depend on their faith when they hit rough patches. Audiences have cried and belly-laughed during her keynote speeches at women's conferences, banquets, churches, sporting events, and business expos. Listeners have found practical hope through her stories about her family, her work with special-needs children, her triumphs over obstacles, and the blessings and burdens of being a celebrity wife.

Brenda is also vice president of the First Things First Foundation, an organization she cofounded in 2001 with her husband, NFL player Kurt Warner. In 2009, Brenda joined Kurt in coauthoring her first book, *First Things First: The Rules for Being a Warner*, which debuted on the *New York Times* best-seller list.

Brenda is also a gifted photographer who specializes in portraits. Her photos have been published in the *New York Times* and other publications. She particularly enjoys taking pictures of the babies she rocks at a local rehabilitation hospital where she volunteers. You can learn more about her and the work of her foundation at kurtwarner.org, or follow her on Twitter @WarnerBrenda.

About Jennifer Schuchmann

J ennifer Schuchmann loves her job of helping incredible people tell their stories. She is the author or coauthor of eight books, including the *New York Times* best seller *First Things First* by Kurt and Brenda Warner, and is the host of the television program *Right Now with Jennifer Schuchmann*. She holds an MBA from Emory University and has an extensive public speaking background. She and her husband, David, have been married for over twenty years, and together they have a teenage son, Jordan. You can find her online at wordstothinkabout.com and on Twitter @schuchmann.

About the First Things First Foundation

In 2001, Kurt and Brenda Warner established First Things First as a 501(c)(3) public charity. The foundation's mission is to have an impact on people's lives by promoting Christian values, sharing experiences, and providing opportunities to encourage people that all things are possible when we seek to put "first things first."

First Things First has actively initiated ongoing projects that bless people in communities in Arizona, Missouri, Iowa, and beyond. Programs include trips to Walt Disney World for ill children, building recreation centers in children's hospitals, teaching the football basics to Special Olympics athletes, and rewarding single parents as they achieve their dreams of home ownership. Each program promotes the Warners' life theme of putting faith and family first.

These programs would not be possible without the support and generosity of corporations, organizations, and individual donors. In order to expand its outreach, the foundation is seeking to build a network of businesses interested in supporting the work of First Things First with product/service donations, sponsorship of events, financial resources, or percentage-based donations on product sales. We invite you to join our team by calling 602-385-0840 to discuss partnership possibilities.

To learn more, visit the First Things First website at www.kurtwarner.org.